To Fifi Nous.

CONTENTS

SCHNAPPS FENDERS AND FLARES

Steve Martin

ISBN: 978-1-5272-7155-5

Warning

This book is based on a true story set in the early 1970s. It contains strong language and references to gender stereotypes that reflect the attitudes of that time which some readers may find offensive.
Reader discretion is advised.

Acknowledgements

A special thanks to:
John, Roger, Wolfgang, Kassy and Donald without whom this story
would not be. Also to Sue Samuelsson for her editing skills and
proof-reading the manuscript.

Prologue

There's just the faintest whiff of sin about the place after midnight. Not that it screams out vice and licentiousness, or even hints of excessive wickedness. You just sense that after twelve the majority of the clientele belong to a rather shifty ensemble Roger fondly refers to as *freunde der nacht*: small-time criminals, pimps, prostitutes, cabaret artistes and musicians. The kind of nocturnal characters who don't set alarm clocks or worry unnecessarily about getting to work before the boss. In fact, the kind of people we had recently become.

Glancing along the bar, I could see all the regulars in their favoured places: Pavel the shock-haired Pole chatting quietly to Claudia the cool, imperturbable bar lady. A decorated fighter pilot for the Free Polish Air Force during the war, Pavel makes a comfortable living – well, comfortable might be pushing it – smuggling diamonds up his arse into various European capitals.

Sitting companionably beside him is quiet-spoken Addie, who works as a waiter in a nearby restaurant. Addie has the discreet demeanour of a gentleman's gentleman and wouldn't appear wholly out of place in one of London's finest houses. But he has a past that still haunts him. Addie is a German Jew who survived three years in Dachau. He doesn't talk about it but Pavel once let slip that Addie had been a kapo: a prisoner who had to collaborate with the guards in order to survive. I've no doubt it was an extremely grisly business as behind his polished exterior you sense a dark melancholy. That and a vaguely sinister rictus smile and you've got an all-round fun guy. Each evening he comes here after work and sits at the bar listening to the band. Occasionally he'll send a tray of Asbach – a German brandy – up to the stage with a request for a tango. On a good night he might even find a willing dance partner. Other nights he just stares into the middle distance, lost in his thoughts.

A couple of tables across from a pair of diamond-encrusted cross-dressers – one whose six o'clock shadow is inconveniently starting to show – are Hans and Werner. Werner used to play football for TSV 1860 München, the city's other major football team. They say he might have been a star midfield player until he was dropped for excessive drinking and gambling. He's always skint and seldom sober, but he's in the fortunate position of having Hans as his best friend. Hans is a pimp. Possibly not a good one, as his stable of filles de joie has certainly seen better days. Nevertheless he always seems to have cash and is generous with it, picking up Werner's drinks tabs and keeping the band fuelled up on schnapps and beer.

And then of course there are the ladies. But I'll get round to them a bit later.

Yes, all in all another sparkling showbiz evening entertaining the crème de la crème of Munich's insomniac community. We're in the midnight hour with another set to play and Roger's making his way over – which means it's time to get up on stage again.

The hours are brutal and the job's not remotely what I imagined it to be, but strangely enough I can't decide whether I'm hating it or secretly loving it. It's certainly very different from everything we left behind in England, but I'm running away with myself. Let's rewind to a couple of months ago: to the day we received the letter.

PART ONE

DEUTSCHES HOUSE

CHAPTER ONE

The Letter

It was a mid-afternoon in December and my friend John and I were in another club, more sedate this time and located by the River Thames.

Skinners occupied the first floor of an attractive Regency building on the Windsor side of the bridge leading to Eton. It was a private members' club popular with trendy twenty-somethings, stylishly draped in the latest Carnaby Street fashions and driving MGBs and E-Types. Actors working across the road at the Theatre Royal could be found here and on occasion you could spot sixties icons like Honor Blackman, Donald Pleasence and Billie Whitelaw having a quiet drink. We were grudgingly accepted as members because we had played at dances for Young Conservatives around the area. Reasonably priced drinks were available outside normal licensing hours and at weekends it boasted a fairly lively disco playing Rod Stewart, Hot Chocolate and even Isaac Hayes – OK, not exactly a hot, throbbing evening at the Marquee Club but still quite risqué for the Royal Borough.

Labi Siffre's *It Must Be Love* was playing on the stereo system. As the song reached the chorus we gave it a shot at adding our own vocal harmonies, but gave up just as quickly when we received some conspicuously unfriendly looks from the barman.

John shrugged impassively and said, "Don't know what's wrong with that bloke. You'd think they would appreciate a bit of live music in this mausoleum."

John had recently returned from Germany where he had been playing organ in a quartet together with two Turkish gentlemen and a female singer of indeterminate ancestry. Performing in some low-rent venue in Mannheim his German adventure hit an inconvenient punctuation mark when he realised he wasn't getting paid. Down to his last few deutschmarks he had wandered into a distinctly smarter nightclub uptown and had, either by luck or astonishing skill, managed to sell one of his own original songs to the resident band. With this money he raised enough cash to catch the next train home. It was now almost a month since he got back.

This afternoon his demeanour was less laid-back than usual. He was excited about something but was taking his time telling me what it was. Finally he extracted a packet of Players No 6 cigarettes from his jacket pocket, carefully lit one and said, "You remember me telling you about the band in Mannheim that bought my song?"

"Yea, you've talked about nothing else," I replied lazily.

"Huh! Well they're looking for a new organist and asked if I was interested."

"You want to go back to Germany?"

"Yes, possibly. I wrote back and told them I'm in a songwriting partnership now and if my partner can come too – then yes I'm interested."

I stared at him questioningly. "Songwriting partner? You mean me?"

"Yes you! Dummy." He grinned and took a long drag on his cigarette. "Anyway I got another letter today and it's a big yes – they want us both to come. So what do you say?"

Before his stint in Germany we had played together in a local band and even had a record released on the Pye label which had garnered a few plays on Radio 1. We were both budding composers and since his return had combined our talents, writing songs together. Various plans charting a fast track to success had been floated but none of them so far involved Germany. In fact, if there was a road to instant fame and fortune, ours was still stuck at the planners.

"I don't know," I replied, somewhat taken aback. "I've never been abroad... well apart from a day trip to Calais with the school. I suppose that counts. Come to think of it, the only one in my family who has been abroad is my dad. And he spent most of his time there blowing bits of it up."

"But you've never wanted to go and work there?"

"Well yes I guess so. But in the other direction. America. You know – hit record, Ed Sullivan Show.

"Yea, but before they got that far, even The Beatles did their apprenticeship in Germany. Listen, have a think about it while I get a couple more drinks in."

He ambled over to the bar and ordered two halves of Watney's Red Barrel while I digested his offer. I stared out of the window across the Thames towards Eton College. Although it was early December, the weather was still mild and a couple of boats chugged jauntily up the river towards Maidenhead. A group of Eton boys in their tailcoats were hurrying across the bridge back to their dormitories, the sun was setting and it was picture perfect.

Beyond Eton was Slough, which was anything but picture perfect. Nevertheless, it was home and where our families and friends lived. Was it really where I wanted to stay? No, probably not but that elusive breakthrough as a composer might be just around the corner, and London was where everything was happening, not Mannheim.

"Well what's this band like?" I asked when he returned with the beers. "I mean are we talking Fleetwood Mac?"

"With or without Peter Green?" he replied, wiping froth off his chin.

"I don't know! You're supposed to be telling me."

He thought about it for a moment. "Nope. Nothing like them."

I threw some more names at him: "Deep Purple, The Moody Blues...?"

His face remained expressionless.

"Come on throw me a bone," I complained. "The Osmonds, Nina & Frederik… Gerry and his Pacemaker?"

He chuckled and said, "No, they're a bit more in the style of those bands you see on a Sunday evening at the Adelphi Ballroom." He noted my look of disappointment and quickly raised his hand to reassure me. "Only a lot more professional. They play some chart stuff and quite a lot of black music but mainly a bit of everything. When I saw them play it was in a really cool club. Smart stage clothes, very chic. I watched them do a couple of sets: The Isley Brothers, James Brown quite a lot of Neil Diamond…"

"OK so they're a cover band," I concluded glumly.

"Well no, not technically as they now do one of my songs."

"Nice try mate. Trust me they're a cover band."

"Come on Steve it's Germany. Think of it, we will be following in the footsteps of The Beatles. Even they were playing covers when they played at the Star-Club."

We stopped for a moment and listened to the next song on the stereo. It was James Taylor's version of *You've Got a Friend* and we prepared to join in. We got about as far as the second verse before our friend, the barman, shouted over at us.

"Oi! Give it a rest! Every time you come in here it's the same. It's like having the bloody Beverley Sisters crooning on everything!"

"Philistine," John muttered under his breath.

"OK so where would we live?"

"The first month we'll stay in the village where the band lives. Apparently it's a really cool place near Frankfurt. They'll organise a room for us, then when we start touring, the clubs will arrange accommodation. With a guaranteed ninety quid a week though, we'll soon get our own place."

The money was certainly tempting as neither of us was earning more than a tenner a week at the time.

After Germany John had returned to his job in Datchet selling illuminated ceilings and I had recently quit my job in a London recording studio because of the unsociable hours and lousy wages. I was now doing a temporary job at an insurance company. We both lived at home.

"So what's the name of the band?"

Subtly avoiding my gaze he mumbled, "The Statesmen Singers."

"Who?"

"The Statesmen Singers," he repeated, still avoiding my gaze.

"That's not a band name." I said scornfully. "Uriah Heep, Black Sabbath, Iron Maiden – they're band names."

"Yes I know it's a bit poncy."

"Poncy! It sounds like an Ivy League college choir."

"Well think of The Staple Singers or the Edwin Hawkins Singers. You never know, it might be a bloody brilliant name in Germany."

As he took a swig of his beer I took a moment to study my friend. If he had been born into a wealthy family he would have been labelled a prodigy and wheeled out to perform something classically tasteful on the piano as dinner guests arrived. In actuality, he had grown up on the tough Britwell Estate on the other side of Slough and from an early age had to earn his pocket money playing old standards in local pubs. He had a rare ability to hear something once and be able to busk it.

By contrast I was a competent guitarist but no Jimmy Page. My dad was a big Glenn Miller fan and persuaded me to learn the clarinet when I was at school. By the time I was fourteen I realised a bowler hat, striped waistcoat and saloon bar was the most likely career path for a liquorice stick virtuoso, so I wanted to quit and take up something cooler like the guitar. At first my dad was having none of it but finally agreed if I was prepared to take piano lessons as well. By the age of fifteen I was in a band playing guitar – even writing songs – and now imagined my future as a songwriter rather than a performer. Any reservations I had about Germany were more about my abilities than anything else.

John was much more upbeat about it. "We'll have a great time, see the world, meet some sexy *fräuleins* and write hit music. Think about the alternative. You really want to stay in Slough your whole life?"

And that of course was the clincher.

CHAPTER TWO

I Just Want to Celebrate

The following day John wrote and told the band we would be delighted to accept the offer and could fly over on 1 January.

After we had posted the letter I went home and announced the news to my family. Their reaction was unusually mixed.

"Good idea. Make a man of you," my dad decided, glancing keenly at me over the top of his newspaper.

My mum was less enthusiastic. She came over and hugged me then, running her fingers critically through my shoulder-length hair said, "Germany? But that's abroad! You don't speak the language and they'll hate you because of the war."

"They didn't hate The Beatles when they played in Hamburg," I protested.

"Yes, but they were from Liverpool – that's different. Well if they turn nasty you must promise to come straight home."

"Yes mum. What about you nan? You don't mind me moving abroad?"

My grandmother had been living together with us since my grandfather died.

"Of course I'm going to miss you dear. I'm going to miss listening to you write your songs and play your guitar. But maybe this is an opportunity for you to do what you really want to do."

"Yea, I hope so nan. Germany isn't my first choice, but I haven't had a lot of other offers."

"Don't worry dear, you're not even twenty yet. Plenty of time for all of that. Go off and have some fun."

Although the UK would soon be joining the 'Common Market' we were still required to apply for permits to live and work in West Germany. I also needed to get a passport so there was a fair bit of running around. I handed in my notice at work and managed to sell my car. Then before we knew it, Christmas was upon us and a group of our friends organised a going away party for New Year's Eve at Skinners.

We arrived at the party to find school friends, musician pals and girlfriends past and present all in the mood to celebrate the New Year and wish us goodbye. The drinks were flowing and of course much of the talk was about our imminent departure. While most of the boys were convinced we'd be back in a month, the girls were certain we were going away forever.

One of them was Annabelle. She had been my first serious love. We were seventeen when we met in the saloon bar of a pub in Beaconsfield. At the time she was living with her parents and two sisters on a very posh private estate in near-by Gerrards Cross. Despite me being the boy from the back streets of Slough her family were wonderfully welcoming and I spent many happy times together with them. Then about a year after we met she moved to High Wycombe and began sharing a flat with Elaine, a cheerful redhead from Liverpool. Unfortunately, like most relationships at that age, ours had a 'best before date' and it wasn't very long after, when she was introduced to Elaine's brother Anthony, that ours rather inconveniently expired. But we were still great friends and tonight the two girls were there together.

I was chatting to Allan, the leader of the first band I was in, when Annabelle pulled me aside and asked, "Why? What can Germany possibly offer that you can't find here? I thought you wanted to be a composer, not some touring musician."

"Yes I do. But maybe that's how I become one? Anyway, I'm in no doubt it will all end in tears so I'll probably be back in a couple of weeks."

She looked at me carefully then caressed my chin. "Hmm I hope so. I've kind of got used to you being around." She arched one eyebrow and whispered, "And Slough just won't be the same without you."

I kissed her fondly on the cheek and turned around to find Adrian – one of my oldest school friends – grinning at me. We'd known each other since we were both eleven and had been in the school orchestra together, him on second trumpet and me third clarinet. We both shared a passion for rock music and while more recently my taste had been veering toward the West Coast sounds of Crosby, Stills, Nash & Young, he had become a mad-keen Led Zep fan. He was of course very curious to know all about the new band.

"So what do they play? Hard rock? Metal? Prog? Don't say they're some cheesy glam outfit like T.Rex or The Sweet?"

"Nooo definitely not," I replied, feeling my nose begin to twitch. "More eclectic than that, I would say. I wouldn't like to stick a label on them though."

"No of course not," he agreed, eying me thoughtfully. "And what's their name? If they're German, and I'm thinking of course Tangerine Dream and Kraftwerk, I bet it's something amazing…"

"Er yea…well they did tell me but I can't remember. Apparently it's very symbolic in Germany."

"Oh wow! What? Like The Bad Adolfs? Or maybe more gothic? Götterdämmerung! Yea, I bet it's something profound like that."

"Er yea... something like that."

Thankfully, before we could get into any more specifics, John came over and grabbed my arm. "Come on. It'll be midnight shortly. Let's get everyone together and out into the main bar."

We hustled our group of friends out into the bar and joined the rest of the Skinner's crowd who were counting down the minutes towards twelve. I gazed around at all the excited, familiar faces and thought about my family, my life in Slough and the job I'd just given up and wondered when we would be back again, and exactly what tomorrow's adventure in Germany would have in store for us.

In the distance the bells from Eton College began to ring in the New Year.

Oh well. Welcome to 1972.

CHAPTER THREE

How Do You Do?

Our BEA flight to Frankfurt left Heathrow at noon the following day. This was my first experience of flying and it was fascinating to gaze down upon the area I grew up in from above. The runway runs parallel to the A4 road so from the moment we took off we could track our progress over Colnbrook, Langley and Slough – even spotting the street where I lived. Then somewhere above the Slough Industrial Trading Estate we made a sharp left turn and headed off towards the continent.

During the flight John filled me in a little on the other band members. Roger, the bandleader, was from London. He played drums and also sang. Kassy was Dutch-Indonesian and the lead singer. There were two Germans in the band: Donald, who played lead guitar and Wolfgang, a tall, blonde bass player. The organist leaving the band was Karl and he was from Hungary.

"That's a pretty mixed bunch. How did they all meet up?" I asked.

"The original members were American servicemen who stayed on in Germany. As people left, the line-up changed and over the years it became more international, I would imagine."

I raised an eyebrow. "No doubt that's where the fab name comes from."

It was quite a short flight and no sooner had the flight-attendants served us some snacks and cleared them away again than the seat belts sign went on and the plane commenced its approach into Frankfurt.

"Well, we'll soon know more about The Statesmen Singers," John said. "There should be a couple of them down there to meet us."

We descended through the clouds and I had my first glimpse of Germany. What immediately struck me was the difference in colour. The part of England we had just left, with its plethora of evergreens and verdant pastures, was a vibrant shade of emerald. By comparison the land beneath us was dusky olive-green, peppered with autumnal shades of brown. I couldn't see Frankfurt so we must have been a fair distance from the city centre. To the left of the airport was a military air base and as we got closer the pilot announced it was the US Rhine-Main Air Base. Running beside it, a busy network of autobahns conveyed speeding VWs, Opels, Mercs and BMWs in every direction. The plane dipped low over one of the autobahns and the pilot executed what I thought was a very decent landing, and then we immediately taxied over towards the terminal building.

After disembarking we collected our bags and went through customs to the arrivals hall. Standing in front of a small crowd was a tall, handsome chap with dark, smartly brushed-back hair. He was wearing a stylish sports jacket and aviator sunglasses. From his appearance I guessed this might be Donald. Beside him was a shorter, slightly rotund character with wild, unkempt hair and a round jovial face, wearing what looked like the uneaten remains of a sheep. John followed my gaze.

"Ah, there they are. Roger!"

"John, you scoundrel!" the jovial face shouted back. "Drop those bags and come over here and give me a hug." He then turned to me. "And you must be Steve." His face split into a wide grin. "Welcome to Germany!"

It was impossible not to be completely charmed by this ebullient character. He was extremely likeable, full of enthusiasm and we immediately got swept up in the warmth of his welcome. Donald was also exceedingly charming, offering each of us a solid handshake and a bright halogen smile that could have lit up a small town. Then following the two of them we made our way through the arrivals hall out into the car park.

To match everything else that was sleek about him, Donald owned a beautiful Mercedes Coupe. It was a few years old but in immaculate condition: white, with a light-blue roof and dark-red leather seats. Roger noticed me admiring it.

"Yeah, we like to travel in style with The Statesmen. All that schlepping up and down the M1 in the back of a Ford Transit – cold tea and burnt sausages at some greasy spoon by the Watford Gap. Done it, seen it and have no plans to do it again, thank you very much."

We loaded the cases into the boot of the car and then while Donald and John got into the front, Roger settled himself into the back seat.

"Steve, come and sit back here so we can chat." He looked me over keenly. "So, you write songs as well? Excellent, because I think we might need some more original material. John's song is going down well with the punters and Kassy sings it great." He patted John on the shoulder then gave me a conspiratorial wink. "But now we need something maybe a bit more Neil Diamondish for me to sing."

Purring like a contented cat, the Mercedes cruised gently out of the airport and onto one of the busy autobahns we'd seen from the plane.

"Righto," said Roger. First stop is Stockstadt so we can get you boys settled in your new digs.

"Is that where you guys live?" I asked.

"Yea, me and Wolfgang have got apartments there. We both have families so we need a proper base to come home to."

"And I live in the village as well together with my girlfriend in my parents' house. No kids yet." Donald added.

"Not for want of trying I imagine," Roger quipped, flashing me a rather filthy smirk.

"And what about Kassy?" John asked.

"He's just moved in with his new girlfriend in Worms," Roger replied. "It's quite close by. In fact we'll be going there later this evening as that's where we've been playing this month: The Imperial nightclub. Tonight's our last night. It's going to be brilliant to have some time off now while we rehearse the repertoire with you boys. Gives me the opportunity to see the wife and kids."

"How many have you got?" John asked.

"Two young boys. Actually you'll meet Mausi, my wife, soon enough. She works in the place where you'll be staying."

As he was explaining all this I was gazing around with interest at the surrounding countryside. We had left the autobahn and were now zipping down narrow country lanes passing farms and some light industrial units. There wasn't much livestock in the fields however, just row upon row of what looked like woody vines.

Roger followed my gaze. "Yes we're in the land of plonk now. They're vineyards."

"Wow. I didn't know they looked like that. They're like zombie arms poking out of the earth."

"The vines are hibernating for the winter." Donald said. "Just wait. In the spring, when the leaves begin to grow and the grapes pop out, you'll see how beautiful this part of Germany is."

After a few more kilometres we passed the sign for Stockstadt. On the flight over I had created a mental image of what the village might be like. I imagined it as one of those photos you see on a jigsaw puzzle box: a picturesque alpine village on the shores of a blue lake encircled by snow-capped mountains. Colourful, flower-bedecked chalets nuzzling companionably beside cosy bierkellers. Possibly a group of chesty blonde *fräuleins* limbering up with some gentle aerobics on the lakeshore.

That illusion quickly evaporated as we drove down the main street. I noted with disappointment the lack of mountains, lakes and chalets and realised that Stockstadt would even have trouble competing with Slough in a beauty contest. A depressing mixture of old farm buildings with attending farmyard clutter, featureless apartment houses, lock-ups and shops selling either hardware or hunting paraphernalia made up the village centre. There were a couple of locals going about their business but otherwise the place was deserted. Shit! What a depressing dump. We drove the full length of the main street in silence before pulling up outside a tired-looking bar called Deutsches Haus.

I still vividly remember my first impressions of that place: a lot of dark wood and a grim assortment of stuffed animal heads glaring balefully down from the walls, opaque windows facing the street and around a dozen scrubbed wooden tables with chairs. A bouquet I was soon to recognise as ubiquitous in German drinking establishments – a sour miasma of detergents and hops – assailed the nose while the ears were equally insulted by some ghastly German pop song blaring from a small jukebox. God, it sounded like a triumphal military march to a disco beat.

Half expecting a few stiff-armed salutes in welcome, I checked out the clientele. It was the middle of the afternoon but there were already ten or twelve people drinking at the bar. As one they swivelled around and warily inspected us. Was it just me or had the jukebox mysteriously turned itself off? Now it was eerily quiet and the atmosphere had a distinct chill to it. A middle-aged lady behind the bar shook hands with Roger, said something warm and inviting to Donald then stared impassively at John and me. A moment later an odd-looking fellow hopped up from somewhere behind the bar. He was small and stocky with a slight stoop and one of his eyes was deformed and a peculiar red colour. I couldn't make my mind up if it made him look comical or sinister. Staring blankly at the two of us, he made no attempt at a smile or greeting.

Donald waved a tentative hello and whispered in my ear, "That's her son, Berndt. He's a bit weird so try not to stare at his eye."

Oh fuck, he might as well have asked me to start speaking German. I smiled brightly at the lady but I could feel my eyes being drawn to that hideous splotch to the left of his nose. Fortunately Donald said something to them both and they entered into a discussion in German which diverted his attention. Standing to one side, we tried to be unobtrusive while the other customers slowly went back to their drinks.

I turned to John and whispered, "Wow! This is a festival of laughs. The only thing missing is a wreath of garlic around the door and something with fur and fangs howling at the moon."

We started giggling nervously.

The others concluded their little chat and came over to us.

"Nice place, eh? And great people too," Roger said enthusiastically. Getting little response from us, he kept going. "Anyway, you lucky boys are going to be staying here for the next two months." A quick look of horror passed between us but Roger continued obliviously. "The really good news though is the first month's for free. They have a large hall upstairs the locals use for weddings and the deal is we can use it for our rehearsals while you chaps will live like kings on the third floor in the honeymoon suite. We'll play at a couple of dances they're going to organise, and that way they make some moolah from the whole thing. Right, let's get the bags up."

Roger and Donald stayed in the bar drinking pils with the landlady while we grabbed our bags and followed our red-eyed host up some flights of stairs. Eventually, we arrived on a small landing. Berndt took one last suspicious look at us before choosing a key from a large fob.

The door swung open and the honeymoon suite turned out to be a dingy room meagrely furnished by what appeared to be the local chapter of the Salvation Army. It contained twin beds, a wardrobe and a chair, a number of mysterious brown stains on the ceiling and a large sink. All that was missing was a rope and noose hanging in the corner. He handed us the key and without a word stomped off back downstairs.

Glumly, John gazed around the room and said, "Oh, what the fuck, it's only for a few weeks. Hey, you never know, there may even be a couple of gorgeous girls sharing a big house just up the road."

"What, one of those glamorous pig farms we passed on the way in? If the women around here are anywhere near as welcoming as that bunch downstairs, then we're in for a tough two months."

We unpacked and rejoined the others. A tall, pale, thin chap with shoulder-length blonde hair and sorrowful blue eyes had joined them and was sitting there puffing disconsolately on a cigarette. As we entered he jumped up and welcomed us warmly.

"John, how nice to see you again," he said.

"Hi Wolfgang, and you too. This is Steve."

"Pleased to meet you, Wolfgang."

"No, the pleasure is mine, and please call me Wolly."

While we found chairs, Wolfgang went off for a pee and Donald mumbled something in German to Roger, who looked at us seriously.

"Wolly's having a pretty rough time of it at the moment," he explained. "He and his wife have only been married a year. They moved to Stockstadt after the wedding and they've just had a baby. The wife's from Bavaria and she's really homesick. Wolly's getting the blame and he's at his wits' end."

Donald chimed in, "And when he gets depressed he drinks."

Roger gave him a sharp look and said, "So excuse him if he's not himself at the moment." He rubbed his hands briskly together and started to get up. "Right, we've kindly been invited over for *abendbrot* by Donald's parents, a kind of German version of teatime. After that we'll have it away on our toes to Worms. We start playing at eight and it will be good for you two to watch and get a feel for the repertoire."

"Eight? So what time do you finish? Around ten or eleven?" I asked.

They looked at each other in surprise and both burst out laughing.

"Funny man," Roger chortled. "I like a bloke with humour. No, three a.m. It's a breeze."

For a moment I believe I was speechless. Eight till three? A seven-hour gig? With just a hint of sarcasm, I managed to croak, "Oh, that's alright. I promised myself I didn't want another nine-to-five job."

"Oh, don't worry," he said. "We get those as well!"

***

Wolfgang returned and the five of us walked through the village to Donald's home. Away from the main street the residential roads had much more appeal. The houses and gardens were all neatly laid out and well tended. It wasn't as pretty as a typical English village but what it lacked in beauty it made up for in solid dependability. There was no fancy brickwork or fussy pergolas, the houses were quite plain, but they all looked very well maintained.

Donald's home was a medium-sized house with a small courtyard and something resembling an outside shed. Whereas in England the shed would house a couple of bikes, a pair of shears and a lawnmower, this one had a bloody great dead pig hanging from a hook, and by the looks of it the creature had only recently passed. Blood was still dripping on the floor while its sightless eyes stared at us through the open door as we crossed the yard. I could swear the poor sod was grinning too, its snout tilted at a jaunty angle and its mouth drawn back in a cheerful smirk. I dragged my eyes away just as Donald's mother and father came out of the back door to greet us.

His mother was a plump, middle-aged lady with a kind and friendly face, while his father – a heavily-built, tanned gentleman in rolled-up shirtsleeves – had the look of a man who enjoyed spending his working life outdoors. They shook hands with us and ushered us into the house while playfully admonishing Roger for being late.

It felt larger and more muscular than a similar type of property in England. The ground floor wasn't any bigger than my parents' house in Slough, but the house had three floors, a full basement and significantly higher ceilings. The furniture was big and sturdy and many pieces looked like they had been in the family for generations. Framed black-and-white photos were dotted around the room and I noticed some of them were of men in uniform. With interest, I looked to see if there were any Nazi uniforms amongst them. There weren't.

Food began to arrive. First it was thick slices of *bauernbrot* followed by spicy sausage, salami and some kind of coarse pork pate, which I imagine had been donated by a former resident of the shed. I watched as the others took large daubs of the pate and spread it thickly on the bread. Nobody asked for butter. For somebody brought up on Wonderloaf, beans and sausages, the cuisine on the table was a new and exotic experience but I was determined to try everything and it was surprisingly good.

We were just finishing when a strikingly attractive brunette entered the room and rushed over to Donald, urgently whispering something in his ear. Noticing the way she had ignored the rest of us, he admonished her sharply and for about five milliseconds she exhibited the slenderest hint of contrition by projecting a rather filthy pout towards Roger and Wolfgang. Turning to the rest of the table, she primly said hello while Donald introduced her to us.

"John and Steve, this is my girlfriend, Margit."

We both said hello and in reply received an unusually forthright appraisal before she rewarded us with the kind of look that should really have carried a parental warning. With her artfully applied makeup and carefully farmed cleavage, she was certainly different from anyone we knew back in Slough, but she also looked to be quite a feisty number. Just as quickly as she had arrived she turned, blew Donald a kiss and hurried out. I caught a funny look between Roger and Wolfgang but Donald was smiling indulgently.

"Sorry about that, but she's late for work. She works in a bar in a village a few kilometres from here and is getting a lift from a neighbour."

"Wouldn't want her to be late for her adoring public, would we, Donald?" Roger commented mischievously.

Donald ignored him and said we should get a move on or we'd be late too.

Teatime was over, so we thanked his parents and walked back to Deutsches Haus and the car. Five minutes later we were on the road again – Wolfgang up front with Donald and three of us in the back – on our way to Worms.

CHAPTER FOUR

Help Me Make It Through the Night

The car journey took about forty minutes but it was too dark to see anything of interest. We crossed a river which somebody said was the Rhine and, as we entered Worms, a magnificent, floodlit cathedral in the Romanesque style dominated the skyline and bathed the car in light. It soon got dark again though as we bumped and shimmied our way down narrow, cobbled streets until we arrived at our destination: the Imperial nightclub.

A wide neon staircase led us down to a pair of smoky-grey tinted glass doors that Roger pushed open with a flourish. I'm not sure what I was expecting but it wasn't anything as grown-up as this. It was glamorous in a faux 1950s New York style. The kind of establishment where martinis and daiquiris would be served by ladies sporting bouffants and bunny suits while Mel Tormé or Bobby Darin headlined the floor show. Velvet curtains and a dark-red carpet enhanced the luxurious feeling while a large, low, semi-circular stage with a raised podium for the drums dominated the back of the room. In front of that was an equally spacious dance floor surrounded by elegant chrome tables and chairs, and at the rear, a long bar displaying what must have been every conceivable brand of liquor. John and I looked at each other wordlessly and then started giggling. Donald stared at us in confusion.

"Sorry Donald," I said. "It's just so different from the last gig John and I did together, a working men's club in Slough."

A moment later a door beside the stage opened and a short Asian chap, dressed similarly to Donald in a sports jacket and slacks, came striding out.

"John, nice to see you again. Did you have a good journey?"

"Hi Kassy. Yes a very good flight thanks."

"And you must be Steve. I'm so happy to meet you."

We shook hands vigorously and sat down for an impromptu meeting.

Roger opened the proceedings. "John and Steve are now living at Deutsches Haus and this afternoon we made the deal we spoke about with the owner. Heinz has already organised a two-week residency for the beginning of February. That's when we need to be ready with the repertoire."

"Who's Heinz?" John asked.

"Heinz Bachmann: he's our manager and arranges the bookings. The gig in February is a US air base in Hanau."

"Hanau?!" I exclaimed with some alarm. "Aren't the Americans bombing that place?"

"They'd better not be," Roger replied easily. "You're thinking of Hanoi in North Vietnam. This place is a bit nearer, just outside Frankfurt in fact. We've played there a few times and it's a nice gig. But you are right, the Yanks are at war in Vietnam and the guys we'll be playing to will either just have been there, or will be going there soon."

That will be a slightly different audience to the working men of Slough I decided.

"Bachmann is still planning the rest of February," Roger said, "but he's confident he'll get us a few more gigs. Then in March we go to Munich for a month."

"And after March?" Kassy asked.

"You know Heinz," Roger replied, "he never books too far in advance.

"Yes, we do know Heinz Bachmann," responded Kassy. "And as

usual everything will be booked at the last minute or not booked at all."

I glanced over at John. From his expression I think he was thinking the same as me. Maybe the ninety pounds a week wasn't such a sure thing?

As the staff drifted in and began preparing the club, there was a loud disturbance in the kitchen. An excited man's voice was shouting animatedly, and whatever he was complaining about, he was seriously worked up. On top of that he appeared to be having some trouble breathing. His choleric outbursts were punctuated by wild choking sounds.

Roger saw our anxious expressions. "Oh, don't worry, that's just Schmiegel, the owner. Lovely fella, but he can be excitable. It sounds a lot worse than it is."

"It sounds like he's choking," I said uneasily.

"Yeah, he does that a lot," said Wolfgang.

The door to the kitchen banged open and the owner of the excited voice entered the club. He was a short, dapper man in a well-cut suit with thinning hair, small anxious eyes and a prominent nose. His eyes darted around the club before coming to rest on our small group. He was massaging his temples as though forcing himself to relax. Finally, he came over to our table and in a high-pitched, sibilant voice sprayed us a short welcome speech.

"So you are the boys joining The Statesmen Singers? Well on behalf of the Imperial nightclub I welcome you to Germany and wish you much success."

Turning to the others, he mentioned that he had been talking to Bachmann about booking the band for June, which was greeted by eager nods of approval.

He got up and was just about to head back to the kitchen when he abruptly stopped and looked around. "And Karl, where is he?"

Roger replied rather casually, "Probably just on his way. He doesn't live far. You know him, he's always—"

"Yes, I do!" Schmiegel snapped, his voice rising a couple of octaves. "And no, it is not acceptable! The orchestra must begin at eight on the dot. My customers demand this. Anything less and they will be most disappointed!"

I gazed curiously around the empty club while he continued to rage.

"Most disappointed!" he squeaked.

Conveniently, Karl arrived at that moment smiling happily at everyone. Schmiegel, who had worked himself up into another major coughing fit, had to content himself with simply staring furiously at the band while tapping wildly at his watch. He stomped off towards the kitchen.

I whispered to John, "How nice, a German barking orders at us."

Totally unfazed by the goings-on, Karl came over and shook our hands. He was stocky, with dark hair and a stylishly trimmed beard. He had a thick Eastern European accent and his English vocabulary was limited, but he made an effort to chat to us, which I thought was nice.

The clock was ticking towards the hour when Donald wisely suggested, "Boys, we need to go and get changed."

While they made their way to the dressing room, John and I found a table close to the dance floor. By now I was keenly interested to hear what our new band sounded like.

Right on time they stepped out onto the stage and began turning their equipment on. While Donald and Wolfgang checked the tuning on their Fender guitars, Roger sat down at his drums and Kassy gave a pair of congas a tentative slap. The club was still empty but Roger counted in the first number. It was a little-known song by The Temptations called *My Baby*. This was followed by a cover of *Celebrate* by Three Dog Night. I was quietly impressed. They sounded good and it wasn't the run-of-the-mill repertoire I was expecting. It was a shame there was no audience to appreciate it.

They were very strong vocally: Kassy, Roger and Donald all had commercial voices and sang beautifully together in harmony. I was particularly knocked out by Kassy, who for such a small guy had a huge voice with a big range. His vocals were reminiscent of Sammy Davis Jr. – happily without the louche, limp-wristed razzmatazz. But they all sang well and took turns. Roger seemed to prefer ballads or jazzier standards while Donald had quite a pure, high voice which I found very attractive. He did a great version of *Roundabout* by Yes as well as more of their pop repertoire.

Even though it was New Year's Day and Germans, like the British, would have been partying until late the previous evening, it was a Saturday night so guests soon began to drift in. By the time the band took their first break the club was about a quarter full. Looking around, it was interesting to get a glimpse of the people we would now be living amongst. No doubt I was expecting a few caricatures of Herman the German: brutal, fleshy, no neck, closely cropped with a toothbrush moustache – the full Erich Von Stroheim. But no, most of the guests appeared to be youthful, friendly and extremely well mannered.

They returned to the stage for the second set and picked up the tempo, performing decent versions of The Isley Brothers' *It's Your Thing* and James Brown's *Sex Machine*. Kassy sang both these numbers brilliantly while Roger, Wolfgang and Donald formed a very tight rhythm section behind him. The only thing I thought was at odds with the modern American sound was Karl's organ. He had a beautiful Hammond B3 that he'd plugged into a Leslie and reverb unit which produced the kind of result you were more accustomed to hearing inside an ice rink. I think John and I were both quietly pleased that the member of the band who for us was the weak link, was the one who was leaving.

The playlist wasn't totally contemporary though, and as the evening progressed they interspersed the pop and soul stuff with ballroom.

A tango swiftly followed by a rumba prompted me to lean over to John and remark disparagingly: "You didn't mention Joe Loss when we were discussing who they sound like."

"You didn't ask. Anyway, we can work on that part of the

program. But otherwise, not bad, eh?"

"No. Not bad at all."

Each forty-five minute set was followed by a fifteen-minute break when the band would come and sit with us, often bringing regular guests who were interested in meeting *die zwei Engländer* who were joining the band.

One particular character, dressed in a slightly old-fashioned checked jacket with a white shirt and bow tie, introduced himself as Peter. He didn't say much and seemed content to just sit quietly with us. To break the ice I asked him if he liked the band.

"Oh yes, they are very marvellous. I am their number one favourite fan," he announced proudly.

He was an odd-looking bird. There was a rather startled quality to his gaze, his eyes just a little too wide awake, and he seemed to be constantly glancing around while perched bolt upright on the edge of his seat. At one point John reached into his pocket for a cigarette. Quick as a flash a lighter appeared in Peter's hand and with great panache he diligently lit the cigarette. The second time he did it I found it amusing. By the third and fourth time it was getting weird and when I finally realised that he didn't smoke himself, it was plain spooky.

Doggedly the band worked their way through a couple more sets and as we moved into the early hours of Sunday morning I could feel my eyelids getting heavier. I noticed John was also semi-comatose, slumped in his seat and snoring softly. The only one at our table still wide awake was Peter who, either through excitement or dementia, was furiously slapping his legs along to the beat of Roger's drums.

It was two forty-five when they reached the last number. After seven hours on stage I expected them to be knackered and ready for bed, but were they? No chance.

"There's an all-night bar up near the cathedral that does a wicked goulash soup. Anyone fancy it?" Roger asked.

"Super idea Roger!" responded Peter excitedly, still full of beans.

"Yea why not?" agreed John, half-heartedly.

Drowsily we roused ourselves and made our way outside, then five of us in Donald's car followed by Peter, Kassy and Karl in a little VW Beetle headed back up the cobbled streets in the direction of the cathedral. When we arrived, a table was quickly found in a busy bar not too dissimilar to the one in Deutsches Haus. The main difference was the decoration which instead of gloomy animal heads consisted of black-and-white photos of 1950s pop singers. A round of beers quickly arrived followed shortly after by the soup which was really good. This was the first hot food we'd had since leaving Slough so we quickly gobbled it up.

While a second round of beers was being served, Kassy rose from his seat and tapped his glass.

"Gentlemen. Tonight we're saying goodbye to our dear old friend Karl. We've travelled a long road together and now he's off to travel a new one with the Blue Tramps. Here's to Karl."

We raised our glasses in a toast and Karl responded by loudly ordering a round of schnapps for the table. When they arrived Roger noticed my look of hesitancy.

"You better get used to this stuff. It's the currency for getting requests played by the band."

"You mean we have to drink it every night?"

"Not every night. It depends. In US bases they send up trays of beer. But when we get into the top clubs – and that's where I intend to get us – it'll be bottles of champagne. Anyway, drink it down and relax. It's Sunday so you can sleep in and take it easy all day. Monday morning is going to be busy. We need to get you guys some equipment and start rehearsals."

CHAPTER FIVE

I'd Like to Teach the World to Sing

Monday morning John and I woke up at about the same time, our eyes growing accustomed to our new surroundings. Outside the window there was a sprinkling of frost on the trees, but it was certainly nice and warm in the room. I lay back and enjoyed the comfort of the bed.

Much is said about German manufacturing and efficiency but somebody should give a shout-out for their practicality too. A good example is the duvet or continental quilt. For the first nineteen years of my life I slept in a bed made up with sheets and blankets all folded up tight like an overstuffed envelope. Here, for the first time, my feet, and indeed any other odd lumps or protrusions, were free to move and position themselves as they pleased. I was lying under a giant cotton marshmallow but it was a warm cocoon that lightly hugged each part of my body. I loved it and looking across at my roommate he appeared to love it too.

"Fancy going down to see if there's some breakfast?" he asked. "I could really murder a couple of eggs."

We hadn't eaten much the day before. In fact we hadn't done much of anything. We woke around three p.m. and as the bar downstairs had been closed we'd taken a walk around Stockstadt. It hadn't looked any more inviting than when we arrived but we found a small cafe serving beer and sausages and spent a few hours in there.

Later we took a couple of beers back to the room and read our books and chatted until we fell asleep again.

Anyway, today was a work day so we quickly took turns at the sink and then made our way downstairs. The dining area was empty although three or four of the regulars were standing at the bar sipping small beers and chatting with a female.

She turned to face us and said. "You must be John and Steve."

She was speaking English with a German accent, but did I detect a slight sneer? We nodded cautiously.

"I'm Mausi, Roger's wife."

We relaxed and began to say how pleased we were to meet her but one of the regulars was also saying something and she turned her back on us to answer him. It gave me a moment to study her a little closer. She was about the same age as Roger – around twenty-six or seven – but there was still something of the fifth form about her. Not really jolly hockey sticks, more like the back of the cycle sheds with a packet of Silk Cut in one hand and a pimply sixth former in the other. She wasn't ugly, in fact she had probably been very pretty once, but the last few years looked like they had taken their toll.

Thinking she had forgotten about us, we were preparing to go and find a table when she turned and enquired sweetly, "You like your room? Well, remember your mothers are not here to clean up after you." We nodded uneasily while she went on, "And the bathroom, I hope you keep it clean. Or maybe you think it's OK to leave a dirty brown ring around the bathtub after bathing?"

We quickly shook our heads but by now she appeared to have lost interest in us and was broadcasting to the whole bar: "Oh, I thought maybe all Englishmen did and not just that idle bloody husband of mine! Anyway I can't stand here all day yapping. I had better get home and check that the lazy bastard is awake."

This was followed by loud laughter from Redeye, who had just entered the room, and puzzled smiles by the other customers who didn't understand English. There was no point in answering so we mumbled something polite and waved goodbye as she left.

"What the fuck was that all about?" John whispered.

"You tell me."

"Anyway let's get some food."

I quietly hoped that somebody young, slim and beautiful would come and take our order but unfortunately it was Redeye who eventually ambled over and truculently demanded something in German.

Before we left Slough, John had started a beginner's course in the language, but I couldn't imagine he had a clue what had just been said. Then to my astonishment he turned to Redeye with a confident smile and said, "*Zweimal Kaffee bitte und Spiegeleier mit Speck für zwei.*"

Redeye stared at him curiously for a few moments, scratched his head and then stalked off towards the kitchen.

I was impressed and asked, "What did you say?"

"I told him to get that fucking eye fixed as it's really bugging me." I gaped at him and he grinned. "No. Actually I've been rehearsing a few phrases that might be useful, and that was one of them. I ordered some coffee, eggs and bacon for two. Either that or I just asked what a nice girl like him was doing in a dump like this. We'll soon find out which."

A few minutes later coffee arrived followed by the eggs and bacon. John was delighted and I think we both realised it was going to make things a lot easier if we learned the language.

As we were finishing up, the band began to arrive.

"Morning chaps," said Roger brightly. "OK it's rehearsal day and we need some instruments for John and Steve. We'll go over to Knapp's place and choose a few things. But first of all, let's get the other equipment out of the van and up to the rehearsal hall. Wolly, you can hang around here and keep an eye on it."

We left in Donald's car, heading in the direction of Darmstadt with Kassy following behind in a beat-up VW Kombi with '*The Statesmen Singers*' printed in large letters on each side. After about twenty minutes, Roger pointed to a distant building on a hilltop.

"Just up there is Frankenstein's Castle."

"Really?" I said, raising an eyebrow. "I thought that was fiction. Mary Shelly and all that."

"No, that's his place up there. We can go and check it out one weekend if you want."

John piped in, "Bloody long way for Redeye to get home every night."

Roger looked sharply at him and asked, "Something wrong with Berndt?"

"Yeah, he gives me the willies."

Roger thought about this for a moment, then changed the subject. "I hear you met Mausi?" He chuckled tentatively. "Hope she was on her best behaviour." Nobody said anything so he continued, "I know she can be a bit hard going sometimes but…"

I was sitting behind, but noticed in the rear view mirror that Donald was looking quietly amused. Roger glanced at him and battled on, "But she's got a heart of gold and would do anything…"

Donald raised an eyebrow, and appeared to be on the point of saying something when Roger burst out, "OK, I admit it, she's a fucking nightmare! Happy?"

Continuing to smile enigmatically, Donald didn't say a word.

Roger looked at him defiantly. "But she's the mother of my kids." He turned and stared out the window. "And that's all I'm going to say on the subject."

We drove into the hills to a small village where we pulled up in front of a shop window full of accordions, zithers, cow bells and brass band instruments. As we climbed out of the car the owner, Herr Knapp, came out of the shop to say hello and, getting into the continental swing of things, I went to shake his hand. Too late I realised with a jolt that there wasn't one to shake – the bloody thing was missing! I was horribly embarrassed but he just laughed it off. Later, Donald told me Herr Knapp had been a useful guitarist in local bands until he lost his right hand in a car accident. After that he turned his energies to selling musical instruments.

We entered the shop and told him what we were after and he

swiftly got down to business sorting through his stock. There was quite a selection of guitars and I tried a few different ones until choosing a white Fender Stratocaster. I picked out a Vox amplifier, microphone and stand and was good to go. Herr Knapp rooted around in his stockroom and found an ancient Hammond B3 organ for John. It was bruised and scarred with cigarette burns but would, Donald and Kassy assured us, produce exactly the sound we would need in the clubs.

Herr Knapp was nodding in agreement but added, "You should bring along a hair dryer to gigs during the winter months as the motor in the organ might freeze up and you'll need warm air to coax it into life.

"And what about a reverb unit John?" Donald asked. "Karl always liked to use one."

"No I think I'll skip that for now." John replied.

Roger grinned. "Hello, young John, weren't you impressed by Karl's orchestral sound? Didn't you close your eyes and imagine sixty Jewish gentlemen scraping away with their bows when his fingers danced lightly across the keys?"

"No, Roger, I closed my eyes and imagined sixty ice skaters gliding gracefully across Streatham Ice Rink."

Roger laughed and said, "Yeah, good man. OK, we're ready."

Back in the bar, we found a rather worse-for-wear Wolfgang sitting with a couple of the locals at a table full of empty beer and schnapps glasses. It looked like they had been drinking pretty heavily since we left.

"Wolly, not good – not good at all," Roger seethed through gritted teeth. "Rehearsal days mean work, not sitting here getting pissed."

Wolfgang carelessly lit a cigarette and said, "I'm fine. I'll be able to work."

"No, you should go home and lie down for a few hours and come back later this afternoon."

"Roger, I just can't face going back there at the moment. I'll be fine." He gave him an imploring look.

Our bandleader continued to stare levelly at him but then shrugged and told him to get rid of the drink and join us upstairs.

The hall was surprisingly large with the capacity for three or four hundred guests. It had a light wooden vaulted ceiling which matched its dark wooden floor. The whitewashed walls were bare apart from a couple of high windows which flooded the room in daylight. There was a stage at one end and a long bar at the other. As a rehearsal room it was perfect. We quickly set up the gear while Donald disappeared, returning shortly after with a small tape recorder.

"I've been recording potential new songs off the radio," he announced proudly. "There's some great stuff around."

We listened to the tape, chose some songs and the rehearsals began.

The band wanted John and me to sing a couple of songs. Not because of our angelic voices, which they hadn't heard yet, but to save theirs on seven-hour stints like the one at the Imperial. I could understand their thinking, although I was hesitant as I had never imagined myself singing lead on anything. Both John and I had strong voices, as the barman in Windsor could vouch for, and enjoyed doing harmonies together, but singing something on our own? I expressed these doubts to Roger, who immediately pooh-poohed them.

"No, don't worry. Even a rasping donkey would sound good through our sound system."

That was damned flattering. Well, if we were expected to sing lead I fancied something not too brash or challenging, but more thoughtful with a bit of cred for the heads – maybe David Crosby or James Taylor? Leonard Cohen would be nice…

Roger listened with polite interest and half a smile, then duly lumbered me with a piece of nonsense called *Birds of a Feather* by a US outfit called Paul Revere & the Raiders. John didn't fare much better, getting saddled with another forgettable piece of fluff called *Beautiful*

Sunday. Not exactly Dylan, but the band were delighted with the results, Kassy being especially keen on having six singers in the line-up.

To experiment with this new vocal sound, we learned a US top-ten hit by The Grass Roots titled *Two Divided by Love*. John worked out a nice vocal arrangement and during the verse four of us took turns on lead lines. The result was surprisingly good and we were all starting to get enthusiastic.

These days boy bands and girl bands often split the lead parts between their singers, but back then, with the possible exception of The Jackson 5, nobody really did. Maybe it would give us an edge?

To take advantage of the new sound, we changed the vocal arrangements on some of the existing repertoire to fit six voices. It felt good and the morale in the band was high. Unfortunately we couldn't unload the ballroom tunes – the boys were adamant we would need them on some gigs – but apart from that we were happy with how things were coming along.

Much to everyone's delight, Wolfgang chose a song by Neil Young called *Heart of Gold*. He had an unusual voice, soulful with an attractively light German accent, which made it appealing. He did some Creedence material and could even pull off Wilson Picket songs, giving them an interesting Teutonic twist. For this song he would also play harmonica, so I'd play the bass.

If that was to everyone's delight, the next choice was to everyone's amusement. The Carpenters were big at the time and their latest hit was called *Superstar*. It was a mournful ballad that required a top-class female to do it any justice.

Roger looked at me and declared, "Steve, this is a brilliant song for you!"

My jaw dropped. Was he joking? "Me? No, I don't think so."

"Nonsense, you'll be perfect," he persisted.

"No, really Roger, I think this song calls for a safer pair of hands." I looked hopefully at Donald but Roger was adamant.

"And I can't think of a safer pair than yours," he purred. "Just wrap your tonsils around it and we'll take it out for a quick test drive." He smiled. "Just to hear what it sounds like."

It was hopelessly high and right on the break in my voice, but I made the effort and struggled manfully through it. It was a disaster, of course it was, but when I looked at the others I was surprised to see five smiling faces. Or were the buggers smirking?

Roger moved us briskly along. "Great, that's another hit in the repertoire. What's next on the tape, Donald?"

The second weekend approached, and Redeye and his mother prepared the hall for the first of the dances. Word of the event had quickly spread around the area and on the night the locals started streaming in early. Mausi was helping out behind the bar and Donald and Kassy's ladies were there to lend support. Surprisingly we still hadn't met Wolfgang's wife.

We opened the evening with *Two Divided by Love* and steadily made our way through the new numbers. At first the audience were content to just drink and chat, but after a couple of tunes a few people took to the floor. Being an agricultural community, it was an eccentric mixture of dance styles, with the older generation opting for well-rehearsed ballroom moves: quickstepping and foxtrotting their way gracefully around the hall to *Sex Machine*. Amongst the younger crowd, the girls had some quite funky disco moves while the chaps were less fleet of foot. Their wild, oscillating hand-movements, bent knees and lead feet appeared to be more useful techniques in a milking shed than on a dance floor. But generally people seemed to be having fun which was the main thing.

When we took a break, John and I wandered into the hall. Several of the older guests studied us with undisguised interest but then shook hands enthusiastically. Words like *wunderschön* and *spitzenklasse* began flying about with accompanied nods of approval so we must have been doing something right.

I spied Donald's girlfriend Margit, who quickly beckoned us both over. We hadn't seen her since that first day and I was reminded what a stunner she was, and how popular. A couple of male admirers were hanging around her – one getting her a drink, the other lighting her cigarette – while she talked animatedly to a couple of females.

"Ladies meet John and Steve from England," she proudly announced.

We eagerly greeted them and John struck up a conversation with one of the girls. Her name was Birgit and she spoke half decent English. Sadly I didn't have as much luck. Her friend began chatting happily to me, but it was all in German.

"You speak a little English?" I asked, my smile pitched somewhere between ingratiating and lustful.

"*Nein,*" she said, shaking her head sorrowfully.

Kassy brought his girlfriend Sonja, a divorcee in her early thirties, over to say hello. She was another very attractive lady and like Margit she spoke good English. Well there were certainly a lot of pretty girls, even in a dump like Stockstadt. If I could just find one that understood English things would be looking up.

CHAPTER SIX

Rainy Days and Mondays

After another full day of rehearsals on the Monday, John and I were invited to dinner and to watch TV at Roger's apartment. John declined the invitation as he was seeing Birgit, and my being away for the evening would give him an opportunity for some privacy in the bedroom. On my way out, I noticed Mausi was hard at it behind the bar serving customers. Excellent – I definitely didn't fancy an evening with her.

The smell of something exotic was emanating from the kitchen when I arrived at their apartment.

"I'm fixing some bongo nosh for us," Roger said. "It's a sort of bastardised nasi goreng that Kassy taught me to make."

His kids – a couple of smiling young boys, still pre-school age – were playing with toy cars in the living room together with an elderly lady who was watching the TV.

"That's Mausi's mum. She's been living with us for the past year ever since her husband died. She's from Northern Germany, a nice town on the coast called Lübeck." He lowered his voice. "The northern Germans are quite different from the good folks down here. A lot cooler, a bit more like us British."

I followed him into the kitchen and as he began dicing onions and garlic and tossing it into a frying pan, the subject turned to music and the band.

"There are four or five dozen professional bands playing on the club circuit in Germany," he explained. "Out of those, maybe about two dozen are in the top-flight, playing high paid gigs in ski resorts and luxury hotels. But the Indonesian bands have cornered that market recently."

He carefully sliced some pork and added it to the pan. "The punters love them. I mean, you've seen what Kassy's like. They're extremely professional, have great voices and are disciplined on stage. The Tielman Brothers and the Timelords are the best and have been for years." He paused, then made a face. "Personally I can't stand the Timelords. Their bandleader also sings and plays the drums – bags of swank but all the musicality of a dung beetle, unflinchingly mediocre and an arrogant cheat to boot."

"Arrogant cheat?" I asked.

"Yes indeed. They come and listen to us play, pat us on the back and nick half our repertoire and arrangements."

"It's the sincerest form of flattery," I said.

"Yeah right!" he growled, stirring the pan more fiercely. "But they get to play in those better-quality clubs before we ever do so it looks like we're just a copy of them."

Oh brilliant, I thought. Now he's telling me we're a cover of a cover band.

He added some vegetables to the pan, finally finishing it off with sambal spicy sauce. "Anyway, that might be changing now. I get the impression club managers are starting to tire of them and they're on the way down. I'm seeing them more and more on the same circuit as us." He winked. "The difference being that we're on the way up, and with our new six-part vocal harmony we're going to knock 'em dead."

After dinner, when the kids were asleep and Roger's mother-in-law had gone to her room, we went into the living room and watched a dubbed version of *Bonanza* on the TV. It was curious and mildly disconcerting to hear Hoss, Pa and Little Joe waffling away in German. I was fascinated and asked a bunch of stupid questions.

Was it the same person doing Little Joe's voice in every episode? Or did he have a light north German accent in one and a rich Bavarian brogue in the next?

Roger shook his head. "No, it's the same voice actor dubbing that character in every episode. Famous actors usually have the same dubbed voice in all their movies."

"Wow! a job for life," I said. "Come to think of it, it's not much different from us. I mean, you guys seem to stick to the same artists that you cover. Kassy's the self-proclaimed godfather of soul, while you're the white man's Ray Charles—"

"And Neil Diamond," he quickly interjected.

"Er, yeah, and Wolly's Wilson Picket…" I continued, but stopped, an uncomfortable thought occurring to me. "Bloody hell! I hope that doesn't make me Karen Carpenter!"

Before we knew it, it was eleven p.m., so we walked back over to Deutsches Haus together. We planned on having a beer before he escorted Mausi home, but when we arrived it was already closed and everything was dark.

"That's funny, we didn't pass anyone on the way here. I wonder where she's got to?" He made light of it and joked, "She might be a bloody pain but she's part of a set and I don't want to lose any of the pieces." He took another quick look up and down the road. "Oh what the hell… She must have gone another way home. Oh! And tell John we are going to see Bachmann in the morning. We'll meet you guys around nine a.m. down in the bar. Goodnight."

I had a door key so I made my way upstairs and found John still awake and reading.

"How did it go with Birgit?"

"Nice. We came up here and messed around. Nothing too naughty though. She was probably put off by the goings-on in the next room. A new couple have moved in and some seriously athletic shagging was going down."

"I would have thought that would put her in the mood."

He sighed and said, "Yeah, well, hopefully next time."

* * *

In the morning, Roger and Wolfgang were already in the bar when we came down to breakfast. Wolfgang was sitting there morosely smoking, being his usual worried self, and I got the feeling all wasn't right with Roger either. He was tapping his fingers impatiently on the table, moaning that Donald was late.

"It's going to be a bummer if we arrive late at Bachmann's office," he complained. "Heinz is a stickler for punctuality."

A breathless Donald rushed in.

"I'm so sorry," he said. "I've been helping my mum and dad chop up the pig and I couldn't leave until it was done."

"I hope you changed your clothes," Roger warned. "We don't want to turn up stinking like an abattoir." He inspected Donald's perfectly laundered beige flares that looked distinctly smarter than his own shabby jeans and grudgingly said, "Hmm... OK. Let's go."

We piled into the Mercedes and headed off towards Mannheim. The road led us through Worms, which in the daylight is not particularly beautiful but has a lot of appeal. It sits on an attractive stretch of the Rhein and is peppered with interesting architecture dating back to medieval times. The city centre is one of the oldest in Germany and ringed by a wall. Within it, historical monuments and buildings in the Romanesque, Gothic and Baroque styles rub up against less attractive utilitarian buildings erected in the immediate aftermath of the war. During the Battle of the Bulge the town was the scene of particularly fierce resistance by the German army and as a consequence, heavily bombed by the RAF.

Leaving Worms, we motored on through vineyards and passed another noteworthy church, this time in the Gothic style: The Liebfrauenkirche, where the first Liebfraumilch wine was produced. After a few more kilometres the surrounding countryside gradually changed from dozing vineyards to a faceless urban sprawl as we approached the outskirts of Mannheim. The buildings were similar in architectural style to Worms but this was more industrial. The city is one of the largest inland ports in Europe. It also sits on the opposite bank of the Rhine to Ludwigshafen, home to BASF, the massive chemical plant.

The road widened and we picked up speed as we passed a dull assortment of factories belching grey smoke into an even darker grey sky while giant cranes loaded and unloaded large ships in the container port. Finally we arrived in the town centre where we found a parking space close to the Paradeplatz.

Making our way down the main street, it struck me how differently people dressed for work here compared to London: smart but not as conventional. Passing a large bank, the cashiers weren't wearing suits or ties and seemed to favour open-necked shirts and pullovers in a kaleidoscope of pastel colours – some even had jeans on. Businessmen carried soft satchels instead of briefcases and looked nowhere near as formal as their British counterparts.

The smells were also different. Germany's fast food stands had a much richer assortment on offer. *Bratwurst, bockwurst* and *currywurst* competed with roasted nuts, kebabs and generous slices of pizza to grease you on your way to a dicky heart. The one fast food you couldn't seem to find however was a hamburger. Strange, as I would have thought it was a German creation.

Roger hurried us along to a modern office block where we took the elevator to the second floor, then made our way down a brightly lit corridor, before arriving at a pair of expensive looking double doors with a sign on it that read:

Heinz Bachmann International Artist & Booking Agency GmbH

The office was bigger than I expected, with several rooms and a staff of around five. Kassy was already there with Heinz. From Roger's references to him, I was fully expecting a cigar-chomping blowhard or at least someone a bit fly, upholstered in camel hair and driving a Jag. But with his perfectly trimmed goatee, short crinkly hair and designer shirt, Heinz Bachmann was a surprisingly gentle spirit. When he greeted us he was softly spoken and I think possibly a little shy. First he introduced John and me to the rest of his team. The ladies greeted us warmly and mumbled a few words of welcome in English, while an older gentleman solemnly shook hands and grunted something in German. Heinz politely asked his secretary to get us some coffee then ushered us into his private office.

Roger lit a cigarette and got straight down to business. "So Heinz, when are you coming to hear us play?"

The secretary came in, served us coffee and handed Heinz a pile of papers.

He glanced at the top page and replied absent-mindedly, "Yes I was just discussing that with Kassy. You are playing in Stockstadt again on Saturday next week? I will be there for that."

"That's good Heinz," said Donald. "We think you are going to be surprised. The band is now sounding quite different."

"Different?" Heinz responded, putting down the papers. "How so?"

"Better. Much better than before. Two guitarists, six-piece vocal arrangements…"

"Spectacular vocal harmonies," added Kassy.

"Hmm OK. You have me intrigued. But you are going to need new band photos." He called out to the next room, "Hannah! Can you book a photo session for The Statesmen next week?"

He turned to Roger, "Tell me. Are you prepared to travel down to Stuttgart one evening to audition for a new club that has just opened? They need a band for the first two weeks in April."

"I guess so," said Roger. "When?"

"I can arrange it for later in February. After you have played in Hanau."

"OK. Sounds good. What kind of club?"

"It's called Happy Night and it's already the top club in Stuttgart. Busy every night and a very fashionable clientele. But I would strongly recommend getting new stage clothes. Shirts and trousers are needed for John and Steve, but if you want to aim for more establishments like Happy Night then maybe evening suits with bow ties?"

I quietly hoped that suggestion would get the thumbs down but unfortunately the others were all dead keen on it. Only John and I had any reservations and I could imagine what Adrian back in Slough would think.

Roger saw the look on our faces. "This is Germany boys and if you look like a million bucks you'll make a million bucks."

"We really need to get into these top clubs," added Kassy, "and to do that we have to look the part."

We both shrugged and I said. "Sure. You know this business better than us." I winked. "Just don't ask me to cut my hair."

We made our goodbyes and arranged to see Heinz the following week in Stockstadt. On the way down in the elevator Roger asked me what I thought of the older gentleman working with the ladies. I hadn't thought anything about him so shook my head.

"He's a strange character," Wolfgang confided. "He came to Mannheim in 1939 and joined the local army regiment. He hates the British and refuses to speak English."

"That's not so weird," I replied.

"It is if your name is Graham and you were born in Bristol!"

CHAPTER SEVEN

Funny Funny

A couple of days later, we returned to Mannheim to visit a tailor's shop where a small Jewish gentleman named Josef was waiting for us. Well known in the German music business for his ostentatious stage costumes, Josef was a cheerful character with a merry gleam in his eye. The others knew him well, and while introductions were made his eyes darted over our torsos, mentally calculating inside leg measurements, which side of the zip the Jolly Roger resided and any physical peculiarities. He would be making shirts and trousers for John and me to match the bands' existing stage uniforms and the new evening suits for the band, which was why we were all present.

Josef took out a large ledger and studied his notes on The Statesmen Singers, then methodically measured every contour of our bodies.

All six of us standing there in only our underpants occasioned Roger to puff out his chest and comment, "Look and admire, Josef. A body women love and men fear."

"And restauranteurs love to feed. You've gained three centimetres around your waist since you were last here."

"A mere detail, my friend. Once we're on the road I'll be back down to my fighting weight in no time. They don't call me snake hips for nothing."

After our measurements had been taken, we were shown some

54

photos of different styles of suits. The seventies was of course the era of cliched flamboyance, the decade that style and good taste slept soundly through. It would have been easy to fall into the trap of autobahn-wide lapels, gold buttons and nut-crunching polyester flares, but Kassy and Donald subtly took charge, steering us in the right direction and exhibiting commendable restraint.

"OK boys, a good choice – timeless and chic," Josef said. "You'll need to return next week for a second fitting but I'll try and have the shirts and trousers ready in time for your concerts in Hanau. The suits will be ready in about a month."

We said goodbye to Kassy and on the journey back to Stockstadt the five of us decided to have dinner together at Deutsches Haus. Mausi was working behind the bar but this evening made a valiant attempt at being welcoming, although she was quick to tell Roger that he shouldn't stay out too late as her mother was looking after the kids.

Wolfgang had dropped in at home to tell his wife where he was going to be and for once came back smiling. "We've decided she's going to take little Sven down to her parents' for a few weeks. I think it's what she really needs." He ordered a large bourbon and Coke and lit a cigarette.

"Wolly, take it easy with the drinking," Roger said, "if you want her to be even happier."

After an enjoyable dinner of *jägerschnitzel* washed down with glasses of pils, we chatted happily for an hour. That evening Wolfgang must have felt like a weight had been lifted from him as he was suddenly another character, happily regaling us with stories about his teenage years in Hamburg. More drinks were ordered but it wasn't long before Mausi began making gestures at Roger.

"Oh fuck, I'd better go," he said. "Wolly, you coming?"

They both got up to leave and Donald said he had to go too and fetch Margit from work. We didn't fancy the honeymoon suite yet so we asked if we could tag along.

The drive took about fifteen minutes along winding country lanes.

The moon was full and in the silver light the zombie arms in the vineyards looked even more spooky. We entered a village on the outskirts of Nierstein. It was similar in style to Stockstadt although the shops and businesses appeared to be more heavily involved in the wine industry than pig farming. The bar was located on one of the back streets.

Pulling into the car park, Donald glanced at his watch and said, "She's still got to work for another half an hour, so we can have a beer while we're waiting."

The interior was quite dark with only a few meagre lanterns on the walls. Faded posters promoting the local wine could just about be discerned. On the tables, flickering light from candles protruding from the stems of empty wine bottles illuminated the faces of the mainly male clientele. We went and sat at the bar and John and Donald ordered beers while I asked for a glass of wine.

Across the room we spotted Margit and – whoa – there she was sitting on some bloke's knee! I hoped she was whispering in his ear because she was certainly doing something in it. Bloody hell, what was that all about?

To top it all off, Donald was positively beaming. "Isn't she great?" he said. "All the customers love her."

I took a peek at John who looked like he was trying to frame the right sort of question. "Don't you get jealous sometimes?" he blurted out. "I mean, what the fuck…?"

His question faded out as Margit sauntered across the room and bent down to whisper something flirtatious in another customer's ear. It was really difficult to see in that light, but I could swear her hand had disappeared down around his privates.

Donald appeared surprised by the question. "No, not at all. She's a pro and knows how to handle the customers. Nobody takes any liberties. Steve, how do you like the Niersteiner? Personally I like it as it's a little drier than Liebfraumilch…"

In the car on the way back home, Margit and Donald were laughing and joking and behaving as though it had been just another boring day at the office. John and I both shrugged philosophically and returned our attention to the zombies in the fields.

Back in Deutsches Haus, the lights were already out, so we made our way silently up to our room. As we lay in our beds we were distracted by the sounds of another round of shagging going on in the room next door. What started as a few dull thumps, accompanied by male grunts and female sighs, soon built in intensity until even our room was shaking. Neither of us had actually seen these guests, and most nights they were quiet as mice.

"Maybe it's the local mayor and his secretary checking in for their bi-weekly shag," I suggested as they reached their climax.

Reflecting on what we had just witnessed in the bar in Nierstein, John said, "Well it's either that or it's Mausi showing a little hospitality to the diners. Nothing would surprise me after tonight."

The following week flew by in a flurry of rehearsals, photo sessions and fittings for our stage clothes. Then it was time for the second of the Saturday dances at Deutsches Haus. It was also the end of the month and on Monday we would begin our first paid gig. Earlier Donald had helped Wolfgang take his wife and son to Darmstadt station. He was now looking much more relaxed, sitting at the bar chatting to Redeye's mum.

Word must have spread following the last dance as there was an even bigger audience in the hall waiting for us to begin. I noticed Birgit and Peter were sitting with a large crowd at a table, while across from them, Margit was standing with another group of girls. When she saw me she eagerly waved me over and introductions were made. All the girls appeared to have names like Uschi, Schnuffy, Sushi and Tuschi which demolished another myth that German women were all lumbered with monikers like Brunhilde, Gretchen or Hildegarde. They were pleasant enough; in fact a couple of them were stunners. Naturally it was the least attractive one that spoke any English.

She stepped forward and asked primly, "Are you Stiff?"

"I beg your pardon?"

"Are you Stiff? Birgit said you are Stiff."

"Actually, the name's Steve," I responded coolly. "Rhymes with leave."

Margit, who had become interested, grinned wickedly and gave my arse a playful pinch. "Don't worry, Uschi, he'll soon be stiff if you press the right buttons!"

Not if I have anything to do with it, I thought grimly. A few moments later Bachmann arrived so with some relief I joined the others on stage and we began the first set.

It was a similar repertoire to the last time, plus some new songs we had rehearsed during the last two weeks. Kassy was doing a nice version of The Temptations' *Papa Was a Rolling Stone* and Donald was singing Cat Steven's *Morning Has Broken*.

When Bachmann joined us after the last encore he was generous in his praise. "*Ja*. I like it. I like it a lot. Maybe we have a chance now to get the band into some of those top clubs we've spoken about. As you know, they mainly prefer the Indonesian bands, and to get into the big Swiss ski resorts you really need sax and trumpet, but this vocal sound you have is very commercial and maybe we can do something with it."

Roger smiled. "Good. We'll hold you to that."

PART TWO

US BASES

CHAPTER EIGHT

American Pie

One thing you couldn't fail to notice when driving through the southern part of West Germany in 1972 was the US military. On autobahns you were certain to pass a lumbering convoy of tanks and jeeps and at most exits or *ausfahrts* you would see road signs adorned with Stars and Stripes stickers giving directions to the nearest *kaserne* or air base. What the Germans thought about it I don't know, but for us it was great as we could tune the car radio to AFN, the American Forces Network, which was much more entertaining than any of the German stations. And now that we were in February the US military were also going to be our employer.

About twenty kilometres from Frankfurt lay the town of Hanau and close by was the Langendiebach US Air Base. For the next two weeks, we would be playing at the enlisted men's club – or the 'EM club' as it was called. We arrived at the base around six p.m. on the first evening and began unloading the equipment. Before we got to the heavy amplifiers, Roger disappeared, explaining he was going to make our presence known to Brad, the manager.

The club was surprisingly big and looked like it could comfortably seat a couple of hundred men. At one end facing the kitchen was a roped-off area with around twenty dining tables, and across from that, a long bar attended by white-jacketed staff mixing cocktails and dispensing drinks. At the other end of the hall was a high stage framed by dark-red velvet curtains with golden tassels. Rather like in a theatre it had wings and backstage there were dressing rooms. Between the stage and the bar were row upon row of tables and chairs where GIs sat in groups and chatted quietly. It had the appearance of a venue that could attract a big audience. But all male? What was that going to be like?

Urgently needing a pee, I went off in search of a loo. When I eventually found it, I was surprised to see it was nothing short of a temple to defecation. It was absolutely massive with yards and yards of urinals. What made my jaw drop though was where you went for a number two. There were thirty or forty lavatories in one row, but alarmingly no dividing walls between them. No doors – *nada!* No doubt the enlisted men had got used to the lack of privacy but I was appalled. Five or six of them were in fact sitting there happily enough, doing their business. One was solving a crossword while another was just staring at the wall opposite. There was of course also one wild spirit who thought it was great sport to give everyone a running commentary on what was happening down below.

"Oh boy, here comes a bad one, better take cover everybody!" This was followed by the noisy arrival of a loud and evil-smelling fart. Delighted with his work, he asked for marks out of ten for pungency and duration.

Very suave, I thought, as I stepped up to the urinals. On the wall behind in large print was a sign that read:

FLUSH TWICE – IT'S A LONG WAY TO THE KITCHENS.

I quickly peed and left.

Roger was back so we took the opportunity to order food. When it arrived, it was a revelation: the hamburgers we couldn't find in Mannheim, rib eye steaks, BBQ chicken with fries, and everything incredibly cheap.

Financial transactions on the bases were in US dollars and, as I would later find out, German shops and restaurants in military towns would accept both currencies. The only downside for us was that we were being paid in dollars while working for the Americans and the exchange rate against the deutschmark was poor, and getting poorer by the day as the German economy was thriving. Not so great for the band, who had to pay German bills.

After dinner we discussed the repertoire for the evening.

"Playing to the Yanks we have a few extra novelty songs." Roger explained. "Nothing complicated, just simple stuff, but listen out for them and follow us. Wolfgang will tell you the key."

"And remember," interjected Kassy, "these guys are at war and none of them are here willingly. They've been drafted and things can get a little wild if we're not careful. We need to keep an eye on what's going on."

Starting at nine p.m. and finishing at eleven thirty p.m., it was an easy gig, more like the ones we had played back in the UK. We began the first set and, as most of the audience were still dining, started slowly with a couple of instrumentals. We followed that with what I thought was a throwaway country and western medley, but it piqued the interest of the guys sitting near the bar and they moved to a couple of tables up front by the stage. Roger followed with *Your Cheating Heart* and suddenly we were a hit – well at least with the cowboy community. He then introduced *The Green Green Grass of Home*. This was one we hadn't rehearsed. Wolfgang shouted across the key and John and I just busked it. It was interesting to hear the lyric Kassy was singing as it differed quite a lot from the Tom Jones' version on my dad's record player.

"The old home town looks the same as they kicked me off the train…"

The boys in front clearly knew this version and were ready and eager to join in with the chorus:

"It's good to smoke the green green grass of home."

There weren't more than twenty of them down there but they made up for it in volume, slapping the tables and cheering when the song ended. A round of beers promptly arrived on stage and we played *Ruby Don't Take Your Love to Town*. In this environment, the significance of the lyrics, about an ex-soldier wounded in action whose wife goes off downtown in search of the satisfaction he can no longer give her, really hit home. When Kassy sang the line *"If I could move I'd get my gun and put her in the ground"*, the place erupted in a deafening roar of approval. After that we took a break.

When we returned for the second set, more servicemen had arrived. Some were young, white guys who went to sit with the others down at the front of the stage, but there were also a group of black and Latino men who occupied some tables further back on the left hand side of the room.

Kassy and Roger had a quick chat, and as we had exhausted our country repertoire, decided we should move on and play a couple of soul tracks to get the black guys involved.

We kicked off with *It's Your Thing* followed by *Papa Was A Rolling Stone*, and sure enough they began to take an interest. Unfortunately down below us the country fans had already started talking loudly amongst themselves.

It was tricky trying to maintain a balance as the tension was palpable. We tried a few pop tracks, a little rock and some Motown, but it became clear we could only satisfy one of the groups at a time.

Finally Roger winked at John and said, "Oh fuck it. Why don't we just piss them all off and do *Beautiful Sunday*?"

That received a two-finger salute from John.

On work days, we would start the day by taking it easy in Stockstadt then drive to the base in the early afternoon so we could eat there and rehearse. I enjoyed the drive because it gave us the opportunity to listen to AFN and the latest music directly from the States. The programs were a mixture of networked shows with well-known DJs like Wolfman Jack and Shadoe Stevens intermingled with locally produced programming. It was a curious contradiction in styles and moods. The Wolfman's wild and crazy rock show would be followed by something mind-numbingly bland featuring Fred and his Simpering Strings or Dale and his Wurlitzer Organ. For every playlist featuring The Doobie Brothers and Three Dog Night there was another with anaesthetised offerings from Mantovani and Ray

Conniff. Shows would be presented by Private First Class this or Air Force Sergeant that, who had almost certainly been professional DJs before being drafted. Commercial advertising wasn't allowed, so obscure public service announcements warning about the dangers of jaywalking or stubbing your fag out on live ammunition would be interspersed with community messages promoting good relations with German hosts.

There was also a busy 'What's On' section, giving a detailed run-down of which movies were playing where – thankfully with their original English soundtrack – which bands were performing in what clubs and what special events were on. There would be baseball, bowling, basketball and American football matches on most nights of the week. It was Middle America right in the middle of Germany.

By the end of the first week, our audience had grown substantially and we were now playing to at least a hundred men each evening. It was constantly challenging balancing the repertoire so it appealed to both the black and the white sections in the club, but we seemed to be getting there. The trick was to move between music genres quickly. No more than two songs in any style and then change. Brad, the club manager, was delighted and must have said something to his commanding officer, who turned up for an inspection with a couple of his officers the next evening.

It was a noisy crowd and we had just finished *Green Green Grass of Home*, which had put them in the mood for more bawdy singalong songs.

Kassy turned to Roger and suggested, "Last one before the break. *Popeye the Sailor Man?*"

"Yeah, why not."

"It's in G major," Wolfgang said, "and we do it in a ska rhythm."

Many of the audience recognised it straight away and a loud cheer went up.

"I'm Popeye the sailor man. I'm Popeye the sailor man. I slept with a duck. What a wonderful fuck. I'm Popeye the sailor man."

And so it went on, getting progressively ruder and more sexually graphic. The audience were clapping their hands and stamping their feet to the rhythm and joined in enthusiastically on the choruses. It ended to loud cheering and we took our break, thinking job well done.

"It's bloody hot in here," remarked Roger. "I'm off outside for some fresh air."

"I'll join you," I said.

We got about five yards outside the front entrance before a loud, commanding voice stopped us.

"You there! Yeah, you. That's right, I'm talking to you, mister."

We turned to face the owner of the loud voice and were confronted by a beefy, purple-faced officer with a string of campaign ribbons on his chest. He was surrounded by a group of equally intense junior officers staring at us gravely. He strode over, looked us up and down and demanded in a clipped parade-ground voice, "What's your name, buddy?"

Roger licked his lips uneasily. "What for?"

"OK, Bob Ford, just let me say this. Profane language is not acceptable in this club. Understood?"

"Who's Bob Ford?" asked Roger.

"Don't play games with me, mister," the officer growled impatiently.

Over his shoulder, Brad was making urgent hand signals to calm things down, so Roger mewed up a half-hearted apology. "Yeah, whatever." Turning on an ounce more charm, he went on, "You're absolutely right. Big mistake on our part. Won't do it again."

The officer digested this for a moment then relaxed. "Good. I'm happy we understand each other. Keep it clean, Bob, we don't like profanity."

Unfortunately, the audience chose that exact moment to strike up a lusty acapella reprise of the Popeye song, landing Bob and his boys right back in the shit. The officer's eyes narrowed and he gave us one final, murderous look before turning and stalking off.

Brad smiled apologetically. "Don't worry, he won't come here again. He usually sticks to the officers' club. Anyway forget whatever he said. Keep that song in. You're playing for those guys in there, not him."

CHAPTER NINE

Beautiful Sunday

Sundays were our day off. On this particular one, Birgit came by in the afternoon with a group of female friends. This included Uschi, who greeted me with an intense, sorrowful gaze. Oh cripes, I thought, she's still interested.

The bar at Deutsches Haus was busy but we managed to find the last free table in a corner. Uschi continued to fix me with a manic stare, blowing smoke rings in my face, probably believing that this would make me find her irresistible. It wasn't working.

But I was fascinated by a group of people at the next table. Something was strange about them. Three guys and a blonde girl were sitting in grim silence, all hunched together with body language that broadcast in large text 'do not disturb'. They were all dressed democratically in the same urban guerrilla chic: flak jackets, Palestinian scarves and jeans. As I leant over to get a better look, one of their number – the girl, who was not at all bad looking – saw me staring and glared pure ice.

OK, maybe not. I turned my attention back to our group. John and Birgit were deep in conversation and Uschi had started a second cigarette's worth of smoke rings. Suddenly I began to feel hemmed in. *Mamy Blue* had just come on the jukebox, so I took that as an opportunity to escape.

Mamy Blue by the Pop Tops was one of the most popular songs in

Germany that winter and we had endured the lingering torture of hearing it wherever we went. In a quiet effort to raise the quality of music in the bar I squeezed past the quartet on the next table, strolled over to the jukebox and slipped a mark in the slot. Hmm… *Ride a White Swan*. That should do the trick.

I went back to our group and asked, "Shall we get some beers in?"

Without warning, the door to the street flew open and a small army of police barged in, swarming all over the place, yelling orders, brandishing machine guns and heading straight for the blonde and her friends at the next table. Even Uschi's smoke rings seemed to freeze in terror as the police rushed past us and tackled the flak-jacketed group to the floor. Furniture, plates and glasses went flying as the group fiercely fought back. The blonde resisted particularly viscously, kicking and screaming as she was dragged outside. The others were arm-locked, handcuffed and unceremoniously bundled out onto the street where a fleet of police vehicles were waiting. It was all over before Marc Bolan had time to reach his guitar solo. Sirens screaming, the police cars and vans roared off down the road, leaving the bar in shocked silence.

"Ride a white swan like the people of the Beltane. Wear your hair long, babe you can't go wrong," the jukebox continued, blissfully unaware.

It took a few moments before anyone could react. When they did, it possibly wasn't the most appropriate first line.

"What the fuck does that mean? *Like the people of the Beltane*?" John asked in a stunned voice.

We all stared at him in bewilderment, then someone laughed nervously and we were all talking at once. One of the locals – a snaggle-toothed character usually stationed at the end of the bar nursing a small beer – wandered over and told the ladies that Redeye had been outside in the courtyard a few minutes earlier, having a quiet smoke, when he was approached by a plain-clothed police officer and asked to identify some people in a photo and confirm if they were in the bar. The suspects arrested were thought to be members of the Baader-Meinhof Gang.

Back in 1972, not many people outside of Germany had heard of Andreas Baader or Ulrike Meinhof. The Baader-Meinhof Gang, or the Red Army Faction as they called themselves, were a Maoist terrorist outfit dedicated to the violent overthrow of the state. They'd been responsible for attacks on US bases, bank robberies and brutal murders of police officers. A nasty bunch, bent on mayhem. In the years to come, as I read about their increasingly bloody exploits, my thoughts would drift back to that Sunday afternoon in a sleepy German village and how I had thought that the most dangerous person in the room that day had been Uschi, with her manic look, cloaked in a nicotine fog.

We needed something to calm our nerves, but soon realised Redeye was far too busy being the centre of attention to be bothered with anything as prosaic as serving drinks, so we wandered outside.

John and Birgit hadn't seen much of each other since we started playing in Langendiebach. He was offering her the prospect of going upstairs later so I quietly suggested that maybe I should take a walk.

"Thanks for the offer, but no need."

"Why? Does that mean I have to watch?"

"You wish. No. The room next door is empty. The shagathon contestants have checked out. I tried the door and it was unlocked. Looks like they've gone so I thought Birgit and I could go in there."

The afternoon turned to evening and we stayed in the bar drinking and chatting. Mausi arrived to begin her shift and after listening in breathless amazement to Redeye's account of the afternoon's excitement, came over and took our orders for food.

Later, after dinner, when John and Birgit had gone upstairs, Uschi took me aside and asked, "You want me to come to your room with you, Stiff?"

Oh God, now I was going to have to spell it out. "No thanks, but it was kind of you to ask."

She wasn't a woman to be put off so lightly. "Why? You don't like *bumsen*?"

"*Bumsen?*"

"*Ja. Wie heißt es? Liebe, macht love?*"

Avoiding her stare, I was silent for a minute, which she simply took as me needing further clarification.

"Sex! You want sex with me?"

Her Teutonic directness prompted an equally English polite embarrassment in me. "Oh! That's really, very very kind. But no thanks."

"Very kind?" she snapped. "Are you mad? Stiff, are you *schwul*?"

"*Schwul*?"

"*Ja*, you like men for *bumsen*?"

"No! Look, I'm sorry," I said. "But I just wanna go upstairs and read my book…"

I knew it was pathetic, but she seemed to get the message. Shaking her head, she went back to the others, who were now regarding me with interest. Shit, why couldn't I just tell her to fuck off? Climbing the stairs to the room, I could imagine the conversation around the table and instinctively knew that Stockstadt was the kind of place where lynching a *schwul* wouldn't even raise an eyebrow.

I read for a bit then fell asleep. Some hours must have passed when I was abruptly woken by a loud commotion outside the door. I got up to investigate and what greeted me was a tableau straight from a bedroom farce. Standing in the open doorway to the next room, Redeye was shouting at John and Birgit, who were struggling out of bed, trying to cover themselves up.

"At least fuck off while we get our clothes on. Bloody pervert!" John shouted indignantly.

Just then I spotted someone standing in the shadows, which added more than a little jolt of intrigue to the situation. It was Mausi. What was she doing up here? And what was Redeye doing? He and his mother lived up the other staircase behind the bar. I hadn't seen him here since that first day. And why was Mausi being so quiet? She was no shrinking violet, especially on the subject of dirty Englishmen. I guessed there might be an explanation, but remembering the noises coming from that room during the past week, one theory was going through my mind, and it wasn't a pleasant one.

CHAPTER TEN

There Goes My Everything

Back at the EM club, it was business as usual. Being around US servicemen so much was having an unexpected impact on our vocabulary. We would come out with phrases like 'can ya dig it', 'at ease disease' or 'hang a right Dwight'. Kilometres became 'clicks' and anyone returning to the States was 'going back to the world'. It was weird how easily we slipped into it and I had the uncomfortable feeling that if we played a few more months in this place we would all be jive talking worse than Huggy Bear.

It was at one of these parlays with the guys in the audience that I heard there was a fair bit of excitement about Saturday's show. A sexy female dance troupe from Paris was on the program together with us. As it was also our last evening, it promised to be an interesting finale.

During our last trip over in the car, we had talked about touring and what we would do if, or when, it was time to quit. Donald predicted he would be dragged into the family business raising pigs. His father had been happy doing this and he hoped his son would take over one day. Donald wasn't at all sure that life was for him. He loved being a musician, but if he couldn't be that he fancied working in dentistry.

"Dentistry?" Roger exclaimed. "Pulling teeth instead of raising young pigs to become sausages? That'll please your dad."

Donald looked at him evenly and said, "At least I've got a plan.

What's yours?"

Roger thought for a moment, then said, "Back in England I worked in a shoe shop in Mayfair. Leathering up the great and good. No way I'm going back to that, though. After show business I can't do shoe business. No, we're just going to have to become unimaginably successful."

Wolfgang had been a musician since leaving school so hadn't a clue what else he wanted to do. John surprised us all by saying he could easily go back to the illuminated ceilings business.

"I enjoyed the job, the product was easy to sell and I think I could have been promoted quickly into becoming an area rep." He shrugged. "I can think of worse things. A nice little house in Farnham Common and a company car."

I thought about what I would return to if this all ended. I couldn't go back to the insurance company – that was always a temporary choice – but would I work in a studio again? Roger interrupted my thoughts.

"It's alright for you, Steve, working with The Beatles. Biggest band in the world coming and going, stopping for a chat over the coffee machine about Maharishi, the meaning of life, Hare Krishna…"

"More like Harry Secombe," I teased. "I do however remember Ringo asking me for something very important."

"Oh yea? What?"

"Milk and two sugars."

My first job out of school had been in a post-production studio in West London, working as a trainee sound engineer, which was a polite way of describing making the tea and running errands. We worked with feature films and had studios for recording voices and sound effects, a row of cutting rooms and a small movie theatre for viewing rushes. It was a magnet for art house films, some of which never saw the light of day while others gained critical and sometimes even box office success.

On my first day of work, I remember being hastily recruited to provide footstep sound effects on a hardwood floor for a movie by Lindsay Anderson called *If*, a satirical movie about life in a public school. About a week later Mick Jagger began coming in to view rushes and re-record dialogue for a movie he was appearing in called *Performance*. This was followed by an American movie called *Husbands* which was being shot on location in London by iconic actor and director John Cassavetes. Around the same time, Roman Polanski dropped by to watch his heavily pregnant wife Sharon Tate in her last movie *Twelve Plus One*. I made tea for her while she reclined on a specially rigged-up daybed in the studio, re-dubbing her dialogue scene by scene. She was incredibly sweet and everyone in the crew fell in love with her. Tragically, just a couple of weeks later, after she returned to Hollywood, she was brutally murdered by Charles Manson's followers.

One of the last movies I worked on before leaving was The Beatles' *Let It Be*. Unfortunately it wasn't a happy production as the band were showing signs of splitting up. Paul McCartney, who appeared to have taken on more of a leadership role, came to the studio a number of times to view rushes and talk to Michael Lindsay-Hogg, the director, and Tony Lenny, the editor. Ringo also came by once and I fixed tea for him, but the others didn't seem terribly interested. Shame really, as I was a fan.

When it was completed the film company sat on the movie for about a year while the band argued about how it should be released. During that time I got my own band to cover one of the McCartney songs called *Two of Us* and that was John's and my first record together. It was released on the Pye label and sank without a trace.

Returning to the present, we entered the EM club for the last time and were delighted to be introduced to a troupe of lovely French female dancers. I wondered absently if they would be sharing our dressing room and mentally pictured us all in our underwear having a cosy tête-à-tête. That dream evaporated when they were led off by Brad to their own dressing room on the other side of the stage.

Later we went down to the dining area and ordered some food. Recently I had been getting a bit tired of the constant cheeseburgers and club sandwiches so had been branching out and experimenting with the daily special. This was always something new and often a dish I'd never tried before. Today it was meatloaf. It was pretty damn good as well and when we'd finished eating I decided, for old times' sake, to take a last pee in the infamous open-plan toilet.

It was a similar scattering of guys going about their private business in public, although there were a lot more of them this time. It no longer shocked me as much, so I happily went over and took a pee. Just as I was zipping up I felt a sharp stabbing pain grip me around the abdomen. Damn! I needed to move fast if I wanted to get to the backstage loo. I started for the door but fatalistically just knew I wasn't going to make it and would have to take a shit in this awful place.

With as much self-control as I could muster I sprinted over to the seat at the end. It was still only one away from the next guy but he was busy reading his magazine. Miserably I sat there before erupting in an uncontrollable frenzy of trumpeting farts accompanied by diarrhoea. I knew it was bad when I realised the other guys were staring at me with interest.

My neighbour had lowered his magazine and asked, "The meatloaf?"

I nodded in anguish as I felt another spasm coming on. My insides dissolved and I held on with both hands. I felt wretched. Damn it, why couldn't I be more like these guys about this lavatory business? Instead I was being all English and apologetic. At last the pain subsided and I felt well enough to make a graceful if hasty exit. My neighbour, who was warming to the subject of the crap food, asked what the rush was for so I explained I needed to hurry as I was short on time.

He smiled enigmatically and said, "No problem my friend, I have plenty. Have some of mine."

When I returned to the band table, a minor altercation was going on. Everyone else had eaten but John's food hadn't arrived yet.

"John, we're on in ten minutes," Roger cautioned. "It's time to go."

"Sorry. You'll have to speak to the waitress."

"Why? Does she play keyboard?" he inquired.

"Possibly. I don't know, but she's the reason I haven't eaten yet."

"Look, I know you see these evenings as a social occasion. A time to meet the chaps, exchange some jokes, have dinner and if the muse is with you play a little music. But it's a gig and if we want the money we need to go up and play now."

Conveniently, at exactly that moment, his meal arrived. I looked with interest to see if he was having the meatloaf. That would have been interesting. But no, it was the usual hamburger.

We made ourselves ready and prepared to start playing. The French ladies had come out of their dressing room to watch and I was exchanging admiring looks with a winsomely sexy brunette. She spoke broken English with a delicious French accent which pressed all of my buttons.

It was a full house so we went straight for the up-tempo repertoire, beginning with *Mustang Sally*, following on with *Celebrate* and *Rainy Day Feeling*, mixing soul, rock and pop freely so each side of the club would feel included. Many of the audience knew it was our last evening and between songs trays of beers arrived on stage. When we reached the end of the set the audience stood up and applauded warmly. It had been a pleasant two-week engagement and personally I would be quite sad to say goodbye.

Backstage, we bumped into Brad, who was busy lighting a cigar and grinning wickedly.

"I've had an idea," he announced. "What about if you guys get dressed up in drag to look like these French broads, then go back on stage before them, dancing to their music?" He waited for a response but, receiving only blank stares, continued, "We keep the lighting down low so the boys don't cotton on too quick, but what a joke when everybody realises it's you!"

We all began to object at once, but Brad airily brushed any

reservations aside and insisted everyone would love it. Finally, with some reluctance, we agreed and stripped down to our underpants while Brad's assistant hurried off in search of bras and other female accoutrements. Five minutes later he came back from the ladies' dressing room laden down with enough stuff to open a bordello.

We picked up a few bits and pieces and I ended up with a black bra and some kind of plumage for around my neck. After a quick inspection I could see we all looked pretty dodgy except for Wolfgang who, with his flowing blonde hair, heavily made-up eyes, rouge lipstick and padded bra looked strangely alluring. John by contrast looked downright rough with bright lipstick, a bristling moustache and his two mutton-chop sideburns.

When we emerged from the dressing room it was to howls of laughter from the stagehands and the Frenchies. Oh well. I had probably just blown any chance with the brunette.

Not having much clue about saucy Parisian dance routines, we lined up like the dance troupes you see on British variety programmes and waited while Brad went on stage to introduce the act. With the fat cigar still stuck out of one side of his mouth, he inspected the packed club and began.

"OK boys, it's time for the big one and I really mean big one. There's a gang of gorgeous, sexy babes back here who have come all the way from Gay Paree just to tease you and please you and rock your world. Are you men enough for it?"

A thundering roar was the response.

Behind the curtain, I glanced nervously at the others and whispered, "Roger, are you sure this is going to be alright?"

He shrugged and said, "What the fuck they gonna do? Draft us?" Fussily he pulled his scarlet leather peep-hole bra further down his chest, stuck his chin out and purred sexily, "OK tigers, let's go get 'em!"

When the music began it was a big, blousy vaudeville number and I thought we choreographed it pretty well in the circumstances. The curtains flew open and with big, cheesy smiles in place we kicked and high-stepped our way across the stage. The all-male audience went absolutely wild and jumped up from their seats, cheering and applauding. It was going great. We were a hit… Bastards! We were getting much more applause now than when we played.

We hoofed, we shimmied and shook our bits and by the time we reached the other side of the stage were on such a high we did a smart about-turn, puffed our chests out and began the return journey.

By now the regulars might have recognised us, as I noticed some of them laughing, but the rest didn't seem to realise it was us. However, as they started to get a closer look at all the facial hair, they must have twigged that we weren't what was advertised and the mood changed.

That's about when the first salvo hit the stage. It started with a few martini olives but quickly progressed to side salads and bread rolls. Something soggy flew over our heads and before they could move on to the meatloaf we quickened our pace, all the while trying to keep our sickly smiles in place. Somebody's nerve broke – I think it was Donald's – and in a disorganised rabble we finally scampered off to a mixed reaction of laughter, flying food, boos and cat-calls.

Everyone backstage was in fits of hysterics, especially the Frenchies, who promptly went off to prepare their own opening number. There was a lot of backslapping from Brad and his crew, who were commenting on us being such good sports – for a bunch of Limeys and Krauts. We took that as a cue to quickly escape, before he could come up with any further wild ideas, and retired to our dressing room to recover with some well-earned beers.

CHAPTER ELEVEN

Black and White

Despite Bachmann's optimism, there were only a few one-nighters on US bases and a gala in Mannheim booked for the second part of February. We would also have to drive down to Stuttgart for the audition at the Happy Night.

The one-night stands at the bases started off easily enough with an officers' club in Mannheim, but two evenings later we had to drive to Kaiserslautern for a special Irish evening at an enlisted men's club. Arriving at the main gates, we were surprised and not a little disconcerted to see a large poster with our name on it and a description of us as 'The Fighting Irish'.

The club manager was there to meet us when we arrived. He was a large, fleshy gentleman with a broad smile and a thick Southern accent. He greeted us warmly, but it was apparent he was disappointed by our obvious lack of Irishness.

Staring suspiciously at Kassy, he inquired, "So, where do you good folks hail from?"

Wolfgang grunted something about Hamburg but Roger interrupted him.

"Forgive Mr O'Toole's humour. The Great British Isles, dear chap. And your good self? Do I detect the soft lilt of the Emerald Isle?"

He may have had a Polish surname for all we knew, but he was delighted somebody thought he was Irish. Even so, his eyes kept wandering sceptically back to Kassy, no doubt wishing he could transform us into Johnny Green and The Greenmen. They were an American band with Irish antecedents who had recently completed a tour of the US bases. With bright-green hair and emerald suits, they were hugely popular with the Irish-American crowd. Anyway, there wasn't much he could do about it now so he wished us well for the evening and left us to finish setting up.

As luck would have it, the audience weren't that bothered and seemed to think good music was more important than bright-green hair. John's informal education in the saloon bars of Slough came in handy as we busked our way through Irish classics like *Danny Boy*, *The Wild Rover* and finished with a rousing version of *When Irish Eyes are Smiling*.

Undeterred by considerations of verity, Bachmann continued to market us with just a hint of desperation. A few evenings later this resulted in an encounter with an infinitely tougher audience.

It was another army base near Kaiserslautern, but this time the posters plastered all along the front of the club announced that we were a soul band from Detroit. It didn't say in so many words that we were a black group but the implication was obvious. It was the first time I heard Roger completely lose it.

"Fucking Bachmann!" he exploded. "What that bastard won't do for his lousy ten percent."

The club was empty when we unloaded the equipment so there was nobody to talk to about it, although I doubt it would have done much good. The club manager, when he did arrive, was another beefy, good old boy. He took one look at us and did a quick double-take before smothering a huge grin and asking how we all were.

"We're not feeling very black today, sir," Roger said with a hint of sarcasm. "But apart from that, everything's delightful. And how are you?"

"Good, good." He beamed, ignoring the irony. He was clearly having trouble keeping a straight face and quickly made an excuse and left. As his footsteps faded down the hall we could hear him hooting with laughter.

We built up the stage in silence and went off to get ready, feeling like turkeys when the Christmas decorations are going up.

For once Roger wasn't his usual cocky self; he was biting his lip and seemed deep in thought.

"OK, chaps, we can do this," he said. "Let's just get focused on the soul repertoire. I think we'll leave Hank Williams and Johnny Cash for another occasion." He scribbled on a notepad. "Kassy. *Papa Was a Rolling Stone, My Girl, Sex Machine, It's Your Thing.*"

Well, this all made a lot of sense.

He carried on, "Wolfgang. *6345789, Mustang Sally.* John!"

"*Oui, mon général?*"

"Hmm, John." His eyes darted down our song list. "Of course! *Beautiful Sunday.*"

"Are you joking? It's by Daniel Boone. They'll murder me!"

"Er, yeah, OK. *If I Were a Carpenter.*"

I looked at him in surprise and said, "What? Tim Hardin?"

"No, the Four Tops version."

"Yeah, but if you follow that reasoning we may as well do *Besame Mucho,*" I argued. "I once heard The Black and White Minstrels do it."

"There's a thought," he said. "Maybe we could black up?" He considered the idea before his eyes came to rest on Wolfgang. "Maybe not. No, fuck it, we'll just have to wing it. Right! Eyes and teeth, *meine herren.*"

The curtains flew back and we started the riff to *Papa Was a Rolling Stone.* Oh shit, the place was packed to the rafters and there wasn't another white face to be seen. They weren't exactly hostile but there wasn't a lot of *gemütlichkeit* on view either. The group closest to me were all sucking sullenly on bottles of Bud, making it abundantly clear we were the wrong band in the wrong club. To gloomy stares we soldiered on, grinding our way doggedly through The Temptations' number.

At least one chap in front of the stage was digging it, and big time. He was smiling up at us with huge teeth and wild eyes while gyrating crazily in circles in front of the stage. When we reached the end of the song and he didn't stop I realised he probably wasn't firing on all four cylinders. He continued to caper about with legs and arms flying, oblivious to the deafening silence from the rest of the room.

Roger took stock of the situation and to our surprise started beating out the same rhythm again, shouting to Wolfgang to join him.

"I'm gonna try something," he said to the rest of us.

Turning to the audience and projecting the oiliest of grins, he began, "Good evening everyone, and thanks for the great welcome. It's wonderful to be here in this fabulous club with you tonight. Just wonderful."

Glancing balefully around at the rest of us, he snarled off-mike, "Just fucking wonderful."

Switching the charm back on, he beamed around and asked, "Anybody here from the East Coast?" He repeated the question and a few hands went up. "Anybody here from Philly?" A few more hands. "What about Detroit?"

Even more hands and a few enthusiastic shouts. They were starting to creep out of their apathetic shells.

"My friends, I'm looking for a guitarist. Have we got any of those in the club?" A few hands went up. "I want a guitarist who's gonna come up here and show us how this song really should be played. Where is that man? Come on, send him up here!"

There was movement and joshing around amongst the group in front of me and a tall, skinny boy was thrust forward.

"And here he comes. Come on, give that man a big round of applause."

He climbed up on the stage to claps and cheers and Roger signalled to Donald to give him his guitar. The new arrival quickly picked up the groove.

"OK, I got me a guitarist, do I got me an organist?" Roger continued, his voice rising in pitch and sounding more and more like an Alabama preacher. "Where's my Booker T? Lord show me the brother who's gonna tickle my ivories!"

I thought he might be getting too evangelical, but the audience seemed to be enjoying it, the atmosphere becoming perceptibly warmer. If he carried on like this we would be doing baptisms and speaking in tongues next.

A lively looking young guy came up and took over from John; he was shortly followed by a replacement for Wolfgang on bass. Kassy quietly excused himself while I looked over at the group the other guitarist had come from. A cheerful character looked eagerly at me. I nodded and he made his way up. Now it was only the Reverend Roger we had to find a replacement for. A big, stocky guy climbed up and smoothly took over, laying down a solid, funky beat. With one last, crazy salute to the crowd Roger joined the rest of us at the bar.

As the drinks were arriving, John asked, "What happens when the song is finished?"

Roger took a sip of his beer and said, "They'll carry on all night now they've got the keys to the candy store."

Sure enough, that's exactly what happened. Another guy who turned out to be an excellent singer joined them on stage and from then on there wasn't much else for us to do, other than order another round of drinks, sit back and relax. By closing time it was impossible to get them to stop so the MPs were called to disburse the crowd, after which we were able to pack up and go home.

CHAPTER TWELVE

A Family Affair

For the next gig we would be playing to a German audience. February is the carnival season and in Germany that means *Fasching*. In the predominantly Catholic southern part of the country it's an important festival with extravagant costume parades, parties and masked balls. Being a last-chance saloon before the arrival of Lent – with its associated fasting, moderation and spiritual discipline – *Fasching* is the perfect opportunity to eat your own weight in meat, drink a tank of alcohol, shag your neighbour's wife and generally let your hair down. We would be playing at such a *Fasching* ball in a large auditorium called the Rosengarten in central Mannheim. One of four different acts on at the ball, it promised to be a lively evening.

As we arrived at the stage door, we spotted Josef parking his car. With the help of his assistant he unloaded a number of suit bags and waddled over. He gamely tried to shake hands with each of us while holding on to his precious load.

"Heinz has been on to me to get these ready for you by tonight. I worked *mein verdammter arsch* off!" he said.

"I'm surprised he didn't ask you to run off a set of lederhosen, so he could book us into a couple of bierkellers as well," Roger remarked drily.

But I could see he was delighted to get the suits in time for the audition in Stuttgart.

Josef couldn't stay as he had another appointment, so he hastily said goodbye as we unpacked the van.

We organised the equipment and located our dressing room where the new suits were waiting to be tried on. Paper tags with our names on were attached to the lapels but a couple had come adrift, so there was an uncomfortable few moments when Wolfgang tried to get into Kassy's trousers, but that was quickly sorted. At last we stood back and admired ourselves in the mirrors. Well we did look devilishly smart but mentally running it past my mentor 'Whispering Bob' of The Old Grey Whistle Test, I wasn't sure the prog rock crowd would have approved.

I realised it could have been a lot worse though when I saw the first band troop on stage. It was a traditional folk act wearing white, embroidered shirts, lederhosen and trilbies with small feather plumes in the hatband. They oompahed, yodelled and slapped their thighs and the audience just lapped it up. Their vocals had that typically echoing sound that created an illusion they were singing to us from the darkest corner of the gents' toilet, but it was perfect – we were back in Germany.

From Mannheim the next stop would be Stuttgart and the audition at the Happy Night. We set off in the afternoon. Kassy and Wolfgang took the VW while the rest of us followed behind in the Mercedes. It was still a novelty driving on the autobahn and there were countless numbers of them criss-crossing the country. Many were old, dating back to Hitler's time, so were not up to the job of carrying the amount of traffic that was now using them at such eye-watering speeds. Two-lane highways were the norm, and the lack of speed limits added more than a dash of terror as crazy-eyed drivers weaved their way through fast-moving traffic with the desperation of getaway drivers fleeing a bank job that had gone horribly wrong.

After about an hour we stopped to calm our nerves, drink some coffee and refuel. I think that was the first time I noticed the Gypsies.

The common conception in Britain at that time was that Gypsies lived in beaten-up old caravans and came round your house hawking clothes pegs and lavender. But these people looked like they had won the lottery. Their clothes were still a giveaway, but they were driving big Mercs and flashing huge wodges of cash.

Wolfgang saw me staring at a group of them as they crossed the car park. I commented that they looked surprisingly well off and he explained that they received money from the German government as a form of reparation for their ill treatment under the Nazis.

"And they're dangerous buggers," said Roger grimly. "So stay the hell away from them."

The Happy Night was a much more modern establishment than the Imperial. Black carpets and walls with chrome and full-length mirrors, illuminated by studio spotlights, gave it a very funky appearance.

The resident band's equipment was already in position on the stage and we were told we could use it for the audition, so after a quick soundcheck we went off to find the nearest Wienerwald restaurant. These were a nationwide chain serving primarily chicken dishes – usually decent quality at a reasonable price. As we were in a hurry, we all ordered the same thing: half a roast chicken and fries. When the chickens arrived, served up cheerfully by an attractive waitress, five of them were perfect, plump and succulent, while the one Wolfgang received was thin and scrawny.

"Excuse me, dear lady," he said. "Don't you think my bird looks a little undernourished? Either that or it's clocked up too many flying hours."

She inspected his plate and then him, taking in the long hair and thin face. "It's got a damn sight more meat on it than you have!" she remarked casually.

Expecting him to respond with something rude, he surprised us all by grinning and saying, "I knew it, the woman fancies me! It's the old Wolly magic."

Winking at him, she strolled off smiling to herself leaving him, despite the Wolly magic, to eat the scrawny chicken.

Back at the Happy Night, we were just changing into our suits when the manager came by to say hello. Scanning the room, he nodded approvingly, so the new stage clothes were doing their job. He told us a little about the club, gave us a bit of a pep talk and warned us that the audience could occasionally be slow to get going.

"No surprises there," Wolfgang remarked after he left. "The Schwaben aren't exactly famous for fun and frivolity."

"They haven't heard us yet," Roger said. "Righto men, let's get out there and do the business."

Promptly at nine p.m., we went on stage and began a set of our most modern dance songs. The audience looked like a hip crowd so I thought they might be difficult to engage with, but it didn't take much coaxing to get them up onto the dance floor. After playing for farmers and men at war, it was good to see a young German audience enjoying the music. We kept the tempo up and the dance floor remained packed for the full forty-five minute set. To top it off we finished to an enthusiastic round of applause.

The manager was delighted. He came backstage with a bottle of sparkling sekt wine and six glasses and said he looked forward to seeing us in April. That was brilliant. We needed a decent job for April and now we had two weeks booked in what appeared to be a great club.

From there it would have been much easier to travel straight on to Munich, but for some unexplained reason it had already been decided we should drive back to Stockstadt to spend the last night there.

Arriving at Deutsches Haus sometime after midnight, Roger asked if he could borrow a book and followed us up to our room. The bar was closed so we quietly climbed the stairs and bumped straight into Redeye and Mausi coming out of the room next door to ours. John and I immediately grasped the situation and it didn't take Roger much longer. I fully expected him to cry 'Infamy!' and invite us to be his seconds. As it was, he did the next best thing.

"What the fuck's this?" he barked. "What are you doing up here?" His gaze swivelled around to the short gentleman beside Mausi. "With him?"

The last two words were delivered in such a derisive tone that Redeye felt obliged to pull himself up to his full five foot four inches and brush his fingers through what little hair he had.

Mausi stared straight back at him, eyes blazing. "What do you think is going on!" she snapped. "You're never home and I don't know what you get up to while you're away! When you are here we never do anything together. Is it so strange?"

The argument continued so John and I tactfully retired to our room. After a while the heated conversation subsided and they must have gone home. There wasn't much else to do but to get some sleep; it was going to be an early start.

A few hours later, probably around six a.m., I woke to hear some stones being thrown at our window. I drowsily got up and looked out. There was Roger, standing in the street beside a couple of suitcases. We were leaving early, but not this early. Grumbling to myself I crept downstairs and opened the door. I doubted he'd had any sleep but he seemed remarkably chipper when we reached our room.

"Morning boys. Sorry about the drama last night. I should have known something was going on."

It probably wasn't a good idea to say anything about our own suspicions, so we just sat and listened.

"Anyway, I'm moving out. She's welcome to all this shit. When I've got something sorted I'll work out an arrangement to see the kids." He walked over to the window and stared out. "Things haven't been right for ages so it's time that we both faced up to it, especially as we're off to Munich now. It'll give me time to get my head around things. But I'm not going to let that knob downstairs have it all his own way, so get your bags packed and let's get everything out of here quietly and round to Donald's. The bastard can whistle for the money we owe."

We shrugged as I don't think either of us had a problem doing a moonlight, and apart from all the meals and drinks, we owed the rent for February.

Roger put up a cautionary hand and said, "Just don't say anything to Donald yet. He won't like it if we skip off without paying." He cracked a smile and rubbed his hands together. "Right chaps, we're getting out of this dump and off on tour. And the forecast said the weather's going to be good, so Munich here we come!"

His enthusiasm was contagious and suddenly we were all laughing as we packed our bags and crept downstairs.

PART THREE

MUNICH

CHAPTER THIRTEEN

Everything is Beautiful

I was captivated. Broad, clean boulevards lined with elegant boutiques serving stylish, well-dressed shoppers. Open-air beer gardens, manicured parks and eye-catching, modern architecture rubbed shoulders with gracious period buildings and what better natural backdrop than a big slice of the Alps. Munich – I was in love.

After a stop for lunch on the autobahn, I had volunteered to accompany Kassy in the VW and we were now driving leisurely down the Leopoldstraße through Schwabing, which was the fashionably hip quarter and dotted with smart bars and cafes. Happy couples sat at outside tables enjoying the warm spring sunshine while toasting each other with bubbling glasses of sekt. It all looked wonderful and felt a million miles away from what we had just left behind in Stockstadt.

We drove on, passing the Neoclassical architecture of the university before arriving at Maximiliansplatz and the bustling Stachus with its pedestrianised shopping area and magnificent fountains. If we had stopped there it would have been perfect, but alas, we had been warned the club was located in a distinctly less salubrious area.

Sure enough we turned right by a large Kaufhof department store and made our way down the Bayerstraße, a nondescript thoroughfare that got seedier by the block. Passing a clutch of fast food joints, X-rated *kinos* and massage parlours, we moved into the city's multi-cultural quarter. At last we pulled up in front of *München Hauptbahnhof* where Kassy made a sudden unannounced, but quite spectacular, U-turn and we were at our destination – Cafe Arcadia. Donald's Mercedes arrived shortly after and Roger, who was still surprisingly bright and eager, hopped out bristling with efficiency.

"OK, chaps, leave this to me. I'll go and speak to the powers that be while you get the gear upstairs."

Knowing looks passed between the rest of us as we wearily began lifting the gear out of the van.

The club was on the first floor, directly above an espresso bar and optician's. It wasn't too bad. Not as opulent as the Imperial or as modern as the Happy Night, but acres of red velvet, subdued lighting and the type of furniture you see in American diners gave it a certain retro style. Plate glass windows faced the street and a small but serviceable stage was set up against the windows. I guessed we could amuse ourselves by watching the comings and goings at the *hauptbahnhof* between songs. Tables and chairs surrounded the dance floor and beside the long, L-shaped bar was a raised platform accommodating a row of more intimate booths.

Ready for a soundcheck, we tuned the guitars while Kassy went off in search of Roger. The two of them eventually appeared together with a lively looking individual called Ivo, who introduced himself as the club's manager. He was a cheerful character in his late thirties with thinning blonde hair and thick, metal-rimmed tinted glasses. He was wearing the kind of loud, brightly coloured sports jacket favoured by ageing jazz musicians and constantly had a cigarette on the go in one hand and a glass of something mysterious in the other. He spoke German and English and had a fondness for the word 'splendid' which he liberally peppered each conversation with. He gazed up at the stage, eyes darting around, taking in every detail.

"*Zwei gitarren, orgel, bass, schlagzeug und congas* – splendid, splendid!"

As for the schedule, we learned we would be playing from eight p.m. until two thirty a.m. with a fifteen-minute break at ten p.m. and again at a quarter after midnight. John and I exchanged looks of surprise. Having watched the band at the Imperial, we were fully aware we were working the same shift as Dracula, but bloody hell! Two hours non-stop on stage? What if we needed a pee?

"When you do these longer sets, you take small breaks on stage. It's called whisky time," Roger said. "It gives the punters time to recover, chat each other up and order a drink. For us it's also a well-earned ciggy break." He winked. "Don't worry, it'll be splendid."

After a short inspection of the stage setup, Roger edged his drums further forward, making a little more space for himself. Satisfied, he proceeded to inspect the stage lighting, which only comprised of five or six meagre lightbulbs radiating not much more than a dull glow.

"Ivo, the lighting's a mite jaundiced, isn't it?" he asked. "I mean, we've got to work up here and I can't even see where I'm banging my sticks."

The manager shrugged apologetically and said he would see what he could do but would need to speak to the club owner.

We soundchecked with *Rainy Day Feeling* followed by a couple of verses of *Sweet Caroline* before Roger abruptly got up from his drums mid-chorus.

"Good enough, chaps. We'll finish this off on their time."

We repaired to the bar while enquiries were made about the band's accommodation.

"You and the boys are going to be delighted, Roger," Ivo enthused. "It's a splendid apartment just for the band: modern, bright and spacious and it's just around the corner."

Probably built shortly after the war, the apartment was located in an unremarkable four-storey building sandwiched between other equally unremarkable buildings at the intersection with the Paul-Heyse-Straße. The ground floor housed a noisy kebab takeaway and a sex shop. The detail escapes me now, but the name of the place must have been something like 'Shags'R'Us' as the shop window was bulging with every conceivable accoutrement for giving and getting a good seeing to. In amongst the hard-school erotica was an astonishing array of inflatable companions, strap-on phalluses, clamps, unguents, lotions and leather ware – I could feel my eyes watering.

"Gosh, you don't find that kind of kit in the House of Fraser. Not in the Windsor branch anyway," I remarked breathlessly.

The apartment was on the fourth floor. It might have been bright and modern in 1946 but now it was tired, gloomy and in need of a paint job. One large room with four single beds, a smaller room with two singles, a bathroom and a small hallway – that was our home for the next month. Donald and Kassy immediately grabbed the smaller room and the rest of us moved into the larger one. We spread the beds around and shifted the furniture to create some privacy. We tried to make it cosy but there wasn't much to do; it was a man cave and a spartan one at that.

After a quick meal at a cheap Italian restaurant we returned to the club. Our changing room was located directly behind the cloakroom which was attended by a lady of advanced years. Wearing a shabby cardigan and an old, misshapen brown beret atop her head, she was half hidden behind a large tome, which looked suspiciously like the Bible. The only sign of life was a mechanical greeting she gave to anyone passing.

At first I thought she asked "'Tis good?" to which I cautiously replied, "*Ja, danke.*"

Roger explained she was making the typical Bavarian greeting *grüß Gott*, which literally translated means 'greet God'.

"How are you supposed to respond?" I asked.

"I usually say 'Yes dear, if I see him."

We changed into our stage clothes and, gingerly squeezing past her, wandered out into the club. The small audience was made up of two or three groups of females sitting at tables around the dance floor while a handful of male guests, who appeared to be regulars, sat at the bar chatting with the staff. As we made our way up to the stage a couple of the ladies looked at us with interest but the people at the bar appeared unimpressed.

We began turning the equipment on and John suggested starting with something big and brash to grab their attention. Roger shook his head.

"No, relax, John, we don't want to climax too early. Let your uncle Roger do the program. That way you'll still have some energy left for one of those luscious beauties."

Leering lewdly towards the front tables, he switched his microphone on and announced: "*Guten abend meine damen und herren. Wir sind The Statesmen Singers.*"

The first night went well – surprisingly well. The audience were quick to get up and dance and every now and then a discreet tray with six glasses of schnapps would arrive on stage together with a request for a song. During the ten p.m. break, Ivo called the band over to the bar and introduced us to some of the regulars who, having heard us, were now noticeably more welcoming. Werner and Pavel were quick to shake hands while Hans was busy ordering a round of drinks for everyone. A tall redhead who had been in quiet conversation with Addie came over, gave us all a big welcoming smile and winked in my direction.

"Wow! She's not bad," I said.

I must have sounded a bit too keen as Roger quickly pulled me aside and whispered, "It's a bloke so don't get too interested."

"A bloke? It can't be. She's got a set of tits on her my mum would be proud of."

"Yeah, and a big, hairy meat and two veg your dad would. Check out the hips and his Adam's apple. Your mum got one of those?"

Oops. He was right. On closer inspection the wig was a giveaway. The thickly applied makeup wasn't hiding his blue chin all that well either.

Ivo made some more introductions: "*Meine freunde,* this sexy, redheaded kitten is Bernhard and the bewitching blonde over there at that other table is his dearest companion Christoph."

I glanced in astonishment at the blonde who I'd also been exchanging flirtatious smiles with during the last set. Hearing his name mentioned, Christoph rose regally from his seat and came wafting over.

"*Dahling, so nass muzeek,*" he gushed, fluttering his eyelids and mouthing a couple of mwa-mwa kisses in my direction. "*I chost loff Englishmann,*" he purred.

As the evening progressed and the club filled up, more and more alcohol-enhanced requests arrived and we downed endless rounds of Asbach and some other lethal concoction called Sour Fritz. The only one who didn't seem to be weaving was Wolfgang, who maintained that glassy-eyed expression he often had after a lot of alcohol.

If I hadn't been feeling so squiffy I might have had a stab at chatting to the gorgeous blonde who arrived just before midnight. She had been sitting together with a group of girls by the dance floor and had given me a couple of long, low, sultry looks during the last set. Working on the proposition her name wasn't Franz or Reinhold, I thought I might be in with a decent chance, but at the last moment my English reticence surfaced and I let it go by. Just after two a.m. she left, throwing me one last flirtatious pout. Well, at least she knew where to find me.

CHAPTER FOURTEEN

Top of the World

The next morning I was surprised to hear someone moving around quite so early. Cautiously opening one eye, I spied Roger. Just as I was about to close it again he said, "Ah, Stephen you're awake! How splendid, to quote my dear friend Ivo. And what a wonderful morning. Let's get John up and hit the shops. I feel Munich is calling us!"

Apart from basking in unseasonably warm weather, Munich was in a state of feverish excitement preparing for the Olympics. A brand new, futuristic stadium had been constructed to the north of the city and there were posters, decorations and an array of souvenirs promoting the Games everywhere. It was all so positive and festive; we were delighted to be there and to be a part of it. We spotted a small cafe with a couple of outside tables and ordered coffee, eggs and *brötchen* then proceeded to enjoy a leisurely breakfast in the sunshine before moving on to the large Kaufhof by Stachus.

It was my first real shopping trip in Germany and I was just staggered by the quality and breadth of choice of the merchandise on sale. If aliens had landed in 1972 and you showed them around Birmingham or Manchester, then took them over to Munich and asked which country had recently won the war… Well for an English boy it was certainly an eye-opener.

We went from floor to floor ogling colour TVs – my parents and all our neighbours still had black-and-white ones – home entertainment systems, contemporary Scandinavian furniture, leather beds, silk sheets, fashionable ladies' and men's boutiques and a sumptuous food hall offering live lobsters in a tank. We stared open-mouthed; I felt like a refugee who'd just got off a boat. It was all so much richer and more plentiful compared to what we were used to in England. And the people: beautifully dressed in clothes that looked like they were being worn for the first time. And they were all so attractive. The women were just drop-dead gorgeous and even the ugly ducklings seemed to make a fist of it with artistic uses of makeup, hair extensions and, if necessary, a touch of light surgery.

"Stop staring, Stephen, and close that mouth, John. Pursue me, chaps, we have purchases to make."

Roger scurried down some stairs leading to the basement. We ended up in the kitchen department where he navigated us along countless aisles until we arrived at a collection of small, one-ring cooking hobs. The kind you find in a bedsit.

"There's the future, gentlemen." He beamed. "Get yourselves one of those, a saucepan and a frying pan and you're set. Tempting meals whenever you want. Never again hungry."

We stared at him glumly.

"I'm happy eating in restaurants Roger," I muttered, starting to feel like that refugee again.

"Yes, yes, of course but some of the places we'll be playing at may not have much on offer. There are a few one-horse towns on the itinerary that don't feature in the Michelin guide, if you get my drift."

Oh what the hell, he might be right. We both picked up a hob and some pans, plates and cutlery and headed towards the cashier.

That evening we made our way up to the club and, after changing, drifted over to the bar. Ivo was there with a squat, shabbily dressed gentleman who he introduced as Herr Müller, the owner of the Arcadia. Herr Müller had a mournful undertaker's face you sensed had never felt the need to indulge in anything as trifling as smiling.

He solemnly shook hands with each of us and seemed courteous enough, so Roger took the opportunity to buttonhole him about the stage lighting.

"Herr Müller, it's a delight to play in such a wonderful establishment. One of Munich's finest, indeed world-class. But the lighting on the stage…" He made a deprecating gesture with his hands. "We're working in the dark. Guests stare into space and wonder where the music is coming from. I stare and wonder where the rest of my orchestra are." He tried an ingratiating smile. "Maybe a few more bulbs? Nothing extravagant. We don't need *son et lumière*" – he chuckled – "but a couple more bulbs?" He was starting to ramble when Herr Müller abruptly shuffled off over to the stage and glanced upwards.

"*Es ist doch hell? Oder?*"

"Absolutely. Indeed, it is light, and I'm impressed by your immediate grasp of the situation, but there is that subtle, almost infinitesimal line between light and… bright." He cracked another even wider smile. "Two more lights perhaps? One on me and one on the singer?"

Herr Müller stared over Roger's shoulder at the lights reflecting up from the street and said he'd think about it and shuffled off again.

"That went well, I thought," said Roger, shooting his cuffs with satisfaction.

"I thought he was a bit of a cunt actually, Roger."

"Now now, John. Let's not bite the claw that feeds us. Mmm, who is that?"

We turned to follow his stare. An attractive woman had entered the club and was heading towards the bar. She was petite with short, dark hair, a pretty face and a perfectly proportioned hourglass figure. Our eyes tracked her progress as she swept across the room, affectionately greeting waiters with the grace of a minor member of the royal family visiting the poor. Roger observed every move, licking his lips. As she disappeared through a door at the rear he wandered over to Ivo and enquired as to who she was.

"Ah, that's Gina." Ivo said, giving him a knowing look. "She's our star waitress, you'll like her. No, you'll love her. Everybody loves her."

Roger winked at him. "How splendid."

She re-entered the club wearing a short black dress adorned with a white lace apron. At first appearance, it was a bit ooh-la-la and could have been taken straight out of a Benny Hill sketch, but she carried it off with style and in the Arcadia it seemed to work. Seeing it was time to play, we hopped up on stage and waited to hear what the first song would be.

"I'm feeling in a Neil Diamond mood. What about *I Am I Said*?"

"On a campaign are we, Roger?" teased Kassy.

It was one of Roger's favourite numbers and he did it well with his warm baritone voice. Sometimes he could get a little too jazzy, slipping into a sort of Zoot Money, Georgie Fame thing but on straight ballads he was very good. The people around the bar had stopped chatting and were listening, while Ivo was smiling and nodding at something one of the barmen was saying. When I checked out a couple of the ladies who were seated to my right, I noticed Gina had paused midway through taking an order to listen. She appeared mesmerised by Roger's performance. John had also noticed and leaned over towards me.

"Fucking hell, I don't believe that! Never happens when I sing *Beautiful Sunday*."

"Hah! You should try playing the role of castrated cockerel in *Superstar*."

He grinned. "Nah, you make a lovely Karen Carpenter."

"It's still about five semitones too high. I'm going to do myself some damage one night and it won't be pretty."

"You should try my top harmony in *If I Were a Carpenter*. I have to wear special underwear to reach it!"

"Ah. Now I know what you were doing in that sex emporium downstairs!"

We returned our attention to the song. Maybe it wasn't love at first sight but by the second refrain it sure felt like something similar. She stood transfixed while he drilled her with his most meaningful look and crooned on about a frog who dreamed about being a king, or whatever nonsense that song is about, and all of a sudden there were just the two of them. The rest of us melted away into darkness while lush strings mysteriously faded in, the scent of fresh roses filled the room and silver spotlights danced delicately across their wondrous expressions. Müller had really come up trumps with those extra bulbs.

The song ended and reality returned, but it was apparent something was afoot… By the ten p.m. break our leader was a man on a mission. He strode purposely over to the bar, ordered a small beer and began his charm offensive. He was chatting to Claudia the bar lady and Pavel, telling them a slightly risqué joke, when Gina sidled over and joined in. Whatever he was saying was working as she smiled coquettishly and gave her ample bosom a playful jiggle.

A little later, Roger's plans started to unravel when a group of guys came in and seated themselves in one of the booths, noisily demanding attention. Gina went over to take their order and was invited to join them. It appeared she knew them quite well as the leader pulled his chair closer, laid his hand on her bum and rubbed it in a proprietorial way.

Roger was biting his lip and looking down.

"What do you think?" Kassy said. "*Crying Time*?"

"No, I'm in the mood for *Georgia*."

Roger had three or four Ray Charles' numbers in his repertoire and he really transformed himself into the part. Slurring the consonants like Ray, he did a great, soulful impression. I'm probably imagining it but he also seemed to get blacker… and blinder as on occasion he would completely forget about playing the drums, getting more than a little carried away in the role. But he delivered it with panache and the audience enjoyed it.

Come to think of it, Roger wasn't what you would call a physical drummer anyway. He took a breezy nonchalance to the instrument and saw the drums more as props. There would often be a cup of tea and an overfilled ashtray sitting on his floor tom. When he got a new song to sing, lyrics would be taped to his cymbals and the hanging tom was a convenient spot to place whatever paperback he was reading – usually open at the correct page. He certainly wasn't a graduate of the Keith Moon or John Bonham school of drumming.

We launched into *Georgia on My Mind* and he gave it his all. He wrung every drop of sentiment out of it while most of the club stopped what they were doing to listen. Over at Gina's group I could see she was captivated. She had even quietly moved the bloke's hand off her bum.

CHAPTER FIFTEEN

Mama Told Me Not to Come

A couple of evenings later, a striking redhead entered the club. She was in the mould of one of those 1950s movie stars, with sultry Latin looks, pneumatic breasts and a hip-swaying walk that would have made a blind man blush. If it had been a movie, a raunchy tenor sax would have soundtracked each seductive move as she sashayed across the room. Accompanying her, looking pleased as punch, was Addie, who smoothly directed her to one of the booths near the bar, clicked his fingers at Gina, and grandly ordered cheap champagne.

For a while they appeared to be getting on swimmingly, loudly toasting each other, whispering sweet little nothings and generally soaking up the promise of what was to come.

During the midnight break I happened to be walking past and noticed the amorous interplay had cooled somewhat. Addie was shooting anxious glances towards his friends at the bar while the redhead verbally tore into him. She was a fiery creature, and after she erupted in a further stream of invective I think he reached the conclusion a tactical retreat was the better part of valour. Mustering as much dignity as he could, he rose, performed a stiff bow and left to join his friends at the bar. The redhead let fly with one final volley, then just as abruptly stopped, gave me a trouser-melting smile and purred something inviting in German. Realising I didn't understand, she switched to surprisingly good English with what I took to be an

Italian accent.

"Hey handsome, I love your band. Where are you from?"

Without waiting for an invitation, I sat down and she poured me a glass. Her name was Dominique. I was right in that her parents were Italian but she had been living in Munich for the past fifteen years. Close up, I could see she was in her thirties or early forties, although she wore it extremely well. By the end of the break, we were laughing and joking and she said she'd stay for the next set. When I arrived back on stage there was a whole lot of joshing from John and Roger. Wolfgang, however, raised a cautionary hand.

"Just be careful," he said. "Women like that don't come cheap."

She stayed through the next set and was still there when we finished. By that time the champagne was fizzing through my veins and I was feeling a lot more reckless than usual. I asked her what she felt like doing and she suggested going to a club by the Sendlinger Tor where the resident band played until four a.m.

From this point I must admit it all becomes a little hazy. We arrived in a taxi and were led to a small table near the dance floor. A reptilian waiter eyed me with interest and, rising to the occasion, I ordered a bottle of sekt. I may even have sent up a tray of drinks for the Indonesian band. The next thing I remember though is waking up with a monumental hard-on and the kind of hangover you could bequeath to science. I also happened to be in her bed.

I think we were in a boarding house, as I could vaguely make out other people coming and going down the hall. Hearing her still sleeping deeply beside me, I realised I desperately needed a pee. I quietly got out of bed and in the darkness, felt my way out of the room and down a dimly lit corridor. There were noises coming from a couple of the other rooms but with no signs on any of the doors – and there were plenty of them – it was difficult to find the toilet.

A door beside me opened and a scantily clad lady stepped out. Staring at me with undisguised interest, she asked something in German before giving me an appraising once-over, lingering a little longer than was polite over the old fellow who was still groaning inside my pants. Seeing I hadn't understood, she tried again.

"You speak English? What are you after, the bathroom?"

I nodded and she said, "Come on, follow me."

An American voice called out from her room: "Hurry up, baby. I'm not paying you to hang out with other customers."

She made a face but said soothingly, "No worries, honey, I'm just showing him where the bathroom is."

That took me aback. I hadn't realised I was a customer.

Finally able to take a pee I looked at my surroundings, eyeing the condom machine on the wall and signs warning of the dangers of VD. Oh heck, there should have been another sign about the dangers of picking up strange women in the Arcadia. On the other hand, if she was a professional lady, I couldn't imagine she would have let me do anything without some kind of protection, so that was probably OK. But how was I going to get out without paying?

With those troubling thoughts in my head, I returned to her room. She was fast asleep and it was still early so I got back into bed. Despite the shock of knowing I was in a brothel, I noticed with some surprise I still had an inconvenient boner, and it didn't improve matters when she moved closer in the bed shoving her ample bum in my direction. I drifted off back to sleep.

Some hours later, Dominique woke me with a light kiss and whispered there was coffee if I wanted it. She was dressed so I took it as a cue to put my clothes on, then we sat together on her sofa while she poured me a cup. I wasn't sure how to frame the right kind of question but I was intrigued to know whether she thought last night was a professional pickup or something a little more intimate. Happily I didn't need to ask.

"I really like you, *amore*," she whispered. "Even a girl like me wants to have a man who likes her for herself, not just for sex. And no, we didn't do anything." She winked and added sexily, "But maybe this morning your big pork chop wanted more than just a pen pal, eh?"

I was still young enough to blush and started to make small noises of protest, but she was laughing so deliciously it was impossible not to join in.

"I know I'm not the right girl for you, and you are almost certainly not the right man for me," she continued, "but it was fun to pretend for one evening." She laughed and became more businesslike. "And now, *caro*, you need to go and I need to get ready."

I kissed her softly, picked up my coat and left.

CHAPTER SIXTEEN

You Make Me Feel Like Dancing

Despite playing until the early hours we rarely went straight home. Usually we ended up in a bar near the Marienplatz that was open all night and served warm schnitzel sandwiches and cold beer. On the first Saturday all six of us were there together with Claudia and a few ladies who had been at the club that evening. Claudia recognised another group of musicians who played in a band called the Transylvania Express and suggested they come over and join us.

Originally from Romania, where they had all been professors at the Bucharest Conservatory of Music, the band had 'hopped off' on a cultural visit to West Germany and applied for asylum. An eccentric-looking bunch for a pop band, they were bookish and intellectual in a sort of Eastern European way: they had goatees and berets and a couple of them even smoked pipes.

Wolfgang and I were talking to a chap called Dan, who was their saxophone player. His appearance was a curious mix between Soviet spy, Manfred Mann and one of the Seven Dwarfs. He had one of those thin jazz beards without a moustache, dark-tinted, metal-rimmed glasses, a hooked nose and merry, dancing eyes. While chatting to us he was openly leering at one of the ladies sitting opposite. She wasn't giving the impression she was interested but that didn't seem to worry him.

A couple of the others were in conversation with the bandleader: a serious chap who exhibited the air of a long-suffering member of the Romanian aristocracy forced into exile. They were comparing gigs and I got the feeling Roger was impressed that a lot of theirs were in luxury hotels. This month they were playing the last of a three-month residency at the five-star Regina Palast Hotel which was just around the corner. From earlier conversations with Heinz and Roger I knew they wanted to get us on that circuit.

Meanwhile the girl Dan had been ogling got up to go to the toilet. His eyes mentally undressed her as she crossed the room.

"Schau mal," he sighed. *"Wie schön. Ein arsch wie zwei schachteln zigaretten."*

Chuckling, Wolfgang translated for us. "Beautiful. An arse like two packets of cigarettes."

John and I looked questioningly at each other while Roger smoothly changed the subject. "If you're free tomorrow, come and watch us at the Arcadia. We're doing a *tanztee* from three p.m. until five p.m."

"Tanztee?" John asked. "What's that?"

"I told you all about the *tanztee*."

"No, you never mentioned anything about a *tanztee*. What is it?"

"Funny. I could have sworn I did. Have you noticed how your voice goes up an octave when you get agitated?"

John stared at him coolly.

"It's a matinee on Sundays." Roger reluctantly explained. "Just two hours. It's easy."

"Oh, bloody brilliant!" John responded, banging his beer glass down on the table. "Two hours in the afternoon as well as six in the evening. And we were going to go over to Schwabing to visit the English Garden."

"You're much better off working. Too many tourists. Go on Monday."

The Romanians had finished their beers and were getting up so we all shook hands and said we would see them tomorrow.

* * *

Three p.m. on Sunday afternoon and the Arcadia was surprisingly busy, albeit with a subtly different clientele: older but considerably lighter on their feet. Somebody once wrote that dancing is the art of getting your feet out of the way faster than your partner can step on them. By three fifteen a lot of enthusiastic feet were doing exactly that, with German precision.

When I was about twelve, my mum sent me for dance lessons. She thought it was important for a man to be able to 'cut a rug'. So instead of Saturday morning movies with my friends, I dutifully trudged across town to the Adelphi Ballroom where I proceeded to make a complete pillock of myself in front of an unforgiving dance teacher named Miss Munch. It was a futile exercise as I have two left feet and a hopeless memory for movement. Together with my poor, long-suffering dance partner Jeanette, I would grind my way unrhythmically around the floor with one eye on the clock and the other on her feet. Consequently the principles of the tango, merengue and foxtrot are still a mystery but it did develop in me a grudging admiration for anyone who could do it well, and here in Munich I'd noticed that a surprising number of people could ballroom dance extremely well.

We opened with a foxtrot, followed by a quickstep and then something Brazilian as the eager dancers swayed, twirled, swooped, dived and shimmied with style and Teutonic flair. There were of course one or two exceptions: a couple performing a paso doble looked uncomfortably like a mafia hit-man dragging a corpse across an abattoir floor. That aside, it was a pleasure to watch them and I felt a strange desire to be back at the Adelphi and to try and be a better student.

A little while later, the Romanians arrived and seated themselves in one of the booths.

"*Spione, meine herren,*" Roger whispered.

"I thought spies were agents and club owners?" John whispered back.

"And other bands. Word of mouth spreads quickly in this business and I'm hoping we may shortly move into the luxury hotel business thanks to these boys."

At five p.m. we took a well-earned three-hour break. Roger went to chat to the guys from the Transylvania Express while Wolfgang invited John and me to a place down the road called the Mathäser.

I don't know what I was expecting but it wasn't this cavernous beer hall we ended up searching for a table in. You hear a lot about Munich's Hofbräuhaus but that was a cosy tavern compared to this place. There must have been something close to three hundred thirsty customers spread around long, wooden tables. Right in the middle was a stage accommodating a full-size Bavarian band enthusiastically blasting its way through a huge repertoire of drinking songs.

We managed to find seats and made ourselves comfortable while litre steins of frothy beer appeared, served by buxom waitresses in low-cut Bavarian dirndls. An old biddy came by offering sliced radishes. The price was right, as it was free, and it tasted great. It also gave you a powerful thirst and before we knew what was happening another round of beers was ordered. The old biddy came by again and the short story is that we weaved our way out of there in a parlous state about fifteen minutes before we were due back on stage.

As we re-entered the club, we bumped straight into Roger. He looked at us curiously and slowly turned to Wolfgang.

"Enjoy the break? Do something cultural? Deutsches Museum, Nymphenburg Palace? Fucking hell, Wolly, we've got another six hours to do."

Our bass player looked a little ashamed.

"Where did you take them?" Roger asked.

"The Mathäser."

"What a good idea," Roger mumbled sarcastically. "OK, maybe it's an advantage that it's still lit like a mausoleum up there. At least Müller won't see that the two of them are three sheets to the wind."

We gingerly made our way up onto the stage and hunkered down. Luckily there were only a few customers so we started softly by dipping into the Brazilian songbook and playing a clutch of unobtrusive instrumentals like *Desafinado, The Girl From Ipanema* and *One Note Samba*. Roger referred to these instrumental sets as 'beefsteak' music as they were low key and useful if the majority of guests were dining. He also liked to insert these sets later in the evening if the club was quiet so he could tap away softly on the drums while catching up on his book. He had even redirected one of the small lights to illuminate the pages.

The following morning I woke up to the urgent, repetitive sound of squeaking bedsprings. Over in the next corner I was surprised to see Claudia stark naked on her back in the throes of passion with an unusually vigorous Wolfgang bouncing up and down on top. Neither of them seemed to be in the least bit concerned that I was now a spectator.

"Morning all," I called out.

"*Grüß Gott*, Steve!"

"Fancy a cup of tea?" I asked.

"*Gerne*," they both replied brightly.

I took out my fancy new cooking hob and boiled up some water while Wolfgang's arse continued to fly up and down like a fiddler's elbow. Conveniently they both climaxed about the same time the water boiled. As it was nearing rehearsal time I went over to wake the others and was surprised to see Roger's bed was empty.

Wolfgang came back from the bathroom and said, "Yeah, last time I saw him he was talking to Gina. I think they probably went off together. They've been mooning after each other for long enough so it's about time."

By eleven a.m., we were all in the club, ready to go. Everyone that is except Roger.

We waited about half an hour then Kassy said, "OK, we'll start without him. He'll turn up soon enough."

John had chosen *Have You Seen Her*, a soul ballad by The Chi-Lites. He picked out the chords and the harmonies and arranged it for the five of us. It has a big vocal opening and when we tried it, it sounded really nice. Kassy delivered the soulful monologue and we all took turns at the high lead lines. As Roger still hadn't turned up, John arranged some small answering phrases for him to do that he could learn relatively quickly.

By the end of the rehearsal he still hadn't surfaced, so we went off for some lunch at the Wimpy Bar down at Stachus. Everyone was delighted with the result of our morning's work, but a little put out that our bandleader had skipped the first rehearsal. That meant we couldn't play the song tonight.

When he did appear at the club it was evening and he was with Gina, looking extremely pleased with himself.

"Evening, men. Phew, you don't look happy. Somebody die?"

"No Roger, we simply missed you at the rehearsal," John said crisply. "If you recollect, it's rehearsals Monday to Thursday and you're the one who keeps going on about new material."

"Cripes! I totally forgot." He glanced towards the bar and smiled. "Unfortunately, a stiff prick has an awful memory."

"Yea. Well we rehearsed The Chi-Lites' song. I've got some vocal parts for you that we can go through in the morning, and the drums are simple."

"Let's give it a go now. I'll just melt in," he suggested.

"No, I'd prefer that you learn the part I give you."

Roger was still staring dreamily towards the bar, mouthing occasional little kisses either at a surprised middle-aged drunk by the cash register or at Gina, who was standing just behind him, adjusting her cleavage.

"Of course," he said. "Absolutely. But maybe we'll just give it a little run-out now so I can get a feel for it."

John was unconvinced but eventually gave in after some urging from the others in the band. The harmony vocal intro sounded as good as it had during the rehearsal, and the few customers already sitting around the dance floor stopped chatting and turned to listen. Kassy performed his monologue word-perfect and we started the high lead parts. All very beautiful until, unannounced, Roger marked out a lower part for himself. He was in one of his Zoot Money moods and, as he spread out and made himself comfortable, the jazz phrasing became more pronounced. John stiffened and through narrowed eyes glared at him with irritation. Unfortunately Roger was too busy smiling towards the bar to notice.

When the song came to an end, we received a nice round of applause but, realising the rest of us hadn't appreciated his own contribution, Roger quickly announced the next number. "And moving swiftly along, here is John with *Beautiful Sunday*."

Grimly, he did his number, but when we reached whisky time he was seriously pissed.

"Roger!" he shrilled. "What the fuck was that you were singing? *Hit The Road Jack*? I didn't know Bing Crosby sang in The Chi-Lites."

"Now now John, your voice has gone up an octave again."

"Yea! Maybe you could try doing the same thing with yours when we do that song again!"

"Yes, point taken. But nice one. The song's going to be great."

It was approaching the twelve fifteen break when I noticed two attractive girls sitting at a table across the dance floor. As we made our way towards the bar they smiled invitingly so John and I made a quick detour and joined them. One was gorgeous with huge brown eyes, light-brown hair – cut in a Mary Quant bob – and a light, olive complexion. Unfortunately, she didn't speak any English, but as John was keen to try out a few new German phrases he made a stab at chatting her up. There was a fashion at that time for girls to wear a brooch bearing their initials and this girl had the letter 'A' pinned daintily on her left breast. He asked in his broken German what it stood for and she replied Astrid. He pondered that and pointed to her other breast.

"And what's this one's name?"

Both girls giggled and I turned my attention to the friend. She was pleasant looking with long, dark hair and a pale complexion, but no competition for Astrid. However, she had a nice personality and spoke a little English so we chatted for a while until I realised the blonde from the first evening had returned. This time she was sitting all alone at the bar, drinking a glass of white wine. I glanced up at her and she smiled, so I made an excuse and got up.

"Sorry friends, I need to see someone."

Still a little reserved, I baulked at the idea of just going straight up to her, so I began to walk past the bar then changed my mind and motioned to the bar lady. "Claudia, can I get a coke please?"

By now I was right beside the blonde. Everything about her was feminine and smelt expensive. Thinking I'd dive straight in with a witty opening chat-up line, I spun around to face her, accidentally knocking her arm and spilling her wine.

"Oh fuck! I do apologise," I spluttered, tripping over her stool and spilling most of my Coke in the process. I was cursing horribly while dabbing at my wet trousers and just about to make a nervous break for the stage when she placed a calming hand on my arm and in a low, sexy voice said how much she enjoyed the band. And she said it in English.

I was on a roll.

CHAPTER SEVENTEEN

How Can You Mend a Broken Heart

Her name was Marlene and her work had something to do with the Olympic Village, hence the good English. It was just getting interesting when I noticed the others walking back towards the stage. Shit! We still had another two-hour set to play. Happily she said she would stay to watch. When I arrived on stage John wasn't as thrilled.

"Fuck a man who leaves his mate in the middle of a major chat-up session. What am I going to do with two of them? Problem is, I need the second one to translate as I'm having trouble understanding Astrid's German."

To his further dismay Astrid and her friend left shortly after. As they passed the stage she threw me a very odd look which I took to mean she was angry at me for my rudeness towards her friend. I was, however, delighted that Marlene was still there at the end so I quickly got changed and joined her at the bar. I suggested going somewhere else for a drink and for some perverse reason mentioned the club near the Sendlinger Tor where I'd been a few nights earlier.

She nodded and said, "Yes, I know it. Let's go."

We arrived just as the band were starting their last set. While she went off to powder her nose I took a moment to listen to the music. Like many bands in Germany the Indonesians loved to slap a lot of reverb on the vocals and brass. While it masked all kinds of sins, the result was that they all sounded the same. A shame because these guys were pretty good. Anyway, that was somebody else's problem. I was on a date with a beautiful woman, in a great city, and I even had some money in my pocket.

When she returned she told me she was from Düsseldorf and that she had studied English for a year in Bournemouth; now she was working in marketing. Before we knew it the band were playing their last song. We finished our drinks and she asked if I would like to follow her home.

The taxi headed north out of town up the Dachauer Straße. At that hour there was very little traffic and we soon passed the new Olympic Stadium. Almost immediately we made a sharp left turn and pulled into a modern residential complex. I paid the driver while she found her keys then we walked down a floodlit path, through a small garden, leading to a swanky, new apartment building where we took the elevator to the top floor.

She opened the front door and I blinked for a moment, suddenly realising Marlene was doing extremely well for herself. Floor to ceiling windows afforded a spectacular view across the Olympic Park to the main arena while her living room was expensively furnished in a contemporary Scandinavian style. Standing on what must have been an acre of creamy shagpile was a huge, L-shaped leather sofa beside a glass and chrome coffee table. On top of this was a remote control for the Grundig colour TV which stood discreetly in a corner beside a small cocktail bar bursting with premier-label beverages. She invited me to sit down then put something by José Feliciano on the stereo and we got cosy.

Before long, clothes were being hastily ripped off and with some urgency we relocated to the bedroom and got to grips on the king-sized bed, engaging in just about every sexual act that came into this woman's very vivid imagination. I was both thrilled and horrified to find she was such a skilful lover. OK, I was possibly being a little optimistic to think she had been waiting patiently in celibate restraint for my arrival in Munich, but a bit of awkwardness wouldn't have been wrong. But not a chance. She did everything with Germanic precision and wasn't at all shy or inhibited about showing me exactly what to do to give her the most pleasure. I don't know what she made of me but for my part I was hopelessly smitten.

I woke up in the morning and looked at her lovely face on the pillow, not really believing my luck.

She opened her eyes and smiled. "Sleep well?"

"Yes," I said lazily. "You?"

"Of course. But now I must get ready for work."

We had a cup of coffee together – perfectly brewed from a Bosch machine – and made plans to see each other again on Friday evening around eleven p.m. Kissing her gently goodbye I left in a cab. I had only just met her and I could feel I was seriously falling in love.

I arrived at the rehearsal looking a bit like Roger the evening before. I wasn't blowing kisses at drunks but I undoubtedly had the same stupid, dreamy look on my face as we worked our way through a song by Santana called *Evil Ways*. John got Roger to work on *Have You Seen Her*, so we had two new numbers to perform.

It was another beautiful day, and after we finished a few of us decided to do some sightseeing. First of all we headed to Schwabing for our overdue visit to the English Garden.

It wasn't really a garden, more like a large park. In fact it was bigger than both Hyde Park in London and Central Park in New York. The centrepiece was a Chinese Tower surrounded in good Bavarian fashion by a large beer garden. Wherever you looked there were attractive period buildings, Grecian temples, streams and fountains, and a lake with a little island.

We took another route back into the centre via the Italian Renaissance style Hofgarten, admiring the impressive Residenz palace. When we got to the Marienplatz, which is at the other end of the main shopping street from Stachus, we climbed one of the onion-domed towers in the Frauenkirche, the iconic cathedral seen on most picture postcards from Munich. At 99 metres it was a heck of a climb but well worth it as there were some terrific views across the city.

At the end of the war the centre of Munich was almost totally destroyed. When rebuilding it, the city elders chose not to simply replace everything with modern skyscrapers but instead painstakingly restore its historical centre to its pre-war grandeur. Gazing across the city to the distant Alps, still dressed in their winter coat, I could only admire their commitment and vision as the panorama of neo-Gothic, Baroque, Classical and *Jugendstil* architecture before us was enchanting.

The rest of the week went by in a blur but Friday arrived and in the evening I strolled down to the club, full of anticipation. As it was already busy we dispensed with the 'beefsteak' hour and moved straight on to our up-tempo repertoire. The dance floor filled up quickly and the time flew by. Before we knew it we were at the ten o'clock break. John asked me if I fancied going to The Babalu after we finished. It was a new club we had discovered in Schwabing. I explained I was expecting Marlene to come over. He raised his eyebrows.

"That sounds serious. Two dates already. Got any names planned for the kids?"

"Yeah, fuck and off."

Eleven o'clock came and went and I found myself staring at the entrance. Eleven thirty. OK, she was being fashionably late. Then it was twelve fifteen. I wandered over to the bar and listened with half an ear to Roger as he told Werner, Bernhard and Christoph a few jokes. Next to them, Addie was conversing in his usual taciturn style with one of Hans' ladies, who in turn was gazing longingly across the room at Donald.

Twelve thirty and I trudged back up to the stage. In my mind I started to go over where it had gone wrong. Of course it's obvious! You're a lousy shag. What do you expect? You're English. Right, I'd better get down to that sex shop and bone up on improving my bedroom skills. Or maybe it was that terrible fart I let off? Christ, I thought she was asleep. Or maybe I was too…

Roger interrupted my thoughts. "Isn't that one of your constituents, Steve? Very nice too. Want me to put you in a good light?"

She had come. Settling herself into a seat by the bar, she saw me and waved.

"Yes, please," I said, gazing happily towards the bar. "Just not *Superstar*," I warned.

He laughed. "OK, leave it with me." Switching his microphone on, he announced, "*Und jetzt meine damen und herren, direkt aus London, England…*"

When the set was over I got changed and joined her at the bar.

"I started to think you weren't coming," I said.

"Sorry, I got a last-minute booking."

"What? For the Olympics?"

She laughed. "No, silly. You know. My extracurricular thing."

"Sorry, I'm lost. What extracurricular thing?"

"My other job."

I was confused and it showed.

"Steve." She stared steadily at me. "You know what I do."

All of a sudden I could feel my happiness evaporating and I began to get a bad feeling. Shit! Doesn't anyone in this town have a regular day job? I really should have stopped right there, but it was difficult to just let it drop.

"So what are you saying? This extracurricular thing, is it working as an escort?"

She didn't answer immediately, but then said quietly, "I thought you understood. You don't think I could live in that apartment on the wage I get, do you?"

"No, but…"

"Look, I'm not going to make excuses for what I do. I have a good life and I don't do anything I don't want to. Everyone has choices. I've made mine and I'm happy. Now, are you coming with me? I want to dance. Let's go and find somewhere fun."

"No."

"What?" She looked surprised.

I tried to make light of it. "I think it's obvious from my present circumstances that I'm a team player, but there are some things I just don't want to share with the team. I guess you're one of them."

"Oh, for God's sake, that's so simplistic. Other musicians aren't as high-minded as you."

"Oh, so there've been many musicians?"

If she was embarrassed she hid it well. "What are you looking for, Steve? A virgin?"

"No, just a little bit of normality."

She smiled sadly and seemed to be considering something then quietly picked up her coat and walked towards the door. I just sat and stared. I knew I could probably salvage something from this if I was prepared to play along. I could chase after her and say, "You're right. Forget my moment of madness," but it wasn't going to happen. I was going to let her go and I was definitely going to be bloody miserable as a result.

John and Wolfgang watched her leave. They hadn't heard the conversation but guessed something was wrong.

"You want to come with us to The Babalu? It'll cheer you up. Most of the others are coming."

"Thanks but no. I'll head off home."

The next week crept by and it seemed every song I heard on the radio was aimed at me: *How Can You Mend a Broken Heart, Alone Again (Naturally), Without You, Where Is The Love, I'm Still In Love With You* – Christ! It was enough to make a grown man weep. Where were the *Chirpy Chirpy Cheep Cheep*s and *Ooh-Wakka-Doo-Wakka-Day*s when you needed them?

Friday evening came around again and this time Astrid and her friend returned to the club. I was just about getting over the misery of Marlene when John asked if I was ready to be his wingman again.

"Not really." I replied and broke into an impromptu version of *I'm*

Through With Love. "But I owe you for last time, so to quote Phil Shakespeare – after you, MacDuff."

He looked at Roger expectantly and asked if he could do his new song.

"Want me to put you in a good light, John?" Roger said, grinning like a cat.

"Yes please."

"Ah, sometimes, you know, this job," he said, leaning back on his stool and rubbing his chest, "it feels like 'Honest Roger's Dating Agency'. Still, anything for a mate. Like to do your new song, would you? Make a splash? I see."

By now John was gritting his teeth. "Yes please, and could we maybe hurry it along before they go home again?"

Roger turned on his microphone and was just about to announce the next song when just as quickly he switched it off and with a hint of mischief enquired, "Sure you wouldn't like to stay with something a little safer like *Beautiful Sunday*? It's been a winner in the past." Receiving only a dirty look in response, he continued as though passing a benediction, "And so it will be done." He switched his microphone back on and said: "*Liebe gäste*. It's time for the big one. It's John and *You've Got a Friend*."

CHAPTER EIGHTEEN

Sweet City Woman

Astrid and her friend, who I now found out was called Elsa, appeared delighted to see us again. After the way I had left them last time, I thought it was generous, to say the least. We shook hands in that oddly polite European fashion and sat down. Elsa quickly took the opportunity to ask what had happened to my girlfriend from the previous visit. I didn't want to get into details so I just said it hadn't worked out. She translated this for Astrid, who gave me a frank stare and then grinned wickedly, displaying a perfect set of teeth. They started prattling on in German and Elsa asked us if we wanted to go with them to The Blue Door club after we finished. Damn, that was the place down near the Sendlinger Tor. John eagerly said yes so I shrugged and nodded.

As we arrived, the band were playing *She's A Lady*. Recognising me from my earlier visits, the guitarist and bassist waved hello and the waiter came over and shook my hand. This prompted John and the two girls to regard me with new interest.

"What's that all about?" John asked.

"I've got a bit of previous at this place," I replied dismissively.

We found a table by the dance floor and John went off to take a pee. As he left, the band took down the tempo with the Fleetwood Mac instrumental *Albatross*. Astrid touched me on the arm, indicating she would like to dance. Where was this going? I nodded cautiously and we moved onto the small, crowded dance floor and came together in a slow dance. I didn't want to cut in on John so I held her body away from mine, but she was having none of it and pulled me close, whispering something softly. Damn! Why couldn't I understand at least a bit of this language?

John came back into the room, saw the empty seats and took in the situation. Over her shoulder, I gave him my most earnest expression of innocence, but I could see he was not impressed. He glared back while Elsa moved into the seat next to him and explained something. At the end of the song we returned to the table and the partner-swapping exercise was a fait accompli.

While the ladies took the opportunity to visit the powder room, we compared notes. He seemed to have accepted the situation and was even philosophical about it.

"They haven't done anything we don't do. Elsa said Astrid already had the hots for you during their last visit and was very put out that you were with the other girl. Apparently that Marlene is a part-time hooker."

"Tell me about it," I muttered.

"You certainly keep your cards close to your chest. Good God man, you were getting it for nothing with a pro and you turned it down?"

I pretended I was listening to the band.

"Anyway," he continued, "Elsa just gave my todger a twitch and invited me back to her place, and tonight I fancy some uncomplicated sex."

Half an hour later they were in one cab and Astrid and I were in another, heading in the opposite direction. She lived on the Leopoldstraße but at the cheaper end outside of Schwabing. It wasn't a posh area, which lifted my spirits, and they lifted even further when we entered her apartment and I saw it was a small but comfortable bedsit. At least this girl wasn't an escort. If she was, she wasn't very successful.

I looked around, taking in the inexpensive furniture, and saw a photo of her in a nurse's uniform.

"Is that your job?" I pointed at the photo.

"*Ja. Krankenschwester,*" she said, giving me a shy smile and taking my coat.

We sat on the sofa and she poured a couple of glasses of white wine then leaned over and kissed me. Staring into those lovely brown eyes, the ache I had felt since Marlene walked out of the club slowly began to diminish.

There was no bedroom and I wondered where we were going to sleep. That question was answered when she began pulling the sofa apart and rebuilding it as a compact but comfortable double bed. The room smelt feminine and there were nice little personal touches with plants and family photos everywhere. I would imagine as a nurse she didn't have a lot of money but she had good taste and made the best out of what she had, which made me like her more and more.

We both undressed, a little shyly at first, lay on the bed and started to touch and explore each other. Her body was everything I had imagined it to be when we danced and much more. Her breasts were full with large, pink nipples and with her slim waist and shapely hips she had the perfect hourglass figure. But my imagination hadn't prepared me for the smells and the tastes. Her full lips were made for kissing and she gently caressed every part of my body while I lay back, drinking in the scent of her femininity. There was none of Marlene's polished professionalism in her lovemaking; it was much more sincere and romantic.

The next morning she woke me with a kiss and a cup of coffee. I'm still not sure how we communicated – I guess it was a mixture of hand signals and pantomime – but it worked and we both seemed to make ourselves understood.

As it was Saturday, we decided to go into the city centre for a walk. I needed a change of clothes so we dropped by the band apartment where we bumped into Wolfgang.

"Hi Steve. Good, you're back. This place is starting to get lonely. I was the only one in our room last night."

Wolfgang shook hands with Astrid and introduced himself. They immediately made a connection as Wolfgang's wife came from the same part of Bavaria as Astrid. It struck me it might be useful to have him along to do a bit of translating.

"We're going for a coffee, Wolly. Fancy coming along?"

"Yeah, why not? I'm at a loose end."

We walked down Bayerstraße to Stachus and found a *konditorei* where Astrid began asking Wolfgang a whole bunch of questions.

"Wow, she's a character and she's really taken with you." He chuckled. "No accounting for taste, I guess. Anyway, she wants to know how long we're playing at the Arcadia and where we're going after. She also wants to know when we're returning to Munich."

"We know our next stop is Stuttgart, but there's nothing else planned for Munich, is there?"

"Müller wants us back and I think he's looking at October. It's a busy month because of the Oktoberfest."

"Tell her that by then I'll try and speak some German."

The days slipped comfortably by and everyone in the band appeared to be enjoying life in Munich. Roger was in love and made sure everyone knew it. At rehearsals he picked up a couple more ballads for himself and each evening sang them exclusively for one delighted lady dressed in black and white. He appeared slimmer, the sheepskin coat had been discarded and he rarely mentioned Mausi.

Some nights – especially early in the week – it was a slow burn and we often outnumbered the guests two to one but were still expected to entertain like it was a full house. The management, using some extremely dodgy logic, believed that potential guests looking in and seeing us perform as though the place were packed would naturally think that it was.

On one particular evening, even the *freunde der nacht* seemed to have abandoned the place. Hans was on his own at the bar and invited me over for a beer. I asked him where everyone was.

"Addie is probably having one of his moodies," he said. He spoke very good English but with an unusual cockney accent and loved to gossip. "Those years in the camp still get to him and every now and again he just drops off the map. Sometimes he can get very low." Thoughtfully, he took a sip of his beer and lit a cigarette. "I don't know about the others but I think Pavel is off on one of his flying trips,"

"Flying trip?" I asked.

He tapped his nose and glanced around the bar to make sure no one was eavesdropping. "He flies up to Antwerp, collects a small stash of gems which he carefully deposits up his tradesman's then flies on to Stockholm where he delivers them to a contact he's had there since the war."

"That must be painful."

He shrugged, "But lucrative. Avoiding the tedious formalities of import duties and tax, there are big profits to be made. He has a couple of other contacts around Europe too so it's a nice little business for him."

We began the next set, still playing to an almost empty room when a cute blonde looked in and persuaded a group of friends she was with to come and take a drink. After a couple of songs she also got them up to dance, laughed at Roger's jokes and generally brightened up what would otherwise have been a boring night. It wasn't long before she and John began exchanging admiring glances.

Roger noticed and remarked, "That little beauty looks right up your *straße*, John. Better get in there quick though before that dastardly Steve nicks another hot property off you."

I was about to protest but he was already announcing the next song. When we got to the midnight break John took me aside.

"I know you're with Astrid but can you give me support over there?" he said. "Nothing carnal, just laugh at the jokes while I break the ice."

"Sure. But please don't drag me down to that Blue Door club again. I'm getting a reputation."

We stepped off the stage and were making our way to her table when loud voices at the front door distracted us. I quickly glanced at John whose face was now registering something between exasperation and disbelief.

With just a touch of hysteria in his voice, he managed to croak, "Who fucking invited them?!"

"Don't ask me," I said, adding rather unhelpfully, "but she looks terribly pleased to see you,"

"John!" Birgit shouted as she rushed across the dance floor and into his arms. "Ooh, I'm so happy to see you," she squealed. "Have you missed me as much as I've missed you?"

"Of course," he said coolly. "Er… Why didn't you tell me you were coming?"

"Oh, it was a last minute idea of Peter's. He's so clever."

John glared at Peter, who was busy lighting Roger's cigarette. "Too bloody clever," he muttered darkly.

Meanwhile, across the room Wolfgang was already chatting with the blonde and her friends, so I went over to join them. Some introductions were made and she told me her name was Rosie.

We exchanged some initial pleasantries and she asked, "Your colleague, the organist, he looked surprised by his friend's arrival?"

"Yes, he wasn't expecting any visitors."

"Is she a serious friend?"

"No, I wouldn't say that."

"Good. In that case I might come back in a couple of days."

"Excellent. I know he'll be delighted."

For two people who didn't understand a word the other one was saying, Astrid and I got on surprisingly well. Actually, it was a shame I didn't understand her as she talked an awful lot and I guessed it was about interesting stuff. But I was happy to just pretend to listen and hope I'd picked up some German by the time we returned.

When she wasn't working, she would come to the Arcadia and afterwards we would go home to her place, build the bed and delight in each other's bodies. On her free days we would go for walks in the

English Garden or take a coffee somewhere and behave like other tourists. I thought she was wonderful and I noticed how people would stop and smile at us as we walked by. For me it was a happy time.

Then all too soon it was the end of the month and we would be moving on. The thirty-first was a Friday and it was already a full house when we arrived. Ivo watched with interest as we made our way around the room, shaking hands with many of the guests who had now become friends. When we reached the bar he took Roger aside.

"You've really made this month a success. I don't remember many other bands getting this kind of reception before."

Roger nodded, but it was clear he had plans to get us out of clubs like this and into something more upmarket. The only problem was that Herr Müller had spoken to Bachmann and was preparing to make a new deal for October.

After the final song, we agreed to meet up at noon to pack up the equipment and have a drink with the staff. I went back to Astrid's for one last night of passion and left in the morning promising that we'd see each other in Stuttgart in a week or so.

Bleary-eyed and with most of us nursing impressive hangovers, the band arrived only a few minutes late at the Arcadia. The VW needed to be brought round to the front of the club but there were no free parking spaces. While we waited for one to emerge we took the equipment apart and moved it closer to the door.

Claudia and Gina turned up shortly after with cakes and coffee, so while Kassy kept an eye on the parking situation we had a break.

I had only taken one or two bites when he shouted, "Quick, there's a space! Somebody go down there and reserve it and I'll get the VW."

John offered to go so the rest of us continued to enjoy the refreshments. A little later he reappeared looking a trifle twitchy. He went over to Roger, who was deep in conversation with Gina.

"I think we'd better leave."

Roger raised a quizzical eyebrow. "And that would be because?"

"I was keeping the space for Kassy when some bloke in a BMW turned up and tried to reverse in to it. I shouted to him that it was reserved, but he just ignored me. So I stood my ground in the space and the bugger drove over my foot!"

Roger looked at him sharply and said, "That was rather unsporting."

"You think! I wasn't at all happy so I went over to him and the arrogant bastard just waved me away, like I was the parking attendant. Anyway, he wound down his window and I took the opportunity to thump him."

Both Roger and I stared at him in alarm.

"The good news is that he buggered off, and the VW is downstairs." His expression became a little more contrite. "The bad news is he was screaming something about the *polizei*."

Roger reacted at once. "OK, men, we need to pack the gear as quickly as possible. John, did he see you with the VW?"

"No, I don't think so."

"Did he see you come in here?"

"Nope."

"Good. He may not realise you're with us. Hop back round to the apartment and we'll pick you up there."

We got the gear down and loaded in record time, then Kassy and I jumped in the VW and headed off around the corner, just as a BMW followed by a police car came racing the other way.

We pulled up at the apartment and loaded the cases while Roger and Wolfgang walked round from the club. Together with a nervous-looking John, they slipped into Donald's Mercedes and in some haste we all left Munich.

Part Four

Stuttgart & the Rhineland

CHAPTER NINETEEN

Starting All Over Again

You don't see them much these days, but in 1972 a VW Kombi was one of the most popular pick-ups on European roads. Fans of lowbrow, American summer-stock movies will know the model, often decorated with 'ban the bomb' stickers and a surfboard on the roof. It was economical and roomy at the back so perfect for our purpose, but I can still get a jolt of fear at the memory of it fully loaded and careering down the autobahn at speed.

The problem was that the Volkswagen engine was situated somewhere up the back, so the only thing between you and the road in front was a windscreen and a thin sheet of metal. Perched together precariously on a bench seat, with the heavy sound equipment stacked behind us, the sensation was something akin to hurtling down the Colorado River strapped to the front of a fast-moving log.

Seat belts were a luxury this particular model didn't provide, and so the journey from Munich turned out to be a distinctly hair-raising adventure. Near-fatal incidents involving Beamers and Mercs roaring up to within a metre of our back bumper, tailgating us and flashing their lights impatiently as we attempted to overtake slow-moving lorries – which in turn would pull out and try to pass even slower army convoys – were only narrowly avoided.

The whole thing was mayhem and with no speed limit on the autobahn, it was mayhem at an insanely high speed. From the front of our 'log' we finally spotted the blue roof of Donald's Mercedes. It was indicating right, so hopefully we were approaching Stuttgart.

I'm sure it's a vibrant city now – after all, it's home to both Mercedes and Porsche – but back in 1972, Stuttgart felt provincial compared to Munich. It appeared as though they were trying to build themselves out of that perception however, as there was a massive amount of construction work going on. They were also digging the new subway system so the city centre was one huge building site.

Despite having been there only a month earlier, we got hopelessly lost looking for the boarding house where we would be staying, and spent over an hour stuck in traffic. The city centre lay in a deep basin, and when we finally found our new home it was back out of the centre, right at the top of the basin's rim. Located on a quiet, tree-lined avenue, our accommodation for the next two weeks was a modest, three-storey house with a small but perfectly tended front garden. We unloaded our suitcases and rang the doorbell, which was promptly answered by a short, plump lady who introduced herself as Frau Rau.

Her age was somewhere between seventy and seventy-five and she had a kind but world-weary face with grey hair pulled back in a bun. Dressed in a long skirt and an old, moth-eaten cardigan, she had two or three more woolly garments tied carelessly around her waist, which gave her the unflattering profile of a duck.

She welcomed us perfunctorily while explaining there were a couple of other bands living in the house this month, her establishment being the number-one choice for travelling musicians. As such, she would be requiring the full two weeks' rent in advance. Recalling our furtive departure from Deutsches Haus, I couldn't fault her logic.

We followed in respectful silence as she waddled off down the hall listening with one ear as she mechanically read out the house rules. These included no women, no alcohol, no gambling and no loud music.

As he was expecting a visit from Gina, Roger's interest perked up.

"We understand perfectly, dear lady. A world without rules creates only anarchy." He smiled virtuously and went on, "I imagine that doesn't mean wives who—"

Her bored expression was gone and she raised her finger warningly. "No women means exactly that. If I find females in the house the offender will immediately be evicted."

As most of us were expecting a romantic visit at some point, a few anxious looks were exchanged. But, putting that worry aside for another day, we continued upstairs to the top floor in silence. John and I settled ourselves into a decent enough room with a view over the city. It was light and airy and the most comfortable room we'd had in Germany so far. We quickly unpacked, joined the others downstairs and made our way back down the basin to the centre of town and the Happy Night.

The minute we walked through the entrance, we could feel the buzz, and it was a totally different buzz to anything we had experienced at the Arcadia. From the moment guests arrived, lively waiters rushed around finding them tables, serving cocktails and delivering ice buckets filled with champagne. The whole vibe of the place was more electric, professional and exciting.

The guests were also very different to the regulars visiting the Arcadia. In place of Roger's infamous *freunde der nacht* were smart, young professionals interspersed with a glamorous assortment of the Stuttgart in-crowd.

The playing times were from nine p.m. until two a.m. with forty-five minutes on stage followed by fifteen-minute breaks – it felt like a vacation. Our bandleader wasn't going to get much reading done either as there would be no time for 'beefsteak' music. We would be expected to play an unbroken program of dance music and instead of the quiet breaks we were used to, there was a hyped-up DJ playing the latest disco hits, entertaining and annoying the crowd in a curious mixture of transatlantic German.

Rubbing his hands together, Roger said, "OK boys, now we're in a grown-up club. Let's show these people what we can do."

CHAPTER TWENTY

Gypsy Woman

I mentioned our previous encounter with a group of Gypsies on the autobahn. Now we saw some at close hand and, as it turned out, a bit too close for comfort.

It was the third or fourth evening and so far everything was going smoothly. Both the audience and staff seemed to really like us and the general opinion was that it was turning into a successful gig.

A little after eleven p.m., a trio of Gypsy ladies entered the club and were shown to a table close to the stage. They were attractive, expensively dressed – in what I can only describe as *Zigeuner* chic – and began consuming an impressive amount of sekt. One of them, an absolutely stunning blonde, was making eyes at Kassy. When he did his James Brown numbers, she got up to dance and gyrated sexily in front of the stage. Then just before the break a note was delivered by a waiter inviting Kassy over to their table for a drink. Despite Roger's warnings that he was playing with fire, he eagerly accepted.

Personally I couldn't see what the fuss was about. They were exotic but didn't appear particularly menacing. I modified that opinion later though when one of them walked past me on her way to the ladies' room. A couple of girls must have said something to piss her off as she spun around and viciously spat at them. She had exceptionally long fingernails and they were drawn threateningly. The girls, realising they might have made a slight gaffe, hurriedly scuttled off while she gave them one last, venomous stare, then carried on as if nothing had happened.

Wolfgang was watching and said, "Kassy needs to be careful. They're dangerous people to mess with and the women are worse than the men."

It didn't particularly bother me as I had no amorous feelings in that direction. A letter from Astrid had just arrived and Wolfgang was translating it for me. She was missing me already and was working a lot at the moment but would try and get up to Stuttgart in the next few days. Great. I just needed to work out the small problem of smuggling her in and out of Frau Rau's.

The following afternoon a few of us went into the town to do some shopping. We were passing a beer hall when a poster advertising live music featuring 'The Ivy Benson Band – *direkt aus London*' caught our eye. An all-female big band playing daily matinee performances from five p.m. It sounded like fun so we went inside.

Gosh, my dad would have been in heaven. They were playing all the music he loved: Glenn Miller, Tommy Dorsey, Benny Goodman, Duke Ellington – and not badly either. The swing numbers were brilliant and they bopped, boogied and jived their way through *Tuxedo Junction, Take the "A" Train* and *One O'Clock Jump*.

Sadly they also felt obliged to play some modern chart hits which weren't as good. One of the trumpet players handled the vocals in a perfunctory manner, accompanied by the rhythm section, heavily beefed up by the brass and woodwind players all shaking tambourines and maracas. The percussion vastly outnumbered everything else so it was a heck of a racket. There was also something just a tad *St Trinian's* about it all. With the exception of the elderly bandleader, who I imagined was Ivy Benson, the ladies ranged in age, from early twenties to mid-forties. While the older ladies were giving it their all, most of the younger ones were going through the motions with one eye on the music and the other on the males in the audience.

When they took their break, they came sauntering into the hall and as we were the only group of guys there under the age of sixty, ambled over in our general direction. On hearing us speaking English, they eagerly made some space at our table and pulled up chairs.

On closer inspection I guess they were the kind of mixed eccentrics you would expect in an all-female swing band touring the continent: cosy and humorous, with a non-stop stream of double entendres flying across the table. While they all could have been lifted straight out of a Giles cartoon in the *Sunday Express*, a few of them were quite attractive and a blonde clarinet player, who had just performed a cracking version of *Moonlight Serenade*, was a stunner. Sadly she was the one who was the least interested in any of us, although a couple of the others made up for that by coming on strong.

A tall, dark-haired girl was chatting intently to John while one particular live wire from the trombone section slipped her hand onto my knee and asked what I was doing after the show. Well I'm no prude but I found myself behaving uncharacteristically chastely and telling her that no, she couldn't come home with me and wash my hair. She aimed a rather naughty pout at me then just as quickly gave my bum a playful pinch and announced she would bring some friends to watch us play the following evening.

Back at the Happy Night, the Gypsy lady was sitting at the same table but with another girlfriend this time. It was a similar routine to the previous night, with hot dancing washed down with a magnum of something sparkling. This time Kassy didn't join them in the break, preferring to go to the bar with us instead. By the second break the girl made it clear she didn't like being ignored and marched over, angrily asking what was up. In an effort to calm the situation Kassy took her to a quiet corner where they talked for a while, and at closing time – to the clear disapproval of Roger – they left the club together.

The next day John and I bumped into Kassy while shopping

downtown and he invited us for a coffee. After being served he looked at us thoughtfully for a few moments then burst out, "I've really fucked up."

Pricking up our ears with sudden interest, we waited for him to go on.

"That girl. I went back with her again last night and now I just can't get rid of her. I don't know how to end it. You saw what she was like, she won't take no for an answer. And now I've heard that Sonja is coming tomorrow with Peter and Birgit."

John perked up at this news, but then remembered the female band from yesterday. "Shit! What is it with that girl? Can't she at least just once tell me when she's coming? I don't like these constant bloody surprise visits. It puts a man off his stride."

Kassy ignored him and continued, "If she's there tonight I'm just going to have to be brutal. I know Roger's going to go mad but it's the way it is."

We nodded. I was just relieved that Astrid wouldn't be here for a few more days as it sounded like it was going to be a mite crowded up at Frau Rau's.

In the evening a group of the girls from yesterday arrived at the club and commandeered a large table beside the dance floor. The trombone player scrubbed up rather well but was being too obvious, nudging her friends and eyeing me like something on a slab in a butcher's window. I believe she may even have been licking her lips. Well she could whistle for that, I thought. Across the room, Kassy's lady was sitting at her usual table, this time alone.

We started playing and the girls got up to dance, forming a circle around their handbags in that funny English style. It wasn't long though before all eyes were back on the Gypsy lady who was also on the dance floor getting down and dirty while throwing our singer hungry looks.

When the break came the girls all waved, so we went over and joined them. The trombone player, whose name was Dawn, made a space for me beside her. At first, she behaved herself, but it wasn't long before her hand was back on my knee. She wanted to know what I was doing later and if I fancied going out. In an attempt to change the subject, I asked how long she had been with the band.

"Oh, I only joined a few weeks ago. I needed to get away from England for a bit and instead of running away with the circus, I ran away with the band," she said, giggling. "Ivy's a great boss and she makes you feel you're part of a big family. It's a nice gig, very girly but nice."

Wolfgang was listening and said, "Funny, I can remember seeing posters for Ivy Benson's swing band when I was growing up in Hamburg."

"Yeah, she's been around since before the war," Dawn replied. "They were the house band on the BBC once upon a time and even played for Monty on VE Day."

I left them chatting and went over to the bar to get a Coke. Our singer was there, warily eying the room.

"How's it going, Kassy?" I asked cheerfully. "All sorted with your lady? She still looks terribly keen when she's dancing."

"No, no, she's taken the hint," he said, sounding a lot more confident than he looked. Sneaking a cautious peek in her direction, he declared, "No, I'll have no more problems there."

It was time for the next set, so we headed back to the stage. By now the club was full so we kept the tempo up, playing one soul track after another. It was hot work so at the next break I went to the dressing room to change my stage shirt.

I'd only just got it off when the door flew open and Dawn strolled in and drawled, "Hello, big boy. I was talking to your nice friend Wolfhound and he suggested you might be in here."

"Who?" I asked, but before I could get an answer she was halfway across the room and pushing me up against the wall.

She clamped her lips on mine and stuck her tongue so far down my throat I thought she was going to take out my tonsils. Moving swiftly down my chest, her mouth licking and kissing everything in sight, she put a hand between my legs and started pulling on the zip.

No no no, this is not good, I thought desperately. Somebody could come in and not only that, I'm in a bloody relationship!

"Dawn, please stop," I pleaded.

She was oblivious to any protests so I gently pushed her away. At the same time the door opened. Thank God it's only John, I noted with relief. Just as quickly however I realised someone else was with him. At first I couldn't see who it was but as he turned around, there was Astrid, staring straight at me.

What was she doing here? And more to the point, what the hell was Tommy Dorsey doing down there on her knees? Of all the bloody unfairness!

Trying to find a plausible explanation, I babbled something stupid but stopped when I saw the pain in Astrid's eyes. Tears were welling up and in that moment I knew I had lost her. She turned and ran out.

I was too stunned to do anything and then Roger appeared at the door and loudly announced, "Gentlemen! The honest burghers of Stuttgart await. Let's not disappoint them."

John, who had been staring at me with interest, glanced down at Dawn and advised, "And while you're down there, dear, I think you'd better put that animal back in its cage. Some of the audience might be vegetarian."

I was cringing with embarrassment and it didn't help that my two band mates were grinning like a couple of cats.

"You dog!" John said. "Who would have known? Carry on like this and they'll have to change the name of the place from the Happy Night to the Happy End!"

We started the next set and I scanned the club, hoping Astrid was sitting in a corner somewhere, but the place was so busy it was impossible to spot her. The evening dragged on and it became clear she had already left.

Unfortunately for Kassy, his lady wasn't going anywhere. When she realised he wasn't coming to sit with her she picked up some unsuspecting punter, dragged him onto the dance floor and locked him in a tight clinch while licking his ear and rubbing his crotch.

She was all over the poor bloke, but realising how unstable she was he made a hasty exit, leaving her alone to turn her drunken attentions back towards the stage. Sensing that things were about to get out of control, Kassy went and sat with her in the next break. Whatever he said worked because she was on her best behaviour for the rest of the evening. Then once again they left together at the end.

The English girls were keen to go on to another place and our band didn't need much persuading. Someone suggested the Theater Klause, a beautiful late-night bar which shared a turn-of-the-century building with one of the town's theatres. I didn't fancy it as I suspected I would end up being the butt of the evening's jokes so I said goodnight and started off in the direction of Frau Rau's.

I'd only gone a few steps down the road when I heard someone walking behind me. It was Dawn.

"Sorry, I'm not in the mood," I said in my best brush-off voice. "I'm way too pissed as I broke up with my girlfriend this evening. Oh yeah, that's right, because you decided to help yourself to what's in my trousers." I gave her a look of bewilderment. "I mean, fuck me! What was that all about?"

"Maybe you didn't want to," she said, "but the little fellow between your legs was eager and willing. He wasn't little for very long." Gently she put her arms on my shoulders and stared into my eyes. "Steve, I'm sorry, I'm really sorry. I can't undo what's done but let me make it up to you. Why don't we just go back to yours?"

"No, I don't think that's a good—"

She put a finger over my lips to hush me and continued, "I'll do whatever you want. We can read a book, practise German, or if you're up for it have hot, sweaty sex. No limits, anything at all." Seeing me hesitate, she whispered, "Never fancied getting it up at the crack of Dawn?"

"Phew, you're no shrinking violet, are you?" I complained.

"Can't afford to be," she said, clinging to my arm a little desperately.

I detected a change in her manner. The bluster was gone, her eyes were tearful and I caught sight of a lonely little girl underneath. I couldn't leave her like this so I suggested we go and sit down on a street bench. We were silent for a few minutes and then she surprised me by telling me she was married.

"Well married might be an overstatement," she said sourly. "He buggered off at the end of last year with a policewoman from Aldershot." I pondered that for a moment while she continued in a small voice, "It really messed me up. It was like somebody died. For weeks I couldn't do anything, I just stared at the TV. One day I knew I had to snap out of it, so I answered an ad in the *Melody Maker* and here I am." She made an attempt at a smile and her voice became more matter-of-fact. "Now he's been in touch, the grovelling little toad, and wants to come back and give it another try. Trouble is, I'll probably say yes." Her eyes narrowed. "But before I do I want to have lots and lots of sex. I just want to be heroically shagged by someone I fancy." She shrugged. "Then if he does it again it won't hurt as much."

There are times in your life when you know you make the right decision and other times when you know you don't. I had an uneasy feeling I was about to make the latter, but I couldn't leave her on her own so I took her back to our place.

Despite the dire warnings, the landlady was sound asleep so it wasn't difficult sneaking Dawn upstairs. We undressed in silence and got under the duvet but then strangely, I think we both felt a little shy. After all the action in the dressing room it was weird, but we were both content to just hold each other close. She smelt lovely and her body was luscious and warm, so I lay there and was just about to fall asleep when I heard the boys coming down the hall. The door burst open and Wolfgang and John came in.

"You lucky bugger," Wolfgang declared jubilantly. "Look who we found wandering around on her own…" His voice trailed away as they took in the scene before them.

"Oh fuck, not again!" John groaned.

Right behind them was Astrid. Her face was red and blotchy from crying and her mascara had run, but it was those beautiful, sad eyes that held my attention. She stared at me impassively without saying anything then turned and walked out. The boys' faces were a picture of stunned surprise. I shouted after her but it was too late. I heard the front door slam.

With all the racket, we must have woken Frau Rau. We could hear her coming up the stairs, moaning something in German. Oh great, that was all we needed now. I pushed Dawn under the duvet and whispered to her to be quiet. Wolfgang went out to meet the landlady and must have come up with a good story because her footsteps faded as she went back down the hall.

He came back in, clearly pleased with himself for getting rid of her so easily. I wasn't quite as delighted.

"Well done. Twice in one night! What do you boys do for an encore?"

Wolfgang's expression turned to surprise and then hurt. "Oh, that's nice! That's very nice. How were we to know you were all cosied up in here with her? Mr Broken-Hearted with his seventy-six tromboner!"

Dawn emerged from under the duvet and looked up at him sharply. "Oh yeah, thanks a lot! Suave. Not often a girl gets so many wonderful compliments."

She sounded like she might be on the point of crying, but took a deep breath and asked if they could step out so she could get dressed. The other two left and I got dressed too.

"I'll walk you home. You can't go on your own now."

She made an effort to smile and asked, "Want to come back to mine? The girl I share with is a deep sleeper."

"No, I just can't. You have somewhere to sleep while Astrid is out there on her own. I need to see she's OK."

We crept downstairs and headed over to the boarding house where her band were staying. When we arrived at her front door I went to give her a goodnight peck on the cheek but in her usual style she grabbed me for a full-on snog.

"Sorry Steve," she gasped when we came up for air. "I probably taste of wine and fags."

"Well you weren't too bothered about that before," I said with just a hint of malice, but then eased back on the critique… "Listen Dawn, it's been an interesting evening but I've really got to try to find my girl now."

"Yea, I know," she said wistfully. "Maybe another time, another place." She softly kissed my cheek and went into the house.

The train station was my first stop but no one was there so I did a couple of circuits of the town centre in the faint hope I might bump into her. After an hour it became clear she was nowhere to be found. Finally I gave up and walked back home.

CHAPTER TWENTY-ONE

She's a Lady

Too little sleep was compounded by Roger coming into our room early in the morning and asking John if he could lend him some money. Somewhere in the mist of torpor I heard him say, "Three hundred marks, John, if you've got it. Mausi needs it for the kids. It's a desperate situation and, in the words of Monsieur Lautrec, I'm a little short. The red-eyed frog apparently isn't doing his duty and they need money for food."

John was still half asleep but mumbled something and pointed to the bedside table where his wallet was.

"Thanks! You're a prince," Roger said. "I'll pay you back in a couple of days."

I drifted back off to sleep and it was several hours before we both woke again. This time it was to me groaning about the previous evening's shambles. "Wow! What a complete mess. How the hell did I let all of that happen?"

"A good start would be by not allowing strange women to do dirty things to you in the dressing room," John said, yawning.

"I didn't!" I complained, but I could see it was no good pleading my innocence as the die was already cast. I changed the subject. "Is it my imagination or did Roger borrow some money off you this morning? Something about Mausi and his kids needing food?"

"Yes," he said. "Shouldn't Redeye be looking after them if he's moved in? What a charmer he's turned out to be."

We dressed and walked down to the Wienerwald restaurant in town. It was where we had dined on the evening of the audition and it had since become our unofficial home and meeting place. Wolfgang came here every day for a lunch of fried chicken, a couple of beers and a small helping of the waitress who had served us on that first day. He was having some success as she constantly fussed around him and brought him beers that he never paid for.

Kassy was already there, waiting for Sonja, which reminded John that Birgit would shortly be arriving too. Any pleasure he was feeling however was short-lived when our drummer entered, wearing a brand new suit.

"Is that what you used my money for?" he burst out. "A bloody suit? You said you needed it for your kids!"

Roger looked shamefaced – well momentarily – then regained his usual confident composure.

"Sorry about that John. False alarm. I misunderstood the message from Mausi." He paused for effect. "Then I saw this wonderful bargain and couldn't resist it." He shot his cuffs and continued, "I'll pay you back of course, but in the meantime I think we should see it as an investment. In my role as bandleader I need the right togs when negotiating with the sharks that prey on poor, unsuspecting musicians like us."

John was gnashing his teeth in frustration and Kassy didn't improve matters.

"So it has nothing to do with Gina arriving today?" he asked.

Roger gave him a withering look and said, "And I may have to begin my work by negotiating the release of a short, randy Indo singer – or what's left of him when those nice Gypsies find out what he's been up to with that girl. They will find out of course when she runs off and tells them."

Kassy nervously flicked some imaginary fluff from his jacket collar and stuck his chin out, "Well it makes me feel much better knowing you'll come to that negotiation dressed as their bank manager!"

Any scathing response was cut short by the timely arrival of Sonja, Birgit and Peter. We hadn't seen them for a few weeks so it was a noisy reunion.

"Happy to see me, John?" Birgit said. "If it's inconvenient I can sleep on the sofa in Peter's room?"

John smiled at her tenderly but must have remembered he was supposed to be angry with her. "No no, the lovely Peter can sleep on his own, but next time let me know you're coming!"

Roger took the change of subject as a convenient cue to go and meet Gina at the railway station. John's eyes smouldered with resentment as he watched him leave.

"Can you believe that shit? He lied to me so brazenly."

Kassy leaned over and said, "The other thing he didn't tell you was that he used his own money to book a room for him and Gina in some smart hotel. That's why he needed cash for the suit."

I left them shortly after that and went back to our room for a couple of hours. When I returned to the club the ladies were busy fixing their makeup in our dressing room, and the band were hanging around at the bar. Just like the previous evening, Kassy appeared anxious: tapping his foot and glancing nervously towards the entrance. I ordered a Coke and he asked me if we could have a quiet chat. We went and sat down at a table in the corner.

"Look, there's a good chance Sofia will come here tonight. You may have noticed she can be a little headstrong." He chuckled tentatively while I looked at him blankly. "Do me a favour and sit with her and pretend she's with you if that happens."

I almost choked on my Coke. "Are you serious?" I yelped, hurriedly wiping Coke off my shirt. "I haven't exchanged one word with her before. Christ! Does she even speak English?"

"She's actually quite charming and has told she likes you."

"Yeah right," I snorted.

"Evening, chaps! And what a wonderful evening it is," Roger said as he proudly led Gina over to the bar, where they circulated like hosts at a society party. Gina was dressed in something black and clingy and made a big theatrical affair of hugging and kissing everyone. I turned back to Kassy, who was waiting patiently for an answer. Grudgingly I said I'd think about it.

It was Friday evening and the club was packed. Kassy opened the proceedings with *Here Comes That Rainy Day Feeling Again* followed by all of us on *Two Divided by Love*. At the break I joined the others at a table Roger had reserved for the ladies. It was the first time I'd really had a chance to speak to Sonja who – apart from being a good-looking woman – was very sweet, although I got the impression she could be jealous. A couple of times she would ask who a girl was when one of them happened to smile at Kassy in too friendly a way.

Wolfgang, who was sitting across the table, gave me a knowing look and leaned over to whisper, "If you think that's bad, Donald's one's even worse. She believes every woman wants to fuck him, and she can get silly about it. Strange, as he's always faithful." He grinned. "And of course you've seen the wonderful establishment where she works."

A little after midnight, I heard a commotion somewhere to the right of the stage and looked over in time to see Sofia and two friends trying to get their usual table. A couple were already sitting there, and I don't think they had any plans to move, until some unfriendly persuasion from the three ladies convinced them the bar might be more comfortable. Sofia and her friends took their seats and proceeded to order sekt from an anxious waiter. At first Kassy just ignored her but when she moved onto the dance floor and began to make a spectacle of herself, dancing provocatively with her friends, he aimed some nervous looks in my direction. Oh God! I could see where this was going.

John was watching too and said with an evil grin, "Good luck with that. Oh, and stay away from the dressing room!"

"Bastard," I said.

When the next break came, I got a drink at the bar and wandered over to Sofia's table, asking if I could join them. The three of them just stared at me in astonishment. I think if at that moment I'd extracted a chilled bottle of Bollinger from my arse with a flourish they would have been less dumbfounded. Anyway, I took their silence as acquiescence and sat down. I asked if any of them spoke English and was surprised, and relieved, to hear that Sofia spoke it well. She got straight to the point and asked if Kassy had sent me over.

"Yes. His girlfriend's here for the weekend so he asked me to keep you company. I can go if you want?"

She thought about this then replied, "No, that's fine. It's nice to speak to an American."

"Actually, I'm English. Does that work?"

She laughed, but I could see her attention was straying back to where Kassy and Sonja were sitting. He glanced over and smiled at us encouragingly. Quick as a cat, Sofia grabbed me and started kissing me fiercely on the lips. When I came up for breath, I peered uneasily over at Kassy but he was talking animatedly to Sonja. Sofia was watching me and relaxed back into her seat.

"So, Mr Englishman, you like kissing a Gypsy lady?" Bloody hell, she was a cool one. I was just formulating a diplomatic answer when she asked, "What about fucking one? You wanna try that?"

"Why?" I squeaked. My reaction uncomfortably somewhere between interest and panic. "Are we going to do that next? I'm here because Kassy wants me to keep you company, not just to make him jealous."

She looked at me sharply and burst out, "Ha! I don't need your damn company! Maybe I should go over there and make his girlfriend really jealous?"

Oh shit, this wasn't going at all well. Luckily I saw the others heading back towards the stage for the final set so I took my leave. Sofia ignored me, but I bowed politely to the other two and hastily joined the band on stage.

"How did it go?" Kassy asked as I was strapping on my guitar. "It looked like you were getting on great."

"Yeah right. If you have any sense you'll get Sonja out of here quickly at the end. That woman is seriously pissed and could do anything."

"No, I tell you what," he decided. "We're all going to that late-night theatre place you guys go to. You take Sonja and tell her I'll follow along in ten minutes. Make some excuse about me having to talk to the manager."

Anything was better than having to go back to that table. "Sure," I said.

We began the last set of the evening and Sofia sprang up from her seat and planted herself on the dance floor squarely in front of Kassy. It wasn't long before she was performing every conceivable erotic act while keeping time to the music. I didn't know about him but I could feel some lead in my pencil. Sonja had also noticed and was looking seriously pissed. From then on it was like watching a car crash in slow motion.

Sonja said something to Birgit and the two of them got up and danced over to the front of the stage. Now the three of them were in a line, making no effort to avoid each other. One girl – I think it was Sonja – pushed Sofia a little too hard and before we knew it, the two of them were at each other's throats with legs and fists flying.

Fortunately, there were a couple of big guys amongst the other dancers who quickly stepped in and pulled the two girls apart. This gave Birgit the opportunity to grab Sonja by the arm and drag her back to their table. Sofia glared malevolently after them, all the while clawing at one of the guys who was holding her. The club's manager and a bouncer came to his assistance and the three of them lifted her up and carried her kicking and screaming out of the club. A few minutes later her friends picked up their things and left, aiming some unfriendly looks at the stage. I had the feeling we hadn't heard the last of this.

CHAPTER TWENTY-TWO

My Way

The rest of the weekend was relatively quiet. We heard from one of the staff that Sofia was now banned from the club and wondered if there would be some kind of reaction from her friends or family. But nothing happened and by the beginning of the next week we had forgotten about the whole thing.

So we were totally unprepared when half a dozen Gypsies turned up in the club the following Wednesday – and this time they were all male. Every one of them looked like a rascal and no stranger to a little light savagery. Spreading themselves around a couple of tables, they ordered whiskies and turned to listen to us.

We were halfway through a set and I could see the others were already cautiously gauging the distance to the exit. OK, maybe those guys could fight, but could they run? They would have to run bloody fast to catch me. Christ, I hoped that woman had only fingered the tiny Indo singer – the lascivious beast. For his part Kassy was looking pale as a ghost. We carried on with another couple of songs and I took a few cautious peeks in their direction but was surprised to see that after the initial inspection they weren't giving us the evil eye, psyching us out or even looking our way. They were chatting intently to each other.

Sticking close together, we made our way to the bar in the break to discuss our dilemma. It seemed most likely they would wait until the end and get us on the way out. Maybe we could invite the bouncer and the waiters to an after-work drink? Roger went off and suggested it to them, but unfortunately they had other plans. We were on our own.

Making our way back to the stage, one of the Gypsies – a heavy-set villain flashing a mouth full of gold – collared Roger and said, "You have nice band my friend. Very nice." He rewarded us with a twenty-four karat smile. "We have my brother with us tonight and he is great singer. He can come up and sing something?"

Roger looked across the room to their table where they all sat quietly staring straight back at us.

"Yea, why not."

"Excellent. You play any Frank Sinatra? Maybe *My Way*?"

"Yea we can play that. What's your brother's name?"

"Hanzi."

"OK, we'll play a couple of songs and then we'll invite him up.

When he came to do his number, Hanzi turned out to be a small, soulful character. Svelte, with large, sorrowful eyes and a huge beak for a nose. Smiling gratefully, he took the microphone and started to sing.

"*Anda nowa ze end iz nehr and zo ay fass ze final coortan.*" It wasn't only the accent, it was the delivery too. He beat it, pummelled it and buzz-sawed his way through the melody until he dragged it kicking and screaming to the final climax: "*Ayyaah deeed eeet MOIAAY VAAAY!*"

Most of the audience looked dazed while some just laughed, but his friends were out of their seats cheering and clapping. Hopefully they would take that into consideration and be a little forgiving.

In the end we didn't have time to find out as they all immediately got up and left. Wondering what the hell had just happened, we exchanged puzzled looks while Wolfgang quipped that it was in fact the perfect punishment, having to listen to him sing.

The next evening, just before midnight, about ten of them arrived in the club. Had Sofia become impatient and recruited more relatives? Of all the bad luck. Tomorrow night was our last night and if we could have avoided them until after that, we would have been away clear.

The others were no doubt thinking the same thing. Wolfgang shouted over, "Roger, why don't you invite him up to slaughter another song?"

He didn't need to. Six Asbachs promptly arrived on a tray with the compliments of the group of gentlemen, and a request to hear their friend sing *My Way* again. To tumultuous applause from his friends he gave another torturous performance, beating the living daylights out of the melody and causing more GBH to the English language. The audience hated it but were drowned out by the cheers and applause from his own group and, just like before, they left straight afterwards.

During the break the manager came and had a word.

"Herr Kapellmeister. If they come again kindly don't invite him to sing. They are not the type of clientele the Happy Night wants to attract. I hope I have made myself clear?

"Of course," replied Roger biting his lip and rubbing his chin thoughtfully.

Thank goodness it was only one more night and then we were off to Wiesbaden.

The last night was a Friday and by nine p.m. the club was already heaving with customers so I doubted the men would even get in. Maybe we had seen the last of them, now all his friends had heard him sing?

Gypsies however have a lot of friends, and an hour later something approaching twenty of them turned up. If we looked surprised, the manager looked appalled as they rowdily went about trying to arrange a table and chairs by the dance floor.

Hurrying over to the stage the manager told us in no uncertain terms to ignore them. That was easier said than done. Within minutes a tray of drinks arrived with a request for their friend to sing.

Roger stared thoughtfully at their table before checking where the manager was. He was standing close to the stage, resolutely shaking his head. "No. We carry on as usual. Kassy! *It's Your Thing*, if you please."

By the next break Hanzi's brother was waiting for us when we got off the stage. He greeted us warmly, explaining how their friends and family had travelled a long way to hear Hanzi tonight. When he realised it wasn't getting him anywhere, he mentioned Sofia – not too much, just enough to let us know she was still angry over the way she had been treated. All eyes automatically swivelled around to our diminutive singer, who was starting to sweat horribly. That settled it.

When we got back on stage Roger announced, "*Liebe gäste*. We have a young man in the club who, over the last couple of evenings, has stunned the Happy Night's audiences with his fiery version of *My Way*. Let's invite him back up on stage tonight as it's our last evening and his last chance to stun the rest of you. Ladies and gentlemen, I give you Hanzi."

Hanzi leapt out of his chair and bounded up on stage with the triumphal air of a man picking up his third Oscar. I would like to report that he then produced if not a world-class performance at least a respectable one, but unfortunately once again it was the pits. The audience's reaction was mixed. His own group clapped and cheered wildly while the rest of the club remained silent. Some were laughing and there were even a few boos, which produced a small scuffle. On top of that they didn't immediately get up and leave. Bottles of whisky and cognac were arriving at their table and it looked like they were going to be there for some time.

At the next break, the manager, who was deep in conversation with their waiter immediately broke that off and came striding over.

"Herr Kapellmeister!" he called out. His voice sounding ominously close to hysteria. "Thank you for following my instructions. Yes indeed, thank you so much."

His eyes darted anxiously around the club, his gaze coming to rest on the tables full of Gypsies. He was making some unsettling mewing sounds and urgently tapping his foot. Finally he tore his eyes away and glared accusingly at us.

"Any other brilliant ideas?" he demanded. "Maybe you could ask him to come up and sing a whole set? Maybe they all could? Then we can clear the club early and all go home."

Roger was anxiously rubbing the back of his neck. "Yeah, look, we're really sorry about that. They just wouldn't take no for an answer. Bloody difficult people to refuse. Tell us what you want us to do and we'll do it."

For a moment the manager just gazed steadily at him. "Oh! Yes, I like that, I like that a lot." There was a petulant tone to his voice as he continued. "I want you to get rid of them. Yes, that's it. Ha ha! And straightaway please. Thank you." With that he turned on his heel and strode off, muttering loudly to himself.

As if seeking inspiration, Roger turned his attention to our lead singer. "Kassy you're good with Gypsies. Any ideas?" Getting no response, he continued, "Maybe you could take your smouldering sensuality over there and politely persuade them all to fuck off!"

"Calm down," Kassy said. "We'll go over and talk to them. I'm sure you'll think of something."

"Yeah, you never know Roger, it might be an opportunity to try the new suit out?" John suggested helpfully.

Grim-faced, our drummer led the way over to Hanzi's table, where we were greeted like long-lost friends. Chairs were quickly found and glasses of cognac offered. Wearily Roger looked around the table and across to the bar where a thoroughly pissed-off manager was staring balefully at us.

Roger raised his glass in a toast and said, "Drink up, lads. If that bugger's going to hang us, it might as well be for a sheep as for a lamb."

CHAPTER TWENTY-THREE

Break Up to Make Up

Our next stop after Stuttgart was a little further north. Wiesbaden is situated on the banks of the Rhine, just across the river from Mainz. The two towns served as the southern gateway to the Rhine cruises that sailed past the many fairy-tale castles dotted along that stretch of the river. With its manicured lawns, fountains and elegant buildings, it had all the hallmarks of a genteel European spa town, and one of its crown jewels was the Park Hotel and Cafe. A grand belle époque wedding cake of a place, it had been entertaining the great and the good of European society for over a century, and for the next five days we would be supplying some of that entertainment. As this was our first time at the Park Cafe, we would be playing for a slightly reduced fee, but the hotel would accommodate us until the end of the month. For once everyone was more than satisfied with the deal Bachmann had arranged.

After unloading the VW and building the stage up, we took a moment to admire the beautiful surroundings. It ticked pretty much every box on the band's wish list as it was another example of the kind of upmarket clubs they wanted us to play at on a regular basis. It was elegant and could have even passed muster alongside the Ritz or Savoy in London with its high ceilings, golden chandeliers and impressive archways and columns. Several sets of French doors were open to the street and there was an outside terrace facing a park. A huge bar in the centre of the room, packed with well-heeled Rhinelanders, stood across from a grand dining room.

Walking out on the stage later that evening I studied the audience and could see they looked as beautiful and as stylish as the surroundings... well that is except for two people sitting at a table just beneath the stage. I had to look twice but damn it, there they were: Redeye and Mausi. They stared up at us blankly, although I detected a grim look of determination on Redeye's face.

The others saw them about the same time as I did. Donald was the only one who made an attempt at being friendly, giving them a polite wave. Roger, not sure if he should play the role of injured cuckold or guilty absconder, struck a pose somewhere in-between and haughtily arched his back, stuck his chin out and totally ignored them.

Starting with one of his new ballads, we then did something by Neil Diamond followed by Ray Charles. Hold on, was I missing something? Surely he wasn't on a campaign to pick up his own wife?

He introduced another one of his own songs and gave us one of his trademark smiles. "Put it like this chaps, I'm not going to make it easy for that knob. If I go down it will be fighting." He winked and I began to think he was actually enjoying the situation.

I noticed Mausi was smiling too, no doubt reminiscing about happier times when one of his songs could melt her heart. At the other end of the satisfaction scale was Redeye, who was scowling horribly.

By the break, Roger was in the right frame of mind to go over and say hello and the rest of us were curious enough to tag along. He strode over to their table and greeting them warmly, leaned towards Mausi and planted two ambassadorial kisses on her cheeks.

He then turned to Redeye and addressed him like the lazy pool boy: "Now then Berndt, how are you looking after Mausi? I hope you're taking your responsibilities seriously."

For a moment I thought our former landlord might actually get up and strike him, but Mausi quickly calmed the situation.

"That's nice, Roger, and yes, Berndt is looking after me. But he's disappointed that you and the band left Stockstadt owing him and his mother twelve hundred and thirty marks and they would like payment."

"Would they now? Would they indeed. That's very interesting Mausi, but actually, I left Stockstadt with Berndt and his mother owing me one wife and two kids." He paused for effect. "And a dear mother-in-law in small change! I believe that's a lot more valuable than twelve hundred marks."

I think I detected a half-smile on her lips. She turned to her companion for a response but Redeye didn't appear to be in the mood for a negotiation. Reverting to type, he growled something menacing before folding his arms and staring belligerently at the stage.

Roger took his cue. "I see! You obviously don't think my family are worth very much. Well I'll let you explain your reasoning to my dear wife. And in the meantime we'll bid you a good day. Mausi, let me know when I can see the kids. Maybe you could bring them over here for a weekend? We could have an afternoon out together."

With that, he nodded genially to them both then strode off. Not wanting to get into any small talk we made a hasty exit and joined him in the dressing room.

"That sorted his nonsense out," Roger said, grinning in satisfaction. "He's not getting a penny off us."

Sure enough, when we went back on stage their seats were empty and the next day Mausi phoned and arranged for Roger to take the kids for a day out.

CHAPTER TWENTY-FOUR

Travelin' Band

The last gig of the month would be in the beautiful riverside town of Rüdesheim. Before driving there we had to stop off at Bachmann's office as he had some contracts to sign and there were new posters for the band. Wiesbaden appeared to have been a success. The management were talking about re-bookings for later in the year and in spring 1973, so we wanted to hear what had been arranged.

Bachmann was apologetic. "Sorry boys, they wanted the second part of October and I've already booked you back into the Arcadia on those dates."

Although Roger already knew this, he took the opportunity to vent his frustration.

"Heinz, this band's on the way up and playing at the Arcadia is the way down. We're fed up of performing in dumps like that with a stage the size of a goat's scrotum and an audience more accustomed to being interviewed by Interpol than entertained by a world-class orchestra. We need the big hotels and the ski resorts."

Bachmann nodded. "I know, and we will get those, but I have to fill the dates in the calendar and October is usually a quiet month. I thought Munich during the Oktoberfest would be something you would like."

"And indeed we will," Roger said. "But it would be doubly good if it was somewhere more fitting the level we're at now. Possibly the

Regina Palast or the Bayerischer Hof. And Stuttgart? Have they said anything about a re-booking?"

Bachmann looked slightly perplexed and said, "It's curious. The first week the manager called me twice to tell me how keen they were to make new contracts. We even discussed November. But now he doesn't return my calls. Did anything happen?"

Roger was staring steadily at Kassy who in turn had found something interesting requiring his attention outside the window.

"No Heinz it went perfectly," Roger said, continuing to stare balefully at our singer. "Try him again, he's probably just busy."

Next we dropped by the Imperial in Worms to give some of the new posters to Schmiegel to promote the June gig. As we made our way down the stairs, we could hear a band rehearsing so we stopped by the entrance to listen. They weren't bad but nothing special. The drummer was singing something by Neil Diamond, and to be honest it just sounded like a poor imitation of Roger. He was a good-looking guy though. I asked Kassy who they were.

"The Timelords," he said.

"Aren't they the ones you told me about, Roger?" I asked.

"That's them," he said. "They nick our repertoire and arrangements, then have the rocks to bad-mouth us to club owners and managers behind our backs. But it's that arrogant git up there on the drums who pisses me off the most. Jimmie, the cut-price Tom Jones."

Kassy laughed and added, "Yes, Karl took a swipe at him once when he made a joke about the size of his organ. Knocked him flat! Ever since then there's been no love lost between us."

The music stopped and Roger turned on the charm. "OK, eyes and teeth, gentlemen." Beaming genially towards the stage he strode into the club. "Jimmie! Boys! Great to see you again. What a wonderful surprise."

The trip north to Rüdesheim was like driving down the wine list of a

1970s Chinese restaurant. Leaving the ancestral home of Liebfraumilch, we passed through Hochheim, where 'hock' originated. The wandering road then took us on through Nierstein, Oppenheim and Bingen before finally leading us into Rüdesheim.

As it was getting late we promptly looked for Kleins, the venue for tonight's gig. The address was on the Drosselgasse: a well-known tourist street famed for its picturesque drinking establishments. That evening the street was thronged with tourists and impossible to drive down. Not sure what to do next, we asked a local shopkeeper. He informed us that Kleins was located much further down the street, one of three identical cellar-clubs sharing a large medieval building close to the Rhine.

Gingerly Donald and Kassy reversed the Mercedes and VW through the crowd and back out of the Drosselgasse, then found a less busy backstreet which took us down towards the river. After a couple of false turns, we located the building housing the three clubs and parked up by the back entrance to Kleins.

An unhappy-looking man came dashing out to meet us, tapping his watch and asking who the Kapellmeister was. Roger introduced himself and responded rather casually to the man's worries about our lateness.

"No problem, *mein herr*. We'll be in and set up before you've had time to get back to the bar to prepare six gleaming glasses of frothy inspiration for my thirsty minstrels."

The man gaped at him for a moment before crisply responding, "You confuse me with somebody else, Herr Kapellmeister. I am the owner, Herr Klein. The man who will in fact be paying your thirsty minstrels their wages. It's the premier night of the season and we have a full house. Make sure you're ready to start at nine on the dot." With that he turned on his heel and shot off back inside.

We quickly got the gear down the stairs, into the club and set it up. It wasn't a large club but it was busy and the clientele, which was mainly made up of tourists, was already fuelled up on the local wine. Starting with a few up-tempo dance songs we soon switched to our

German party numbers, as they just looked like that kind of crowd. Roger suggested *La Bostella*: a novelty dance in the style of the conga line. We had played it at the Rosengarten in Mannheim and on a couple of busy nights at the Arcadia. It involved one or two members of the band going down to the dance floor and organising the dancers into a line, then leading them around the club in time to the music. Wolfgang and John offered to do the honours and got all the guests lined up.

We began the song and the boys did a couple of circuits of the club with everybody clapping, dancing and singing. Even Klein was clapping his hands and smiling. Wolfgang, who was clearly enjoying all the attention, indicated they would try taking them up the stairs onto the Drosselgasse and back. They wouldn't hear us playing up there but as they were all singing along so loudly it wouldn't really matter. The end of the line disappeared out of the door and the place was suddenly empty.

Klein came over to the stage and joked, "I hope that's not the last we've seen of them!"

Everyone laughed politely while the four of us continued to play the song to an empty club. The minutes went by as we waited for our boys to return with the audience. Glancing over at the bar I could see Klein was tapping his fingers impatiently. He began to look concerned, and to be honest, he wasn't the only one; we were all wondering where they had gone. After about fifteen minutes and countless more choruses of the song, we stopped when Wolfgang and John appeared at the door – all alone.

Shit, that didn't look good – that didn't look good at all. Klein stepped out from behind the bar and appeared bewildered: his mouth was working although no words were coming out. It was John who broke the silence.

"The street wasn't too busy when we got up there, so we turned right and made our way up to the top and danced our way back down again. It was going good."

"Yes, and then?" Roger asked impatiently.

"We got back down this end and… well all the fucking doors looked the same!"

Roger had put on his 'dad face'. "So where did you go?"

"We must have gone through the wrong one. We thought it was the right door. It looked like this club; it even sounded like this one. You were playing *Sex Machine*." He paused. "Although it turned out it wasn't actually you, it was a record on the disco…" His voice trailed away.

"Well which door? Where did you all end up?" Roger persisted.

John rubbed his brow uneasily and blurted out, "The club next door." Klein had joined us as John continued his wretched narration. "We tried to turn them all around again and leave, but it was so crowded and our group just mingled with the others on the dance floor. We tried our best but…"

At last Klein found his voice and turned accusingly to Roger. "So, Herr Kapellmeister, what he's telling me is that your orchestra has stolen my public! Stole them right out of my club and took them to another club!"

Wolfgang tried to shift the blame. "And it didn't help that the *scheiße manager* next door, having realised our small error, made it worse by handing out welcome drinks!"

Klein was apoplectic. He looked fit to either explode, burst out crying or collapse in a swoon.

By now even Roger had to admit defeat. He spread his arms in a gesture of resignation. "Herr Klein, I'm at a loss. That bastard manager next door has obviously stolen our audience. But maybe we're also being premature? Who knows, in a few minutes maybe they'll all come quietly home?"

I wasn't so sure. None of the clubs in Germany charged admission so customers could come and go as they pleased, and it was warm enough outside that people hadn't brought coats. Personally I'd stay where the crowd was, especially if it was a jumping disco with free drinks. Looking around the empty room, I fancied it myself.

A couple of hours later we were sitting quietly in the car driving back to Wiesbaden feeling somewhat chastened. A few of the audience had returned, but nowhere near the large, happy crowd who had left. Surprisingly Roger managed to get paid, although I'm sure Klein resented every *pfennig* of it.

As April turned to May, we once again packed our personal belongings into the van and made our way from Wiesbaden further north towards Dortmund.

CHAPTER TWENTY-FIVE

Every Picture Tells a Story

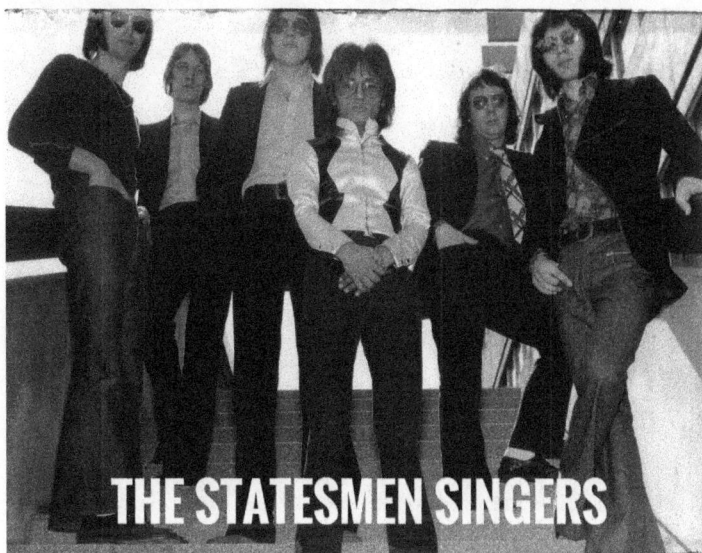

THE STATESMEN SINGERS

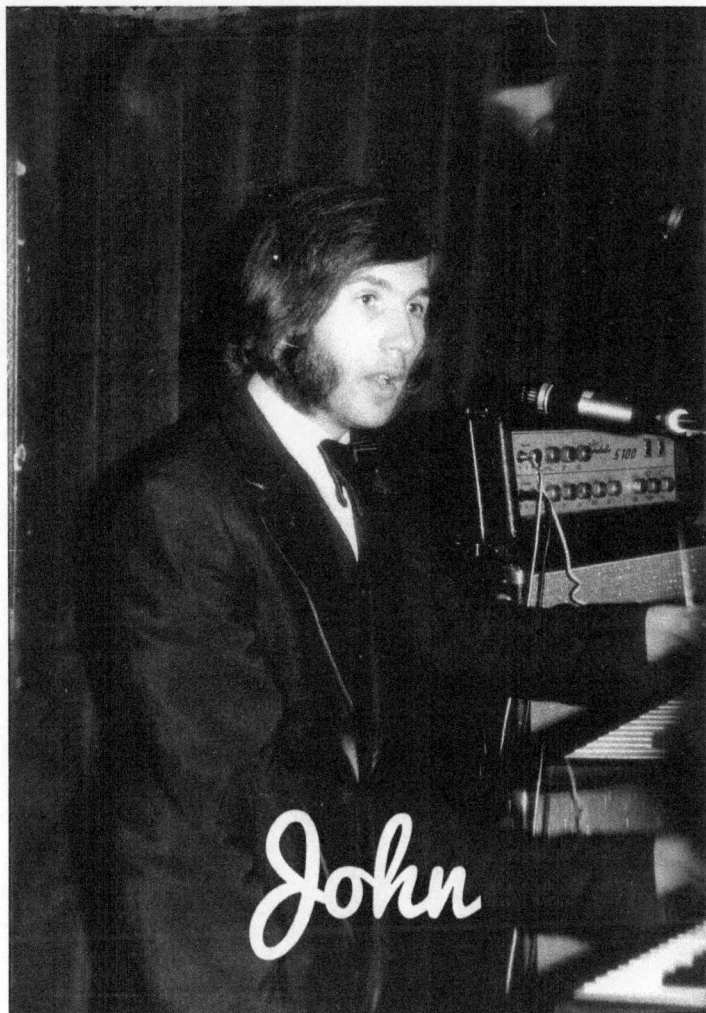

Wolfgang

* * *

CAFE ARCADIA MUNICH MARCH 72

HAPPY NIGHT STUTTGART APRIL 72

PART FIVE

DORTMUND & WORMS

CHAPTER TWENTY-SIX

Life on Mars

Before arriving in Germany, if anyone had asked me about the Ruhr Valley I would have said my knowledge was limited to whatever I'd learned watching movies like *The Dam Busters*: bouncing bombs, flooded factories and a rousing music score. In fact, as we whizzed along the autobahn skirting Düsseldorf, I couldn't resist humming the theme tune and feeling just a bit patriotic.

It was another butt-clenching journey but this time I was sitting together with Roger and Wolfgang in Donald's car while John was taking his turn with Kassy, strapped to the front of the 'log'. After driving through the beautiful Rhine region, the scenery had dramatically changed and we were now in a depressing, bleak industrial landscape full of ugly factories belching out smoke and pollution. It brought to mind the dark satanic mills of another rousing piece of music, so I quickly switched to that and let *Jerusalem* carry me onwards to Dortmund.

Zipping swiftly along the autobahn we passed a massive Krupps factory and then almost immediately came to a screeching halt behind a long line of stationary traffic. For all their efficiency and *vorsprung durch technik*, the Germans hadn't solved the problem of traffic jams any better than the British. As we were often to experience in Northern Germany, 20 and 30 kilometre tailbacks were daily features on these older autobahns that required constant repair. In the end, what should have been a two-hour journey took closer to four before we spotted the *ausfahrt* for Dortmund.

Following signs for the *stadtmitte*, we wound our way through a number of colourless suburbs. Dortmund was one of the most heavily bombed cities during the war and consequently had the architectural feel of somewhere rebuilt in rather a hurry. Entering the city centre, we quickly found the Corso which was situated on a pedestrianised shopping street opposite a couple of big department stores. There were parking spaces at the rear of the club and from there we went inside to make our presence known.

It was a reasonably sized club with dark-red walls and black leather and chrome furniture. A wooden stage stood at one end of the room across from a long bar. Between the two was a rectangular dance floor surrounded by tables and chairs and a DJ's booth which was decorated with hundreds of black vinyl 45rpm records. Unfortunately, after the Happy Night and Park Cafe, it felt rundown and dated. There didn't appear to be anyone around so a couple of the boys began shouting 'hello' but got little response. Finally an unremarkable man in a grey suit emerged unsteadily from a small office beside the bar. It was the middle of the afternoon but it became apparent he wasn't completely sober. In fact he was plastered.

Unperturbed, Roger turned on his usual charm. "Harry, what a great pleasure to be here again. How are you? Goodness me! You look absolutely great. What's the secret? A painting in the attic?"

Harry seemed to be having trouble focusing but made a stab at mumbling something unintelligible while introductions were made.

Roger increased the charm level to ten. "Apart from managing one of the coolest clubs in Germany, Harry is also a famous local disc jockey with a reputation for playing the hottest hits, so we're going to have to stay sharp to keep up."

We were all smiling foolishly, but none of it was registering with our host, who was staring glassy-eyed at a distant point on the wall. He appeared unsure what to do next but then took a deep breath, burped loudly and stepped backwards falling straight over a chair.

Looking even more dazed, he picked himself up and wordlessly shuffled off back to his cubbyhole.

As he closed the door Roger eased back on the charm. "And he was a hopeless drunk and a crashing bore last year and I'm delighted to see he hasn't improved one jot this year. OK, chaps, let's get the gear in and set up."

We did the usual soundcheck and got our personal things up to the apartment, which was directly above the club. It was another three-bedroom setup so we paired off with our usual room buddies. John and I got a room with a view over the main street, opposite a department store sign, its radiance bathing us in a depressing neon glow. Later, we went to a nearby restaurant for dinner and returned to the club in time for the nine p.m. start.

The disco had been going since eight p.m. but only a couple of people were dancing. The choice of music was all wrong and to top it all Harry's repartee on the microphone was a disaster. Not only was he mumbling over the intros, but there was reverb on his voice making him sound like a drunk on a mountaintop.

We went into the kitchen to say hello to the staff. One particularly attractive lady greeted us warmly and Roger introduced her as Harry's wife. The rest of the staff however looked like they had been hanging around the boss too long, lacking any get-up-and-go. It was all rather depressing. The one bright spot was the playing times: nine p.m. until one a.m. on weekdays and until two a.m. on Friday and Saturday. Mondays were our day off.

Promptly at nine we kicked off the first set and a bunch of people immediately got up to dance. By the second break the club was half full, which I imagine was good for midweek, and the audience were dancing and applauding. Harry was back on the mountaintop droning on about tomorrow night's talent competition, then played a song by some *schlager* artist. I got the feeling he only liked to play German music.

"Talent competition?" I asked Wolfgang.

"Yes, every Thursday. It's harmless enough. There's not much talent but it's fun."

By the end of the evening we thought we'd done a decent enough job. The audience were enthusiastic and Harry's wife was full of praise, but Dortmund's coolest DJ was avoiding us. We weren't quite ready for bed so when someone mentioned The Blue Moon – a nearby club with a live band that was open until three a.m. – we decided to go there for a nightcap.

We quickly got changed and stepped out onto the pedestrianised street. Immediately we were hit by the most ghastly smell. John and I screwed up our faces in disgust.

"What did they do?" I asked breathlessly. "Coat the town in shit while we were playing?"

"Yeah, it's a bit of a whiff, isn't it?" Roger said, grinning. He and the others didn't seem quite as surprised as we were by the abhorrent pong. He went on, "It's from the Dortmunder brewery around the corner. It's a massive place and it lets off a powerful stench when they're brewing the beer. It's the yeast or the grain, I don't know which, but they do the smelly part during the night so it's less offensive to the residents. Tough on us night owls, though."

The Blue Moon was situated a couple of hundred meters further up the street from the Corso. As we were led to a table near the stage I noticed a number of guests who had been dancing to us earlier in the evening. As one, they raised their glasses in a toast as a young waitress led us to our table. We began ordering drinks and I took a moment to study the surroundings. The room was bathed in various shades of blue light, courtesy of a battery of movie-studio style spotlights on a gantry around the dance floor. Otherwise it looked very much like the Corso. It was a little smaller but the layout was the same with the stage and dance floor at one end and a kitchen and bar at the other.

A few moments later the resident band emerged from the kitchen and waved hello to us as they made their way back up to the stage for the next set. I realised this was the first opportunity I would have to hear a German band instead of the usual Indonesian. They were a five-piece outfit called the Tonix and with typical German efficiency and thrift each musician doubled on a second and even third instrument. The guitarist had an array of other stringed instruments while the saxophone player was a one-man Latin percussion section. When required, the organist would breezily whip out a trumpet and join the saxophone on brass parts, still playing the organ with his left hand.

They seemed partial to soul music and covered similar things to us from the Isley Brothers and James Brown, although they lacked a vocalist with Kassy's cojones to really carry it off. It was the organist doing most of the heavy lifting on vocal duties, gurning desperately into his microphone in a thin and reedy voice with a fractured German accent. He attempted Joe Tex's *I Gotcha*, but the result sounded uncomfortably like a petulant gay guard in a prison camp as he lamented miserably: "*Aha. You tried to sneak by me now, didn't ya.*"

Next up they did a version of *Guantanamera* which attracted most of the audience onto the dance floor.

A waitress was handing Roger a bourbon and Coke when he asked, "*Guantanamera* – what's that all about? I mean, everyone joins in like it's a prayer to life singing the same stupid word five hundred times."

"If we're going to go down that road," I teased, "what's *Chirpy Chirpy Cheep Cheep* all about?"

"Now now, Stephen, I won't let anyone take Middle of the Road's name in vain. Without that wonderful orchestra, Dortmund's finest would have nothing to sing at tomorrow's talent contest."

The club was already full when we arrived the following evening. Making our way past the disco we were pounced upon by a short, eagle-eyed character with slicked-back hair sporting a bright-purple suit with gold trimmings. Even by the standards of the 1970s it was extravagant. I was just wondering what a Telemundo game show host was doing in town when I remembered it was talent night.

Introductions were made, and sure enough this was the compere. Roger greeted him like an old friend and the two of them went through the program for the evening. Three of the singers had brought sheet music so we would have to accompany them as well as a juggler and there would be three others singing to karaoke tapes.

When it was time for the show, the purple-suited gentleman walked up to the side of the stage. This was a cue for us to play one of those brash Elvis-in-Vegas pieces of walk-on music. He then picked up an enormous amount of speed before bounding onto the stage to enthusiastic applause from what was now a full house.

The whole band were grinning and Wolfgang whispered, "We call it the Dortmund Run. Roger figures he gets from zero to sixty faster than Donald's Mercedes."

The compere's presentation redefined kitsch – oozing every possible nuance of showbiz pizzazz – but the audience loved it. With great fanfare he introduced the first act: a middle-aged lady who lumbered up onto the stage and for the next three and a half minutes proceeded to murder *Mamy Blue,* defiantly wading her way through the lyrics without once landing on one of the consonants.

She was followed by another lady who had also planned on murdering *Mamy Blue,* but had been told she had to butcher something else. She had chosen *Soley Soley* instead and, while seething her way through it, kept throwing resentful looks at the previous contestant, who was standing close to the stage smiling mirthlessly.

Next up was the juggler. We played the *One Note Samba* and he started juggling some small, white balls competently enough. To muted applause he switched to larger skittles. Unfortunately, part way through this routine he tripped over Donald's guitar stand and one of the skittles went hurtling towards Roger. Kassy stepped back, smartly caught it with his left hand and gave an extravagant bow, which prompted applause from the audience and withering looks from the juggler and the man in purple.

After a couple more nondescript vocalists we arrived at the final act, an odd-looking fellow who must have been in his fifties and who projected an aura of dark melancholy that could have given Bela Lugosi sleepless nights. His name was Tchaikovsky and rumour had it he was related to the Russian composer – unfortunately musical talent wasn't part of the inheritance. He was singing some obscure, operatic piece to a playback tape and his performance was truly awful.

"Kein zweifel herabkommend," he wailed, glaring mournfully towards the bar.

Actually, it was laugh-out-loud funny because it was so terrible. The audience all appeared to be in on the joke though as many were hugging themselves with delight while others had hands to their mouths muffling their giggles.

He continued to bray his way lugubriously through the libretto, wrapping his teeth around the German vowels: *"Gefahr ist nicht, doch gut ist's wenn du wachst…"*

Finally he reached his strangulated climax and as one, the audience leapt to their feet, cheering and clapping wildly. Wow! Who said Germans didn't have a sense of humour?

We took a break while the audience voted for a winner. On my way to the kitchen I noticed a group of smiling ladies sitting at one of the larger tables. A couple of them waved so I went over to say hello and was delighted to hear they spoke English.

A dark-haired beauty stood up and said, "Nice to meet you, why don't you come and join us?" She made room for me to sit. "I'm Heidi by the way. We are here celebrating my friend Dagmar's birthday."

She put a glass of wine into my hand and I raised it in a toast to the birthday girl.

Dagmar blew me a kiss and said, "We love your band."

"Thanks, but it's going to be hard to follow Herr Tchaikovsky," I joked.

"Now now, pet, don't be unkind," she giggled. "That silly old sod is here every week with his operas and overblown arias. He never wins but we ladies love to hear a man murder the classics."

I was trying to figure out where she came from. She was in her mid-thirties, and German but with this thick Geordie accent. I later found out she was married to a sergeant in the British Army but was going through a divorce. With the exception of Heidi, who was about the same age as me, all the others at the table had been married to British soldiers serving in Germany. I hadn't really thought about it before but one of the lasting relics of the war was the allied zones in Germany, and we were now solidly in the British zone, having spent the last four months in the American one.

The purple-suited compere climbed back on stage to announce the results of the contest. In third place was a young girl who had sung a German version of *The Night They Drove Old Dixie Down*. In second place was the *Soley Soley* lady, and to her undisguised disgust the first prize went to Miss *Mamy Blue*.

Dagmar saw the look of bewilderment on my face. "Don't worry, pet, those old bags go through this every week. They're sisters and compete as though their lives depend on it."

"Sisters?"

"Yes, and they're both single and live together in their father's house."

I felt a tap on the shoulder and turned to find the juggler staring earnestly at me. He shook my hand and said something in German.

Heidi translated. "He's just been to thank the others in the band and he wanted to thank you as well for the good job accompanying him."

I nodded and smiled. "That's nice of him. Gosh I really must get around to learning some German. I've been here since January and still understand nothing."

"Oh! Well why don't you let me give you a few lessons? I'm doing a course in hotel management at college and I really need to practice my English. I've got a couple of afternoons off each week. So?"

At first I was taken aback by the offer, but thinking how useful it would be I said, "Wow, that would be brilliant. Yes please."

After that evening we got into a regular routine of meeting in a *konditorei* a couple of times a week and in a quiet booth – fuelled by coffee, hot chocolate and creamy cakes – we tackled irregular verbs, masculine and feminine articles and all the other opaque rules of grammar that make up conversational German.

CHAPTER TWENTY-SEVEN

Poppa Joe

Monday was our day off and Roger had spent it down in Munich visiting Gina. He arrived back on Tuesday evening about half an hour before we were due on stage. The rest of us were up in the apartment organising our stage clothes.

"How was Munich?" I asked.

"Yeah, it was great. A long way to go for a short break but worth it." He turned to Kassy. "The Timelords were playing at the Arcadia."

"Oh yeah? That's a step down for them. They used to play at the Regina Palast. Did Jimmie welcome you like a brother?"

Hardly. But he couldn't play his usual games as everyone was still going on about how fabulous we were. Anyway, Gina's got the measure of him so he'll have to behave this month. I also spoke to Bachmann while I was down there and he's managed to book us into the Bayerischer Hof for two weeks in July."

Kassy gave him a thumbs up. "Wow, that's a really smart club. Probably the hottest place in Munich right now."

"Exactly! The only craziness is that re-booking at the Arcadia in October."

Tuesday was a quiet night and for most of it we were playing to tables and chairs. A few regulars drifted in and sat by the bar, but as nobody was dancing we reverted to the 'beefsteak' repertoire while

Roger caught up on his book.

If playing to an empty club was boring at least we got paid. The serving staff, who worked solely for tips, depended on the generosity of the guests and knew that an empty club meant an empty wallet. Even the toilet attendant worked on commission. At the Corso it was a white-jacketed sycophant wreathed in smiles and bonhomie who handed out perfumed towels, packets of condoms and cheap eau de cologne to unsuspecting clients, who really only went in there for a quick pee. In the absence of customers, he smoothly redirected his power-selling techniques onto the band, and by midnight most of us were smelling like the inside of a tart's handbag.

Twice during the evening an elderly lady came in to sell red roses to romantic couples but, noticing the lack of any, briskly altered her sales spiel and managed to unload a rose onto a lonely drunk sitting at one end of the bar. When the lights went up at closing time I noticed he was fondling a beer in one hand and a wilting stalk in the other.

Further along the bar Harry was sitting on his own, morosely drinking brandy. For no obvious reason he had taken a strong dislike to us and, from what I could understand, was making snide comments about the band during his disco spots. Little digs about us not playing enough German songs. It was all very petty, but a few evenings later it led to a major bust-up.

Roger heard him say something to the audience about Karl and his orchestral string sound having been the real star in The Statesmen, and without him the band were no longer as good. When we went back on stage Roger made some remark to the audience about how much better the disco would be if the DJ was sober. A few of the dancers started laughing, which prompted Harry to come staggering over to the side of the stage. We pointedly ignored him and he disappeared, but when we finished and went into the kitchen, Harry was in there ready for a fight. He shouted at Roger, complaining the band was playing too many British and American songs. Roger responded by saying it was to make up for the tripe he was playing in the disco. It was almost at the point of getting physical when Harry's wife stormed into the kitchen and made them stop.

Tempers cooled but the lines had now been drawn and it was a matter of us keeping our heads down and getting to the end of the month without any more trouble.

Away from the Corso, my German lessons were zipping along in some fashion. Heidi was an excellent teacher and before I knew it I was speaking some basic phrases. I was even starting to pick up bits and pieces from conversations I was hearing. Our relationship had slipped into an easy platonic thing: the kind of friendship where you could stretch out and relax. For different reasons neither of us were looking for romance and I think she was content that I wasn't pushing for anything more than friendship.

Stung by Harry's drunken criticism of our Anglo-American repertoire, we started rehearsing again with a view to adding some German hits. This didn't go down so well with John and me. Although we knew we were a cover band, we had avoided the *Mamy Blues* and the *Chirpy Chirpy Cheep Cheeps*, choosing to cover more quality songs. So there was a fair bit of arguing about what new songs to rehearse.

Donald thought we should be looking at the German charts and take songs like *How Do You Do* by Mouth & MacNeal or a new instrumental called *Popcorn* that was playing everywhere. John and I wanted to do *Love the One You're With* by Stephen Stills and *I Just Want to Celebrate* by Rare Earth. In the end Roger and Kassy reached a compromise and from the German charts we rehearsed *(Is This the Way to) Amarillo* by Tony Christie, *Poppa Joe* by Sweet and to satisfy us, Donald handled the lead vocal on *Love the One You're With*.

Poppa Joe was a simple enough pop song with a light, Caribbean feel and we nailed it quickly. The only problem was the drum break before the final chorus. It wasn't all that important but John wanted Roger to play it exactly the same as on the record and Roger, more out of obstinacy than anything else, kept varying it each time he played it. This led to a few crossed words between them.

"Just because all you have to do is *rat-a-tat-tat* your way through a song doesn't mean you can make something up," John complained. "We have to follow the bloody chords. You follow the drum part."

"*Rat-a-tat-tat*!" Roger said indignantly. "I'm as much a musician as you. The fact that I dare to experiment and improvise—"

"Improvise! It's the bloody Sweet not Chet Baker!"

And so it went on. John was on his artistic high horse but there was something going on with Roger, whose heart simply wasn't in it. That evening we played the song for the first time and he made a complete mess of the drum break. The audience hadn't noticed but when we took our break John was keen to get the issue resolved.

"Listen, there's an easy way to remember the rhythm," he said. "Dagenham Dagenham, Fords of Dagenham."

Roger nodded absent-mindedly. "Yeah, whatever."

"You could sound more interested," John grumbled. "It's a simple way to remember the rhythm. Dagenham Dag—"

"Yeah, I get it."

"No, I don't think you do because you're not listening. It's Dagenham Dagenham—"

At that point Roger blew up. "Quite honestly, I couldn't give an ant-sized shit if a burning bush explained it to me! Fuck Dagenham, fuck Fords and, surprise surprise, fuck *Poppa Joe*! I've got other things to think about so just leave it."

Later, while the others went to The Blue Moon, Roger came and joined John and me up in our room. He was contrite, but more than that, he was miserable.

"I'm sorry about all of that earlier," he began. "I called Gina last night and she told me she's not coming on Monday. Says she's been thinking about our relationship and finds it difficult when I'm always travelling." He walked over to the window and stared down at the street. "I thought it was just cold feet so I phoned the Arcadia earlier this evening. She wasn't there so I ended up speaking to Claudia. Turns out Gina's been with Jimmie for the last week." He turned to us and made a face. "Fucking Jimmie of all people! And think what I gave up for her. A wife, two kids, nice apartment…"

"I thought you were already broken up?" I said. "Redeye and all of that business at Deutsches Haus."

"Yeah, yeah, details. Let's not get so specific Stephen." Now he was starting to sound more like his usual self. Unperturbed, he went on, "No, I've come to the conclusion I was just her plaything: a beautifully crafted sex toy for her carnal pleasure. And in my absence she's drafted in some cheap Asian copy."

I looked at him carefully and tried to see if he was joking, but it was impossible to tell.

John changed the subject. "Anyway, not many more days here now and then we've got Worms to look forward to."

This produced a surprising response from our lovelorn leader. "That's it!" he said. "That's what I need. My kids and my family. I'm going to go down there and fix things with Mausi. Get back in the family nest. Perfect opportunity, being in Worms."

It sounded like he was trying to convince himself it was a good idea, although personally I thought it was a terrible one. The look on John's face said the same thing.

When the others heard the news and Roger's plan to win Mausi back they all tried to talk him out of it, but his mind was made up. On Sunday evening, straight after the gig, he jumped in the Mercedes with Donald and together they whizzed off to Stockstadt.

They returned on the Tuesday with Roger looking a lot happier, but there was definitely a mad gleam in his eye. People do strange things when they're on the rebound and he was bouncing more than most. I asked him how it went.

"Good. Very good in fact. I stayed at Donald's but met Mausi for lunch yesterday and again today. We've agreed that I'll stay at the apartment next month and see how it goes."

"What about Redeye?"

"Ha! Fuck him. The cat's back in town and the mouse can piss off back down his hole."

And on that happy note, we prepared for our return to Worms and a month of eight till threes under the iron heel of the irascible Herr Schmiegel.

CHAPTER TWENTY-EIGHT

Get Back

We arrived in Worms during the mid-afternoon and headed straight to the Imperial to unload the gear. Afterwards Donald, Roger and Kassy went to their respective homes while the rest of us moved into the band apartment. It was nice – much better than anywhere we'd stayed so far – and as only Wolfgang, John and I would be living there we each got a bedroom to ourselves.

Later in the evening when we went back to the Imperial, Schmiegel was already in the middle of one of his choleric rages, berating some poor sod about a delivery of beer that was wrong. The moment he saw us though he quickly stopped and made a heroic effort to put on a welcoming smile. After Harry's drunken behaviour he appeared positively ambrosial by comparison, enquiring how we were getting on with our German lessons and if we were comfortable in the band apartment. Hmm, maybe I had been wrong about him.

The Stockstadt contingent arrived shortly afterwards with our bandleader looking unusually smug.

Donald wasn't so happy. "Berndt is going to cause trouble," he said. "He's really in love with Mausi and believes Roger is just messing her around. Trust me, this is not going to end well."

While the others left to get ready, John had an idea.

"Hey, we've got two weeks off next month. Shall we go back to England for a few days? It's July. Could be fun to take a holiday somewhere?"

He was right. We had two weeks free before returning to Munich and it would be nice to visit Slough, tell everyone about our adventures in Germany and go somewhere on holiday.

"We could borrow a car and spend a couple of days in Cornwall?" I suggested.

John looked interested and said, "What about Newquay? That's always buzzing in the summer. Let's check out train tickets to London tomorrow."

A little later I noticed a striking blonde lady sitting at the bar chatting to one of the waitresses. I strolled over, ordered a beer and casually edged my way into the conversation. Hearing my tentative German, she slipped effortlessly into English and asked how I was enjoying Worms.

"I'm not sure really." I replied, "We've just arrived."

Sadly she was no great beauty. The band liked to rate women on a scale of one to ten and from a distance I would have put her at a comfortable seven. Up close she had slipped down to a five, but overlooking her visage for a moment, there was something about her poise, lustrous blonde hair and direct manner that just about nudged her back up to a six. She was flirty, without really trying to be, and let me know she had been married to a musician for five years so knew all about our hedonistic lifestyle with one-night stands, gang-bangs and orgies… Blimey! Which band had he been in? I was about to press for more intimate details when I saw the others across the room, heading towards the stage. Regretfully I left her to join them, hoping I might see her later.

As I'd come to understand since sitting there back in December, the brutal playing times weren't quite so awful when you were up there performing. So even if time didn't exactly fly by, the evening passed relatively quickly. Countless trays of Asbach arrived on stage courtesy of the band's local fans and by three a.m. we were all plastered. So much so that when I returned to the bar I must have drunk the blonde back up to an eight, because now she looked hot and horny.

I'm not sure if she was expecting an orgy but she got me, and after two months of self-denial I was good to go. We got back to my room and she demurely removed her clothes and switched the light off. But after that there was nothing hesitant about her. If there had been any orgies with her husband's band they had certainly paid off as she was up in the same league as Marlene when it came to technical skills. Unfortunately, just like Marlene, her lovemaking lacked any real warmth and by the end I felt we were just ticking boxes. This time it didn't bother me as much, as there was no risk I was going to fall in love.

Eventually I dropped off into a booze-induced coma, and I guess she fell asleep beside me. Actually, I don't have to guess as when I came round a few hours later it was to the sound of her snoring. It was just getting light and the blinds were slightly ajar. I cautiously squinted my eyes open. God, I had a splitting headache and my mouth was as dry as a desert. But all that faded into insignificance as I stared in astonishment at the short, blonde-haired woman staring at us from the foot of the bed. For a moment I was too dumbstruck to say anything. How on earth had she got in? And what did she want? Before I could pose those questions, a little more light filtered into the room and as my vision improved I realised the blonde wasn't a lady. It was a bedpost crowned with the luscious, golden locks I'd so admired last night!

I was appalled. Holy fuck! I've just slept with a three! The boys would never let me live it down. OK, it could have been worse. A set of false teeth grinning admiringly from the side table would have been bad, but the hair had been one of her best assets and now there it was six feet away waiting patiently for its owner's return.

Gingerly I leaned over and took a peek at her slumbering form. Well at least it wasn't a prison cut but it was damn short and a long way from blonde.

Sometime later I felt her get up and move around. I wasn't sure of the etiquette when you woke up beside someone whose hair had relocated during the night, so cravenly I pretended to carry on sleeping, even throwing in a couple of pantomime snores for good measure. I felt her give me a light kiss on the cheek and then she quietly left.

After that I couldn't sleep so I got up and went into the kitchen where I found Wolfgang and John sitting at the table, drinking coffee.

"So who was the tasty blonde?" John enquired, leering lasciviously.

"Oh that was Erika."

Wolfgang asked, "So you're seeing her again?"

"No, I'm hoping I might get it fixed with Astrid." They both stared at me in surprise so I continued defensively, "OK. Even being wildly optimistic I can appreciate that forgiveness might be pushing it, but innocent by reason of diminished responsibility gets a lot of dodgy people off in court. Anyway, we're off to Munich next month so I'm going to give it a go." I changed the subject and asked John, "What about Birgit?"

"I think it's run its course. I didn't appreciate the surprise visits, and since we've been here in Worms she's just been too keen. There are a million great-looking women out there, and it would be wrong of me not to share my unlimited bounty with at least a few more of them."

"How generous," said Wolfgang drily.

Our bass player then surprised us by announcing that his wife was coming this weekend. We hadn't heard much about her since January. Granted, the band had been on the road but it was still an unusual situation. She was coming up on her own so he was pulling out all the stops to arrange a nice weekend for them both.

As the weekend approached we helped transform the apartment into a romantic honeymoon suite. There were flowers all over the place, a bowl of fruit in the kitchen and mood lighting in Wolfgang's bedroom. The usually overfilled ashtrays were emptied and the whole place now smelt like a florist's shop.

On the Thursday we rehearsed a couple of new songs and

Wolfgang asked if he could do Percy Sledge's *When a Man Loves a Woman*. He mastered it admirably in his uniquely soulful way while Roger picked out Neil Diamond's *Song Sung Blue* for himself, explaining that he might need a couple of new songs in the ongoing campaign to beat off his love rival in Stockstadt.

Friday was a busy night with lots happening in the club. John and I got into a conversation with a couple of US servicemen. They had been in a band back in the States and were now serving their time at the army base in Worms. When they introduced themselves I had to concentrate to keep a straight face as their names sounded suspiciously like the heading for a personal ad. Randy and Rich were a drummer and bass player who had been one half of a rock band in their hometown of Austin, Texas. They were fun to talk to and liked all the same music we did. Rich had just bought Elton John's *Honky Château* and was raving about it. We countered with *Something/ Anything?* – Todd Rundgren's fabulous new album, which we loved – and Rich immediately broke into a few bars of *Hello It's Me*. We were getting on so well they invited us over to their *kaserne* the following afternoon to look around the music facility.

Across the room Bachmann entered with a group of gentlemen and found a table close to the bar. They were all in dark suits except for one lively character who was sporting lederhosen. Schmiegel welcomed them with elaborate courtesy, shaking each one solemnly by the hand and smoothing them into their seats while Bachmann signalled to Roger to come and say hello. We were about to begin the next set, but he hurried over to greet them. When he returned he was looking extremely efficient and businesslike.

"*Spione, meine herren*. The ones in suits run clubs in Switzerland and Austria, and the bloke in shorts owns a club in the mountains somewhere between Munich and Salzburg."

This was the first time we'd had a group of club owners come and watch us all at the same time, and Switzerland and Austria sounded like cool places to work, so we took it up a gear. For the next forty-five minutes we played most of our best songs, and a couple of well-placed German hits from our ever-expanding repertoire. For once our leader even got the drum break right in *Poppa Joe*.

One of Bachmann's guests, the chap in lederhosen, was called Herr Markl. His club was somewhere in the Bavarian Alps and he was considering having us play there in September. He invited Erika onto the dance floor and made a clumsy attempt at dancing a foxtrot to *It's Your Thing*. He followed that up by yodelling along with Donald to *The Lion Sleeps Tonight*, while poor Erika stood there squirming with embarrassment.

"Weeeeeeeey ooh weeeoooh weee oh weemaway!"

That put him in the mood for something with a dash of Bavarian *gewürz*, so we played an up-tempo waltz while he chaotically swished her in every direction around the floor. After that he appeared well pleased and sent a bottle of sekt up to the stage with a note saying he would see us in September.

Despite drinking until the early hours, Wolfgang was up before the rest of us making final touches to the apartment. John and I got up around midday and had a slow breakfast before heading downtown in search of the American army *kaserne*.

Until the end of the war it had been the home of the German army garrison and was located conveniently close to the town centre. There was extra security at the front gate because of the recent terrorist threats from Baader-Meinhof, so we had to wait while a sergeant phoned around to locate Randy and Rich. When they were found they promptly came down to the gate to sign us in then took us up to their music room.

With it being the weekend the room was empty apart from a vast array of brass and woodwind instruments as well as a nice selection of guitars, keyboards and drums. Following Randy and Rich's lead, we plugged a few things in and tried jamming together. First we played a simple blues and then at their prompting, we showed them a couple of the original songs we had written back in England. When we finished we were surprised and delighted with their reaction.

"Why the heck are you guys in a place like the Imperial playing Neil Diamond, when you should be pushing your own material?" Randy asked. "No one makes it big playing in Worms. You guys need to be in the States. Play that last song again and let's try it together."

Rich had a warm Californian-sounding voice and could easily have fit in with bands like The Beach Boys or Eagles. He brought something new to the song, making it sound quite different to the way we had imagined. After playing it a couple of times Randy, who seemed to be their spokesman, suggested we go for a coffee so we went to the canteen and found a table. After a bit of chit chat he got down to business.

"We believe you two might be exactly what we've been looking for. We don't write songs and a half American, half British band would go down really well where we come from. We get out of the army in January and we'll be going back to Austin. If you came over and joined us, we could have a go at making it big in the States."

It was tempting. It was also of course a gamble, but we made all the right noises without making any firm commitments and arranged to meet for another session the following weekend.

CHAPTER TWENTY-NINE

Where Is the Love

On our way back to the apartment we passed the bar we visited that first night in January and there, sitting at one of the outside tables with a large beer in front of him, was Wolfgang. He was alone and had that glassy-eyed expression that meant it wasn't his first drink of the day. This couldn't be good.

John was first to ask, "Hey Wolly, what happened? Where's your wife? You haven't chased her off already?"

Wolfgang looked at us curiously, but didn't say anything. We pulled up a couple of chairs and sat down and in a strangely detached voice he said, "Did I tell you I met Heidi in Munich?"

At first I was confused. Was he talking about Heidi from Dortmund? Then I realised he meant his wife.

"We were playing at a club called My Fair Lady. She had just moved from her parents' home to Munich and I met her shortly after."

"So where is she? John persisted. "We'd like to meet her."

Wolfgang continued obliviously, "We fell in love straight away. Sometimes you just know when the right one comes along, and I just knew." He took a long pull of his drink. "The next month we were playing here in Worms and I didn't even need to ask her. It was just understood. She packed her things and came with me." His eyes focused and he looked straight at us. "I didn't need to ask! We were married around the corner at the town hall." Tears were slowly starting to run down his cheeks. "We had the reception at the Imperial. And last year Sven was born, and I had everything I ever wanted." His voice trailed off as he reached for his cigarettes and unhappily lit one.

Obviously things hadn't gone the way he expected, but what to do now?

The waitress appeared and before we could say anything he ordered a round of beers for us. We sat there for a while in companionable silence.

When the beers were finished he came to a decision and said, "No point in sitting here being miserable. We better get to work, or Roger will have something to say. Don't want him angry with me as well."

Roger and Donald were getting out of the Mercedes as we approached the Imperial. From their faces I could see they already knew what was going on. They walked over to Wolfgang and gave him a hug. Roger was talking gently to him as they made their way into the club. Later he took John and me aside and told us what had happened.

"Heidi phoned Mausi from the station. Apparently she had only come up here to get Wolfgang's signature on a divorce document. Her lawyer had been writing letters addressed to their apartment for months, and he hasn't been there since February. Poor sod, didn't even have a clue she wanted a divorce. He met her at the station with flowers, and half an hour later was waving her off again." He stared across the room at two waitresses who were sharing a joke and snarled, "Fucking women!"

Somehow I thought that wasn't only aimed at Heidi.

All the German clubs we had played in so far had a bar bill system for the musicians and staff. They wrote everything you ordered on your private bill and you settled it on the last evening. In the first break I went to the bar and ordered a Coke but unfortunately they had lost my bill, which was causing the barmaid some anxiety.

She called Schmiegel over and asked him what to do, but he just looked baffled, insisting it had never happened before. As we had only been playing for a few evenings he suggested that I try and remember everything I'd ordered so they could make a new bill. That was a bit of a stretch as I got pretty pissed the first evening. But with some prodding from the barmaid I managed to get it roughly accurate.

By the time I'd finished, I saw Erika was sitting a couple of stools away.

"Working hard?" she asked.

"You could say that. They lost my bar bill so I'm having to remember everything I've ordered since Tuesday."

She laughed. "Maybe you should only own up to a couple of glasses of water?"

"Yes, Schmiegel hasn't had a good eruption for a few days," I said, and we both laughed.

Nothing was said but I sensed she knew I wasn't interested in taking up where we left off, so she changed the subject.

"That was a real character last night, Herr Markl. He mentioned he booked you for his club in September."

"Yes. I haven't been to the Alps before so I'm really looking forward to it." I grinned and added, "I don't think it was only us that he liked. He seemed to be keen on you too."

"Yeah, the randy old swine. In the end I had to tell him I don't date men in hot pants."

As the evening progressed, Wolfgang added a good few inches to his bar bill and his mood swung wildly between manic and morose. He couldn't sing anything intelligible, and his usual steady bass playing was all over the place. At one point he made desperate signs to me that I should take over and staggered off in the direction of the toilets.

When he returned, Roger cautioned him to take it easy but he wasn't listening, and in the next break he was sitting drinking Asbach with Peter and some friends. This time when we returned to the stage he fell over his microphone stand and had to excuse himself in a hurry. I switched over to bass and stayed there for the rest of the set.

By the third or fourth break Roger had had enough, especially when he saw Wolfgang standing at the bar.

"Wolly, this stops now," he demanded. "It's simply not on that Steve has to keep taking over on bass so you can go and throw up in the toilet."

I was expecting a drunken response but he surprised us both by taking a deep breath, raising his hand imperiously and, in a rather plummy BBC newsreader's accent announced, "Roger, you're right. Perfectly right. I'm behaving badly." He allowed himself a brief but dramatic pause to burp. "But whatever I've done this evening, and I humbly apologise for that, the damage is done and can't be undone."

Any response our bandleader was about to make was cut short by Wolfgang's finger.

"But tomorrow I'll be sober, so it's best to draw a line under it now and say no more about it." He pulled himself up to his full six-foot height and raised a quizzical eyebrow. "Or...?"

Roger digested this for a moment while we both stared curiously at our bass player, who remarkably now wore the demeanour of some poor, hard-working chap who had just been inconvenienced by a bit of unpleasantness among the lower ranks. Amazingly he even managed to demolish that undeserved image by turning around and grandly ordering another double brandy.

I could see this was going to be a long night. Looking further down the bar John was in deep conversation with Erika, and the body language between them oozed sexual promise. Oh, what fun! I couldn't wait for breakfast tomorrow.

CHAPTER THIRTY

United We Stand

I had just started on a second bowl of cornflakes when I was joined at the breakfast table.

"Morning, John," I said cheerfully. "Have a good night?"

He looked at me warily and said, "Yes. Why?"

"I mean you and Erika." I smiled mischievously. "And the blonde. You always said you fancied a threesome." All of a sudden I couldn't contain the giggles any longer.

"Bastard," he responded, but was laughing. Neither of us could stop giggling.

"When did you find out?" I asked. "Wig on the bedpost?"

"On the bedpost? Fuck no! We were doing it doggie style and I started pulling on it. I must have got a bit carried away cos' it flew off!" Tears were rolling down our cheeks as he continued, "Puts a man off his stride when the hair and the head part company like that, mid-bonk as it were."

"How did she react?"

"Very well actually. She gently took it off me and placed it on the side table, and we continued where we left off. Just with the top off."

"Al fresco you mean?"

We erupted in another round of laughter.

Wolfgang came in and groaned, "Fucking *Engländer*. Have you no respect for the dead?"

"Morning, Wolly. How's the head?"

"What head? I think I left it in the Imperial." He attempted a smile. "But today a new Wolly is born. No more tears over that fucking woman." He sat down at the table and asked, "Steve, that blonde you were with the other night. Mind if I have a go?"

John and I just looked at each other for a few moments before breaking down in another fit of hysterics.

A few minutes later there was a knock at the door and we had a visitor. It was Karl, The Statesmen's ex-organist. His band the Blue Tramps were playing at the Park Cafe in Wiesbaden and had Sunday free, so he had come to watch us in action. Wolfgang brought him up to date on all the news including his own situation. Karl listened sympathetically in silence and then, with a little fanfare, produced a bottle of slivovitz plum brandy from his bag. I was just thinking how that was not going to go with my cornflakes when to my horror Wolfgang took out four small glasses and started pouring. I was appalled.

"Wolly, remember your promise last night. And I'm really not sure I can handle alcohol this early."

"No worries, boys, just one toast," he said reassuringly. It's been six months and we have a lot of history, don't we, Karl?"

We took a polite sip then sat back and listened to them exchanging reminiscences. Karl had been an amateur wrestler as a teenager in Hungary and kept himself in excellent shape, which had come in handy on more than one occasion playing in some of the less agreeable parts of Germany. His English wasn't brilliant and he kept dipping in and out of German but John and I were picking up more and more of the language now so could follow the conversation quite well.

Karl told us a little about the Blue Tramps and the kind of gigs they were doing. They didn't seem to be too different to ours – the Happy Night, Park Cafe, Bayerischer Hof – although they had gigs in Switzerland and Austria too. I think Karl was surprised to hear we were also playing in the better-quality clubs, as part of the reason he left The Statesmen was to get onto that circuit.

Wolfgang took a siesta during the afternoon and turned up at the club in good shape. There were few signs of last night's excess, so we weren't going to have an uncomfortable meeting with Roger. When the other band members arrived they were delighted to see Karl again and gave him a warm welcome.

Roger was particularly pleased and said, "He won't be smiling as brightly when he hears what we sound like now."

As usual the club was empty at eight p.m. but we still opened with all our big vocal numbers and did a whole set of the new material. When the break came and we joined Karl at his table, I imagined Roger was hoping to bask in the warmth of the anticipated compliments. Instead he got an urgent phone call so hurried off to the bar. A few minutes later he returned looking shaken.

"That was Mausi," he said. "Apparently Redeye has just been around to say he's got a gun and he's coming over here to kill me."

A stunned silence enveloped the table. It was Wolfgang who broke it. "Any particular reason why?"

Roger appeared taken aback by the question. "Because he's got the fucking night off and there's nothing on the telly!" he responded indignantly, his voice rising in agitation. "What the fuck do you mean reason why? I don't know. The bastard wants blood… Mine!"

We all fell silent again while I for one pondered what kind of shot Redeye was. It was pretty dark in the club and we wouldn't want him hitting the wrong target. Finally Roger broke the silence.

"OK, boys, we need a plan. It's important we stick together…" He was looking carefully at each of us, but stopped and snorted in disgust. "I see. Fair-weather friends, are we? Every man for himself. Devil take the—"

"Leave it off, Roger," Kassy interjected. "Of course we'll help. Karl, you can hang around near the entrance and head him off, can't you?"

Maybe Karl relished some excitement but had to point out that he didn't have a clue who Redeye was. Donald and Roger spent a couple of minutes describing him.

Karl grinned and said, "Sounds like a real film star, Roger. Mausi still has great taste I see!"

Roger bit back an angry retort and went in search of Schmiegel. When he returned he was slouching and even less happy.

"He doesn't think it's a good enough reason for us to stop playing. I bet the bastard quietly hopes there'll be some excitement. Sundays are usually quiet."

"I always knew he was a wonderful human being," I said.

"Yeah yeah, I know. Unfortunately I don't pick them, Stephen."

A couple of minutes after nine, Schmiegel came out from his office and elaborately adjusted his watch, so we began the next set.

After four or five numbers Roger quietly inspected the stage and exclaimed, "Don't you think I can see what you're doing?"

We looked at each other. Without realising it we had all subtly moved a few feet away from the drums. In fact, if Donald and Wolfgang got any further away they'd be standing in the dressing room. Sitting on his own little island in the middle, our drummer was looking very lonely. Guiltily we edged our way back in.

"That's more like it," he said. "A bit of The Statesmen esprit de corps. It takes more than some midget barman to frighten us."

Brave words. Brave words indeed, and would have been even braver if he wasn't crouching so low behind his drums.

An hour passed and nothing happened. Eleven o'clock came and went, still nothing: no bloodbath, no crime passionnel and worse still, no guests.

For a while any unusual activity by the entrance resulted in most of us nervously scampering to the side of the stage, leaving a fretful drummer alone on his podium. But as the evening dragged on it was so dull I began to quietly hope something thrilling would actually occur.

Then just before midnight we received another phone call from Mausi, this time announcing that Redeye's friends had persuaded him to return to Deutsches Haus. The immediate threat was over but, erring on the side of caution, Roger took some advice from Donald to stay with us in Worms that night.

After all the excitement we needed to come down slowly, so after we finished playing we all went back to the band apartment and polished off Karl's bottle of slivovitz.

CHAPTER THIRTY-ONE

In the Summertime

I thought our month in Worms was going to be a tedious, hard slog, but it flew by. There was always something happening at the club and at weekends we got together with Randy and Rich and played our songs. Once again my love life was non-existent but I was getting used to that.

A couple of attractive girls had visited the club and one alluring, sexy lady had looked particularly interested, but by the time we finished playing at three a.m. she had left and was probably safely tucked up in bed.

At the beginning of the third week she returned. It was after midnight and she was on her own. Maybe that was a good sign? Or maybe not, when I reflected upon my bruising experience with Marlene. I wandered over to the bar, ordered a beer and asked her what had brought her to the club so late. Surprisingly her reply came in perfect English, albeit with a broad American accent.

"My folks own the restaurant at the train station and I work there until late most evenings."

"You're American?"

"No, but I was married to one for five years."

"And now?"

"It didn't work out so I came home."

"Lucky mum and dad."

As usual it was just getting interesting when Roger tapped me on the shoulder.

"Time to be wonderful, young Stephen." He smiled at my companion and went on, "I understand completely why you would prefer to stay here and continue chatting to this lovely lady, but our public are a demanding beast and they require constant feeding."

I raised a quizzical eyebrow at her.

"No problem," she said. "I'll be here in the next break. Go and feed the beast."

Her name was Elena and not only did she stay to the end, she stayed overnight. The following morning she drove me down to the Rhine in a sporty, red BMW where an equally glamorous motor boat was moored. We took a little punt up the river to a village where we had lunch by the water. After that things just fell into place.

Her daily timetable meshed with mine as she started work at six p.m. and finished around midnight. Later she would come over and watch the last set at the Imperial, and follow that up with a seismic sex session with a delighted Englishman back at her apartment.

True to form it all fell apart, in my usual shambolic style.

We were on our way home in her car one evening when she suddenly pulled over and turned off the engine.

"Where are we going with this Steve?"

"I thought your apartment," I said, slightly surprised by the question.

"You know what I mean. Are we just having fun or is this relationship more than that to you?"

"I don't know really," I said cautiously. "I mean, you live here and I live everywhere else."

"Yes, I know. I've been thinking about that."

"You have?" I asked, suddenly alert. I wasn't sure where this conversation was going, but it sounded as though she was keen to tell me.

"I've been talking to my family and I told them all about you. They're really happy for me, my dad in particular. He wants me to stay in Worms and now I've met a man here there's no risk I'll go running back to the States."

"Yeah, but I don't live here, Elena. I live wherever—"

She put a finger to my lips and said, "But you can't do that forever and my dad said he can find a job for you here. He's opening another restaurant in the centre of town soon and he'll need a manager. You'd be perfect."

"Oh yeah, me with my flawless German and vast experience in catering," I said dismissively. "Look, Elena, I know I can't be a musician forever, but I've only been doing it a few months and I don't want to quit now. And as lovely as Worms is, I'm not sure I want to live here. My home is in England."

I could see this was not the response she was expecting and her mood changed.

"So all I'm good for is a quick fuck?" she asked, her voice sounding somewhere between pissed and heartbroken.

"No! You're lovely. But I'm just not ready to settle down." I could feel I was on the point of babbling and might say something I would later regret so I changed tack. "Look, why don't we forget about it for tonight? You come round when you're feeling a little better about things. I can walk home."

She didn't respond. She kept staring out of the windscreen, so I climbed out of the car and walked home.

The next day I was having coffee with Roger and John in a little Italian cafe in the square opposite the cathedral.

"It's the usual nonsense," Roger said sagely when I told them what had happened. "In the beginning it's all billiards and blow jobs then when they've got you where they want you, they lower the boom. Carefree bachelor days over. Take it from one who knows."

Maybe he was right. I tried putting things into perspective. I'd only been together with Elena nine or ten days so it was way too soon to be getting serious, but I had only been together with Astrid the same amount of time when I started to feel serious about her. And maybe that was the problem: I just wasn't over Astrid.

The final week passed by and Elena never did return. Then it was the last night and the day after we would take a short vacation. John and I were returning to the UK for a week. It would be our first visit since coming here in January and it felt both exciting and weird to be going home. But before that we had one more evening to play.

It didn't begin too well. I needed to settle my bar bill and was surprised to see there were now two sheets of paper. Looking closely, I realised one of them was the original bill they had lost. I explained this to the barmaid who immediately called Schmiegel over. The conversation that followed unfortunately confirmed every suspicion I had about the man.

I reminded him about them losing my first bill, which he vaguely remembered. I explained that as I had put all of those drinks on the second bill, the first one was now redundant and should be thrown away. From his pained expression I could see that throwing away a bill was a concept he would have trouble getting his head around; instead he insisted I should pay both.

Dumbfounded, I said, "But the first bill is a duplication of the first four days of drinks, which are now on the second bill."

He examined them both and pointed accusingly at a discrepancy. His voice rose in annoyance. "But they are not the same. See, there's a beer difference here and the fourth drink is not a Coke, it's a 7 Up!"

I blinked at him in disbelief. "That's because I had to do it from memory. I tried to remember the drinks, not the bloody order I drank them in!"

I desperately looked around for some support but across the bar I could only see John grinning like a hyena and Roger looking fretful. He was making subtle hand signals for me to calm down. Seeing I wasn't going to get any help from that quarter, I reluctantly gave up. "As you wish. Next time you lose my bill it's your problem." And with that I stalked off.

If you at that point had asked me for my feelings about Herr Schmiegel and the Imperial in Worms, they wouldn't have been flattering. But as the evening progressed and so many people came and thanked us for such a great month, it was impossible not to feel some warmth towards the place.

I felt I held the moral advantage over Schmiegel until right at the end, just after we finished the last number, when he came to the dressing room and presented each of us with a bonus. It wasn't a huge amount, just a couple of hundred marks, but it was much appreciated by the others and I could see I had lost some of their sympathy.

"Steve, how could you think Herr Schmiegel would try to cheat you when he does something as generous as this?" Donald asked, with just a hint of disdain in his voice.

I was seething with frustration but realised it was a no-win situation so didn't even bother to answer.

In hindsight I still can't make my mind up about Schmiegel. Like many independent club owners in Germany at that time he was a Jew who had gone through all kinds of horrors during the war. He had a number on his wrist and had lost many members of his family to the Nazis. But he stayed in Germany and built a successful business selling drinks to the children of the generation that thirty years before had meant him harm.

In some weird way I think he saw boys like Donald and Wolfgang as sons. And like the patriarch of a large family, he could produce moments of unreasonable unfairness as well as extreme kindness. With the exception of John and me, the band loved him. We could take him or leave him.

But now we were on our way to England.

PART SIX

ENGLAND, MUNICH & THE RUHR VALLEY

CHAPTER THIRTY-TWO

Summer Breeze

In 1972, flying inside of Europe was prohibitively expensive and although we had flown over in January we decided to be thrifty and take the boat train back to London. This was before the Channel Tunnel so it was a long train journey to a bleak point on the North Sea coast called the Hook of Holland, from there an eight-hour choppy boat ride to Harwich and then a train to London. In total the journey took around twenty-four hours – not the kind of thing you plan for a long weekend.

It was Sunday, 2 July when we got off the train in Slough. Somewhere between Paddington and Ealing Broadway we realised neither of us had actually written to say we were coming, so there was a flicker of unease that there might not be anyone home. Hoping for the best, we parted company at the station and I grabbed my case and walked the few blocks to my parents' house.

It had only been six months but I was astonished by how different our street looked. The houses were all so much smaller than I remembered. One thing that hadn't changed though was the friendliness of the neighbours: everyone knew each other and I was greeted warmly by people I'd grown up with as they worked in their gardens.

I reached home and there was my dad polishing his car. The front door was open and when he saw me his eyes lit up. He shouted excitedly for my mum and nan to come quickly. Possibly expecting the worst, they rushed out and there we all were. As was usual with my family it was laughter, a bout of scolding for not telling them I was coming and a nice cup of tea.

Later on, I was sitting in the living room with my dad. He was reading the *Mail on Sunday* and leaned over to show me a double-page feature about Munich preparing for the Olympics. I glanced at it with interest, then froze. It was an article with a couple of photos about the police closing down legal brothels for the duration of the games, possibly to spare the sensitivities of visiting tourists. The working girls were up in arms about this unwarranted interference in their business activities and had taken to the streets to protest. In the newspaper photo, a group of about twenty of them were blocking traffic and provocatively waving placards at passers-by. And there in the centre of the group, striking a haughty pose somewhere between militant shop steward and sexy siren, was Dominique, my fiery redhead.

I looked across the room at my dad and the TV in the corner, which I think was showing an episode of *Love Thy Neighbour*. I took in the sounds and smells of Sunday lunch being prepared and looked back at the photo. I would have liked to explain the feeling I had but I couldn't. It dawned on me that I wasn't part of this world anymore. It wasn't anything specific. I wasn't sitting there in full Bavarian *tracht* whistling *Schöne Maid*. I was still me but I just felt different.

That feeling was reinforced over the next couple of days. I wanted to visit Annabelle and tell her all about our adventures but heard from her family that she had recently moved to Leeds. Adrian and a group of schoolmates had gone down to Spain to work in bars over the summer so were nowhere to be found. John and I went out with some of our other friends, but it wasn't the same. Nothing specific was said, but they couldn't connect with our stories of diamond smugglers, terrorist gangs and US army bases. And it didn't help when, without realising it, we kept slipping German words and GI slang into the conversation.

After a few days in Slough we rented a car and some camping gear and drove down to Cornwall. We searched and found a campsite close to Newquay that became our base for the next few days. Initially the weather was great and we sunbathed, toured around visiting all the sights and generally had a good time. On the third day the weather changed dramatically. For the next forty-eight hours thick sheets of rain relentlessly pounded the tent and the beautiful field we were camped in changed into a muddy quagmire. By the sixth morning we were in a bad state: all our clothes were damp and we were cold and miserable.

We stared out through the tent flap; the rain had stopped but the sky was grey and oppressive.

"Remember that little cafe across the road from the apartment in Worms?" John asked wistfully.

"What, the one with the dark-haired waitress and her magnificent mammaries? Her cream cakes weren't bad either."

"That's the one. What I wouldn't do to be in there now. *Ein kännchen kaffee* and a smile from her lips. I'll never complain again. Didn't think I would say this about Worms, but it was actually quite cool."

"Yes, it was. And Munich is even better than Worms, and that's our next stop."

"Indeed it is." He took one last look at the dark, overcast sky and the soggy field and came to a decision. "Don't know about you but I'm all vacationed out. Shall we hit the road?"

There was no motorway in 1972 so we were going to have to stop somewhere to sleep on the way. We pulled into Bournemouth hoping we could find a room but everywhere was full, even the campsites. Deciding to plough on, we drove for another couple of hours until, overcome by tiredness, we gave up and set up the tent by the side of a quiet road.

It was murder trying to put it up in the dark: the sky was pitch black, it was blowing a gale and more rain arrived. Finally, soaked and exhausted, we managed to creep under the covers and fell asleep.

A few short hours later we both woke to an enormous whooshing sound. Initially we heard it only once or twice but then it started coming regularly, violently shaking the tent each time.

"What the fuck is that?" exclaimed John.

I was starting to get a bad feeling. I pulled back the tent flap and saw in a flash of panic that last night's quiet road was a dual carriageway, and our campsite was the central island. We had been sleeping less than three feet away from fast-moving HGVs.

If it took us an hour to get the tent up, it took us about a minute to get it down as we scrambled to depart. A few hours later we were back in Slough, arranging our return tickets to Germany.

CHAPTER THIRTY-THREE

Mister Big Stuff

Munich sparkled in the July sunshine. All the preparations were made for the Olympics and the city looked stunning in its summer colours. It had been another tortuous train and boat journey but nothing could spoil our delight at being back. Making the most of the warm summer weather, we grabbed our bags and strolled down the Bayerstraße in the general direction of our next venue.

Close to Maximiliansplatz, the Promenadeplatz is an elegant, tree-lined square peppered with muscular buildings, many with more than a touch of Bavarian flamboyance. The Bayerischer Hof Hotel stood proudly in the centre, a grand five-star cream-and-gold establishment built over a century ago.

This morning its only inelegant feature was the beat-up VW Kombi parked outside the entrance. Kassy was busy lifting an amplifier out of the back of it but the moment he saw us he waved and shouted to the others. Was that a look of relief on Roger's face? I smiled.

The club was located at the bottom of a broad, sweeping staircase on the lower ground floor, beside an exclusive Trader Vic's restaurant. Everything about it oozed class and old money – from the dark, wood-panelled rooms dotted with plush furnishings to its gleaming, chrome-fronted bar offering a choice selection of champagne, cognac and single malt whiskies. There was a large, centrally placed stage and an equally spacious dance floor.

That's where we were standing when we heard some activity by the door and watched, intrigued, as another band entered, carrying their own equipment. Roger was immediately on his guard.

"Hello. And you are?" he asked in German.

They didn't appear to understand so he tried again in English.

A response was still not forthcoming until one of them – a short, lively character who looked a bit like the dark-haired one in the Marx Brothers – shrugged apologetically and said, "*Scusa non capisco. Tu parli italiano?*"

Our leader was already thinking the worst. "Fucking Bachmann! I knew it was too good to be true. We're obviously in the wrong club. I bet it's the restaurant upstairs working as singing waiters. I'm going to bloody kill him."

"Roger, calm down, let's wait for the manager." This was the voice of reason from Donald and seemed eminently sensible.

"OK, fair enough," he replied. "Say nothing to them, though. Keep schtum. And don't let them put anything on the stage. Remember, chaps, possession is nine tenths—"

Fortunately at that moment the food and beverage manager came striding down the stairs, loudly bidding good day to everyone. In both German and English he began explaining that it was usual to have two bands playing in the club.

"Il Tempo, from Italy, are a four-piece band and will begin the evening at nine p.m. and play for thirty minutes. After that The Statesmen Singers, who are a six-piece band, will also play for thirty minutes and so it proceeds until two a.m. when you finish. It will be non-stop so you need to organise a takeover song for when you handover."

Roger, who had immediately perked up at this news, shot his cuffs and took charge. "Got it. Understand completely. We have a support act! What a place. Such style…"

The manager gave him a curious look. "I didn't actually say that. Il

Tempo are very well regarded in—"

Roger smoothly cut him off, winking in a conspiratorial manner. "Say no more, say no more, I understand completely. Leave it with me and it will be done."

By now the manager simply looked confused but glancing quickly at his watch realised he needed to get the restaurant ready for lunch so left us to it. Roger cheerily waved him off and addressed the rest of us.

"Bene! Molto bene." He kissed his fingertips and flashed a bright smile at the Italians. *"Magnifico!"*

Chico Marx, who hadn't a clue what had been said but had been smiling happily throughout, took this as a cue to begin gesticulating and waxing lyrically in Italian.

When all the superlatives and continental hand gestures were finally out of the way, we got down to business. Through an interesting mixture of sign language, Italian musical phrases and English song titles, we managed to negotiate how we should set up the stage.

Roger was in his element directing Italian bearers, advising on loudspeaker placement and generally revelling in being there. He had spoken to the kitchen and got them to bring a tray of coffee down. When we stopped for a break he couldn't contain his satisfaction.

"We've made it boys: quality club, top of the bill, support act. Perfect. Just perfect. While you boys finish off I'll just mosey on upstairs and check the billing on the posters." He thought for a moment. "Maybe it should say 'Starring The Statesmen Singers'?"

He was off on another flight of fancy when some more activity by the entrance interrupted him. This time it was in the form of a stylishly dressed character in a powder-blue suit and fashionable pink and canary yellow tie who was accompanied by an attractive brunette in a figure-clinging, emerald-green dress.

"Cor, she looks a bit fit," John remarked.

The man inspected the club critically, wrinkling his nose in disapproval, then said something to his companion. Sensing his territory was once again being encroached, Roger leapt up and went over to meet them.

"Sorry, we're closed. If you come back at nine o'clock the music program commences, although the star act doesn't begin until nine thirty."

The blue-suited gentleman looked him up and down with interest. In perfect English, he said, "No, I don't think so. Yolanda never performs before eleven thirty. And who, by the way, are you?"

"Roger, dear chap. And this is my orchestra, The Statesmen Singers."

"Well Roger dear chap, my name is Figaro Schmaltz and I am the international business manager for Yolanda, the Swiss singing star."

Roger digested this new information. "I see. And you have a contract to work here?"

Figaro stared at him curiously. "Hmm, let me see," he drawled. "If this is still the Bayerischer Hof Hotel, and the sign above the front door said it was…" He made a big theatrical gesture of stroking his chin and surveying the room. "And this does look uncannily like a nightclub…" He turned back to Roger and smiled genially. "Then yes, we have a contract to play here for the next two weeks."

Sensing we were about to slip down the bill, Roger changed tack. "Obviously there's been a mix-up and they've booked two headlining acts. We can of course negotiate some compromise, and I imagine you'll want to talk to Il Tempo, your backing band?"

"No, no our contract stipulates clearly that The Statesmen Singers are accompanying Yolanda. I'm sure I have it here somewhere."

Roger fixed him with a beady stare and appeared to swallow his resentment, no doubt still throwing imaginary darts at Bachmann's photo. Resignedly he said, "That won't be necessary."

Figaro flashed him a wide toothpaste-commercial smile. "Good. Shall we say back here at three p.m. for a rehearsal?"

After setting up the gear we went off in search of our accommodation which was in a guest house a few blocks away, just off the Maximilianstraße. It was a smart area close to The Opera so we really couldn't complain, but that didn't stop Roger trying.

"I tell you boys, I bet Yolanda's comfortably upstairs in the hotel, running a bath and ordering room service. Probably also being given an executive seeing to by that pretentious Figaro character. Swiss singing star – I can't think of a more striking oxymoron."

We had dropped off our bags and were wandering back in the general direction of the hotel when Roger stopped and said, "That's it! It's obvious. If we're going to reach the next level – swan around in these kinds of clubs, go on stage at eleven thirty and just play a couple of tunes – we need a hit." His eyes narrowed and he looked at John and me. "So where is that hit?" he asked. "What have you two been up to since you've been here?"

"That's rich," I laughed. "You haven't asked once about doing any new, original music."

"Oh, I see. I have to ask, do I? Like us to beg?"

John jumped in and said, "Yeah, and nicely too!"

"Now now, do I detect the faint whiff of rebellion?"

"No Roger, you detect the very pernicious stench of artistic revolt!"

He grinned. "Good. Just as long as we've got that sorted. Now, about that hit song."

At three p.m. we were back in the club waiting for Yolanda and Figaro – or 'Yolaro' as Roger was now calling them. A few minutes later his patience snapped.

"Right, fuck 'em, they're late," he said. "I'm going upstairs for a shit. If Yolaro condescend to drop by then be sure to advise them that the percussion department is taking a well-earned shit upstairs and will return at the department's convenience."

With a flourish he swung around and bumped straight into Figaro.

"Good. You go off and have a shit while the music department learn the scores." He grinned wickedly. "But no more than fifteen minutes, or I'll come looking for you."

Roger slunk off and we looked over the musical scores. I think we were expecting some songs we didn't know: Yolanda's hits in Switzerland. But it was the usual cover versions of international stuff like *Soley Soley* and *From Both Sides Now*. It wasn't challenging and we knew within a few minutes what we were doing, so we found ourselves waiting around for the return of the percussion department.

I took the opportunity to ask Figaro about Yolanda's record career. Pressed on the detail, he became a trifle vague and resorted to that classic refuge of a showbiz scoundrel, throwing a bunch of famous names around in the hope we'd be impressed. I started to suspect Yolanda's record career had been about as successful as ours. But she was attractive and would add glamour to the evening. The plan was for her to come on at 11.40 p.m. and at 12.40 a.m. and do three songs, so it was a nice gig for her.

The percussion department finally returned and Figaro signalled to Yolanda to make her way up on to the stage. She took the microphone and gave a professional performance of each of the songs. With the exception of Roger, the rest of us were starting to admire Figaro's style.

Later, over dinner, Roger asked if John and I fancied joining him for a weekend in Prague at the end of the month.

"Are we allowed to just go over there for a visit?" I asked. "Iron curtain, Dubček, Brezhnev, Russian tanks? Or were you planning something a little more clandestine?"

"We'd need visas but we can get those at the Czech Embassy here in Munich. I played in a Czech band before joining The Statesmen: The Tito Pavlik Orchestra. Tito's going to be performing in Prague on the first and second of August and as we don't start in Duisburg until the third it's a great opportunity to visit a cool city."

We were all for it so we arranged to locate the Czech Embassy and get the visas sorted.

CHAPTER THIRTY-FOUR

I'll Take You There

It was the third evening and it was going very well. The management were so pleased with our performances they had even sent a bottle of the house sekt to our dressing room last night. All-in-all the Bayerischer Hof was everything we imagined it would be and more. The audience were eye-poppingly glamorous, many of the younger women looking like they had stepped straight out of some sexy lingerie ad on TV. There was a healthy sprinkling of celebrities too and the champagne flowed like water. The only bummer was that we weren't actually welcome to enjoy any of it.

The hotel regarded musicians like any other hotel staff, so we had to spend the breaks either in our dressing room or in the canteen. The only exception was the 'singing star' who sat at a specially reserved corner table with Figaro in close attendance. Naturally this didn't go down at all well with our bandleader.

"Yes, that's fair. The bloody Barber of Seville and his protégé sitting down there in the club lording it up in magnificent splendour, while we skulk up here in the canteen with the Turkish bottle washers."

A couple of Middle Eastern gentlemen at the next table threw him a dark look.

He casually ignored them and continued, "Where's that hit song, John and Steve?"

It was all very well, but John and I weren't sure we could pull a hit song out of a hat just like that. We listened to half of the nonsense played on the German radio and didn't have a clue where the appeal was. But we said we would come up with a couple of ideas next month when we were back in the Ruhr Valley and were bound to have time on our hands.

That morning we had visited the Czech Embassy to organise visas for our trip to Prague. It went pretty smoothly, meaning we didn't have to join the Communist party, but they stiffed us for seventy-five marks each for the visa and another twenty-five for a photo. We had to leave our passports at the embassy and were told to pick them up in a week when the visas, subject to approval, would be ready.

Afterwards John said he was going to find Rosie and let her know we were in town so I decided to take the bull by the horns and call in on Astrid.

I took a tram over to Schwabing. It was another thing I admired about the Germans: their honesty. You bought a ticket at the tram stop and punched the ticket yourself when you were on the tram. Nobody checked it and from what I could see nobody, except for a shifty young Englishman, was cheating.

From the Leopoldstraße I walked the last bit, quietly working out the correct phrases in German to explain the unfortunate goings-on in Stuttgart. Sadly there was no answer when I rang the doorbell. I waited a few minutes but it was clear she wasn't at home. I decided I'd try again tomorrow.

On my way back to the apartment I dropped by the *hauptbahnhof* and bought a copy of the *Melody Maker*. It had become one of my weekly rituals, since our first visit in March, to pick up the MM from the international newsagents and read it over a leisurely cappuccino in a cafe on the Bayerstraße.

The main story this week was about Paul McCartney's new band Wings and their current European tour, which they were undertaking on a London double-decker bus of all things. I was just calculating where they might stow the gear – up the narrow, windy staircase? No, that was ridiculous – when the bus hove into view. I gaped for a few moments as it steamed majestically down the busy street in the direction of Stachus.

As it passed I did have the presence of mind to look and see if the former Beatle was driving, or clipping tickets at the back. The only faces I could see though looked like roadies.

Returning to my paper, I checked the tour dates and sure enough, Wings would be playing tonight at the Circus Krone which was just a few blocks away.

For the rest of the afternoon I was in quiet awe of this man who I had last seen back in the winter of 1969. He'd been such a major influence on me personally and on popular music in general over the last ten years, and now here he was roughing it on some London bus. A man of the people, going back to his roots and slumming it like the rest of us poor foot soldiers. That's style, I thought admiringly.

On arriving back at the Bayerischer Hof, I had to modify those thoughts slightly as the bus was now parked outside the front entrance and the porter, who I was on nodding terms with, excitedly informed me that the McCartneys had just checked in to the Royal Suite. Well, OK – you shouldn't begrudge the man a few small luxuries, I suppose.

Back in the canteen, Donald was tapping his watch. I think for once we were all keen to get back on stage as there was always a chance McCartney and his band may drop by the club for a nightcap.

A little later, a group of people arrived and joined Figaro at his table. They were all colourfully dressed and looked like they might be in the entertainment business. Sure enough it wasn't long before Wolfgang leaned over and whispered, "*Spione*."

Roger immediately looked interested. "Who is it Wolly? McCartney?"

"No, at the table with Yolaro. It's Peter Maffay."

Although I'd never heard of him he was the new, big name on the German *schlager* scene, and he often appeared on TV. He was there with a group of seven or eight other people including a couple of nice-looking ladies. Figaro appeared to be discussing us as they kept stopping to listen and nod appreciatively.

In the break I bumped into one of the women on her way back from the ladies' toilets. She was an attractive brunette who greeted me with a warm smile as we passed each other. I got the feeling she was about to say something when Roger shouted for me to hurry up as we were needed on stage. I smiled at her regretfully and then the moment was gone. Probably a good thing as tomorrow was Saturday, and with a bit of luck I would be seeing Astrid.

The next morning I was up by ten thirty. I had a quick shower, put on a new Velvet Underground T-shirt I had bought especially and made my way towards Schwabing, cutting through the Hofgarten and the English Garden before joining the Leopoldstraße. I arrived on Astrid's street and looked up to see if there were any signs of life in the windows. Taking the stairs two at a time, I knocked loudly on her door.

After a couple of minutes I realised she was not at home. I was just about to leave when the neighbour's door opened and a young lady, about the same age as Astrid, cautiously looked out. She said in German that Astrid was on vacation in Greece and wouldn't be back until the fifth of August. Damn! We would be up north by then. Seeing my look of disappointment she asked if I wanted to leave a message. I told her my name and realised my reputation had preceded me.

Her eyes narrowed and brusquely she said, "Oh! I don't think she was expecting to hear from you again. She was heartbroken when she returned from Stuttgart."

"I know, it was all my stupid fault but I really wanted to try to explain."

She stared levelly at me for a moment then said, "Well would you like to come in for a coffee and explain to me?"

It seemed like a good opportunity to get my side of the story across, so I joined her for coffee and in halting German explained about all the mix-ups in Stuttgart. Even putting the shiniest gloss on it, I still sounded like a complete twerp but I could see from her expression that her demeanour had changed and she was now having trouble keeping a straight face. By the end of the second cup I think she had got a grip on the situation and she assured me she would talk to Astrid and also let her know we would be playing at the Arcadia again in October.

That evening another ghost from the Arcadia appeared in the form of Marlene, who arrived in style clinging to the arm of some moneyed geriatric. I had no doubt it was a professional engagement and would include a superbly presented bonk at the end, if he survived that long. If she was surprised to see us she definitely wasn't unhappy about it and made a point of getting the old boy up to dance. They ended up by the front of the stage and while he wasn't looking she threw some x-rated looks in my direction, while at the same time licking his earlobe. Two disco songs later he looked set to expire, so they hastily retired to their table where a restorative bottle of Bollinger was waiting. I thought about it and laughed. I might have been more wise to the ways of the world now than I was in March, but I still wasn't prepared to share a woman's bed with paying customers.

Later, someone mentioned that the Timelords were playing at The Babalu, the Schwabing club we'd visited a couple of times in March. Everyone was keen to go and watch them. Everyone that is except Roger.

"What do we want to go and listen to those wannabes for?"

"Come on, it'll be fun," said Wolfgang.

John joined in enthusiastically: "Yeah, I want to hear what all the fuss is about with these blokes."

It must have been around three a.m. when we arrived at the club. There was a small queue waiting to get in but conveniently the bouncer on the door had seen us play at the Arcadia. He smoothly whisked us past the queue and organised a table near the dance floor.

I could see the band had noticed us and presumably they had gone into the same spy mode as we usually did.

They played a relatively flavourless version of *My Girl* followed by something German. If they were trying to impress us, they weren't trying hard. After that Jimmie took a moment to introduce our band to the audience. He was complimentary and asked Roger to come up and sing something. It was a nice gesture and I was starting to warm to the guy. I couldn't understand what was not to like. The expression on Roger's face, however, didn't reciprocate my feelings.

"Bastard. What cheek. I'm not singing with them," he said grumpily.

"Go on man, don't be daft. It'll be good promotion for us and you can show everyone you're a better singer than he is," Kassy urged.

We were all egging him on and finally he agreed.

"Alright, but I'm singing one of your songs, Kassy. Not wasting one of mine on them. *Ruby* – what key do we do that in?"

"G," John said, "but that's quite high for you. Better tell them to do it in F."

"No problem. If Kassy can sing it in G, I can too."

Calmly he got up and climbed onto the stage to cheers from us and a few polite claps from the audience.

After discussing the song and key with the band, Jimmie introduced him: "*Meine damen und herren*, I give you the wonderful voice of Roger and *Ruby Don't Take Your Love to Town*.

"*You've painted up your lips and rolled and curled your tinted hair.*"

Oh God, the bastards were playing it in C instead of G – way too high for him to sing.

"*Ruby are you contemplating going out somewhere?*"

He was trying gamely but it was a desperate, strangulated effort. Abruptly he changed tack and attempted the second verse an octave lower: "*It wasn't me that started that old crazy Asian war.*"

This was in the lower basement of his vocal range and only a morbid drone was coming out. The Timelords were all deadpan, but it was obvious they'd done it on purpose.

Ambitiously he took another shot at the higher octave. *"Oh Rooooooobeeeee."*

I thought his eyeballs appeared perilously close to being shot from their sockets – and the plumbing down his neck didn't look in much better shape. It was not at all pretty but I doubt it mattered much as most of the audience were talking and drinking.

Then we noticed – and from the wild look in his eyes our drummer did too – that Gina was sitting across the room with some friends. The sympathetic expression on her face was almost certainly a worse pill for him to swallow than the embarrassment the band were dishing out. The song ended and we all cheered noisily – even a few in the audience joined in – but Roger was having none of it. In clasped rage he stomped off the stage and rejoined us at the table.

"Any other brilliant suggestions?" he demanded. "Right, I'm off home, anyone else coming?"

We all got up and left.

The following Wednesday our passports and visas were ready to be picked up and we made preparations for our trip to Prague. Kassy would be taking the VW to Worms and Donald and Wolfgang the Mercedes to Stockstadt, so we needed to arrange transport. We searched around and found a rental company where we could pick a car up in Munich and drop it off in Duisburg.

On the final evening, Roger managed to place a phone call to the club where Tito was playing to let them know roughly when we would be arriving. All of a sudden I was really excited about seeing a country on the other side of the Iron Curtain.

It was a noisy farewell as we had become good friends with the Italians and Yolanda. Even Figaro was now a chum and full of praise, promising he would let the club owners he worked with back in Switzerland know all about us.

Then finally, with John driving and Roger snoozing on the back seat, we headed north out of the city. After a few kilometres Munich became a fast-fading memory as we sped east towards

Czechoslovakia. It was the middle of the night and the roads were empty, which was handy as John hadn't actually driven on the right before.

Without too much drama we made it to Regensburg and turned off in the direction of Pilsen, which was the first major town over the border and of course the home of the famous beer.

We reached the border around five a.m. and went through the barrier on the German side. After about a hundred metres of no man's land we arrived at the Czech border which comprised of a guardhouse, a watchtower, a flagpole and a couple of sentry boxes.

The whole setting looked like something straight out of an episode of *Mission: Impossible*. Two or three guards were leaning against the guardhouse wall, lazily pointing bolt-action rifles in our direction while an officer, keeping his hand firmly on his holster, walked over to our car. Up in the watchtower another couple of them, holding sub-machine guns, eyed us with suspicion. All in all, we were seriously outgunned if we wanted a fight. Happily, the only thing we wanted was a warm bed, so we adopted our friendliest demeanour and handed over our documents to the unsmiling officer.

He looked at the first passport and asked, "Who is Steffen?"

"Er that's me," I replied.

He stared suspiciously at me for what seemed like ages before examining my passport and visa. He picked up the next one.

"And who is Rogger?"

"Roger old chap," came the reply from the back seat. "Rhymes with lodger. That would be me."

The officer looked at the visa, at the passport, then back at Roger. "But this doesn't look at all like you! Where is Rogger?"

Sensing things were starting to go awry, our leader got out of the car to explain things better. Immediately the soldiers who had been lolling about were on their guard.

He smiled ingratiatingly at the officer and explained, "Er, yea, my passport's a few years old. And I might have put on a couple of pounds and lost a bit of hair." He paused for effect and tried to hold in his stomach before attempting an even more winning smile. "But it's still the same old engine under the bonnet. It's dear old Roger."

I wasn't sure if the officer understood any of that but he moved on to John, and that's where we really became unstuck. He looked at the passport photo, the visa photo and the beaming organist in the driving seat.

"And who are you?" the officer demanded. "None of these photos are of you!"

John and I looked uneasily at each other and decided to get out of the car too. Leaning over the officer's shoulder, I could see the problem. In his passport photo John had a beard. In his visa photo he had no beard but had recently grown a lustrous moustache. Inconveniently at the present moment, his anxious phiz was clean-shaven.

"Bloody hell John, can't you grow something quickly?" Roger asked. "You're very glandular, it shouldn't be that difficult."

John looked affronted. "Glandular? What the fuck does that mean? What about you, you fat fuck? Can't you lose a few pounds?"

The officer was having none of it. "Enough! You two must go back." He pointed at me. "You can go through."

"I can't go on my own!" I squeaked. "I haven't a clue where we're going or who we're seeing." I pointed accusingly at Roger. "They're his friends."

The officer grinned nastily and drawled, "Then you must return with your friends."

Roger took a new tack and reasoned, "Look, if there were any discrepancies between the visa photos and the passports, why didn't your embassy reject our applications? We've paid a lot of money for these visas and if there was anything wrong, it should have been dealt with. And if it's the small matter of my friend being under-moustached at this early hour, I'm sure we can draw one under his nose with a pen."

The officer was already walking away but said with some finality, "No! The papers aren't in order. You must go back."

I don't know if it was tiredness or frustration or both but all of a sudden we were arguing with them – and for one short moment I think we may even have invaded a small corner of Czechoslovakia – before we were forced into the car and ordered to drive back.

In the end, knackered and feeling totally cheated, we drove back to Regensburg and found a cheap hotel where we morosely kicked our heels for a couple of days before making our way up to Duisburg.

The subject had been tactfully avoided until now, but on the journey north John asked Roger why he hadn't gone home to Stockstadt during this little break.

"We're going to have to move from Stockstadt," he replied. "It's too complicated living in a small village after all that shit with Redeye. In a place like that they're all related to each other and, as we know, he was trying his best to get related to my little family. Mausi's got no friends now and he's threatening violence if he sees me again, so a move is in the offing."

"Any idea where?" I asked.

"Back to Lübeck where her mum still has a small apartment. She's already gone back up there as she hates Stockstadt. Her apartment is too small for us so we'll need to find something of our own but I'll get onto that while we're in Duisburg."

CHAPTER THIRTY-FIVE

Sex Machine

We rolled into Duisburg late in the afternoon. At first glance it looked very similar to Dortmund, although with its commanding position at the confluence of the Rhine and Ruhr rivers, the city felt more open and spacious. That feeling was also reinforced by the amount of greenery we drove through as we approached the city centre. Duisburg boasted one of the largest zoos in Germany and to the south of it was Duisburger Stadtwald – an extended park and forested expanse covering around 10 percent of the Greater Duisburg area.

Zipping airily past this bucolic idyll we continued on downtown in search of the Silberpalais: our next residency. Like the Corso it was located on a pedestrianised shopping street, but whereas the Corso looked like a club, this place looked like it was more accustomed to hawking car insurance or offering unemployment benefits. Sometime in the past it had been a suite of offices before some live wire decided to resurrect it as a nightclub. But it was still all plate glass and parquet floors. The windows provided a lacklustre view of the town centre, while electric signs for Kaufhof, Hertie and Karstadt department stores competed with glaring sunlight to create an uninspiring club vibe.

By the time we arrived, the others had already built up the stage and were sitting quietly in the kitchen drinking coffee. After saying hello to the staff we enquired about the band accommodation and set off in search of it.

The manager had scribbled a rough map for us and, following his directions, we headed back out to the Stadtwald. There, on a quiet street backing onto the forest, we came upon an imposing heap of bricks in the *Jugendstil*.

"That's the place," Wolfgang said, rechecking the address on the paper.

Whatever the building had been before, it had seen better days. Much better days. The ground floor was now a seedy bar that was all locked up. Above its entrance hung an unlit neon sign for 'The Lady Bar' and a card in a first floor window advertised rooms available to rent by the hour.

"How nice," I remarked. "When I tell my mum we're staying at a B&B in Duisburg, I might want to leave out that B&B stands for Bar & Brothel."

A side door led us up some stairs to a small reception on the first floor where a wizened old crone sat behind a counter, eyeing us narrowly through a fog of cigarette smoke.

"We don't open for business until this evening," she said before we had time to say who we were.

"No worries, dear lady," Roger said. "We're the band from the Silberpalais and I believe you have six luxury suites waiting upon our arrival."

She took a deep drag on her cigarette and stared at him, goggle-eyed, for a couple of seconds before cracking up into mirthless laughter. Unfortunately, this also brought on one of those coughing fits only a committed sixty-a-day smoker can produce. We stood there patiently waiting for the spasms to pass.

"*Ja, ja,* nice joke Johnny," she croaked. "You have three double rooms at the end of that corridor. They're reserved for musicians. Any other luxuries cost extra."

She hacked up a ball of phlegm and began cackling with

demented laughter as we took the keys and paired off into the rooms.

Back at the club, black curtains had been drawn across the windows while red and blue mood lighting was creating something approaching a nightclub atmosphere. We took to the stage and gamely opened with *Love the One You're With* and followed that with a succession of up-tempo dance songs. After two hours of playing to half a dozen guests, while bored staff just loafed around, it was becoming apparent we weren't playing in one of Duisburg's top spots. In fact, the place had taken on the proportions of some deathless corporate landscape where Germany's lonely came to drink and die.

A little after midnight, the manager kindly put us out of our misery and allowed us to finish and go home. Whatever guests had been there had left, and for the last hour we had been playing to chairs and tables.

Returning to the lodgings the neon sign for The Lady Bar was now lit, broadcasting to the neighbourhood that they were open for business. It was still early so we went in.

Subdued lighting and heavily made-up ladies, all skimpily dressed, dotted around the tables confirmed our suspicions about where we were now living. An older lady came out from behind the bar, welcomed us warmly and asked where we would like to sit. Donald explained that we were the band living upstairs and would be delighted if we could just come in for a nightcap. I thought we might get the cold shoulder but not at all. She introduced herself as Eva and found a table for us while drinks quickly appeared.

We were recounting our unfortunate exploits on the Czech border to loud hoots of laughter from the rest of the band when some of the ladies, who had become bored sitting alone, came over and joined us. Anyone just walking in could easily have got the wrong impression from all of us sitting there laughing and drinking with these conspicuously professional ladies. So I imagine Roger felt particularly awkward when he turned to the door and saw Mausi and the two kids standing there.

I don't know which one of them looked the most shocked. It took a few moments until somebody came up with the original line, "Mausi, what in God's name are you doing here?"

Actually, that was Wolfgang. Roger still looked way too surprised to ask anything. Eventually he had the presence of mind to get up and lead them over to our table.

She sat down and turned to Donald. "I saw your mother this morning. She told me you and Wolly had been home for a few days, but had already left." Turning to Roger, her voice hardened a little. "Of course it would have been nice if my husband had come to see his family at the same time."

"If your lover wasn't so keen on gunning me down, I'm sure that could have been arranged," he mumbled.

She ignored him and continued, "Anyway, it's become impossible for us to stay in Stockstadt. Donald's parents helped all they could, but Berndt has friends and relatives everywhere and they blank me whenever they see me. It got so bad I didn't even want to go to the shops. There was also the small question of the unpaid rent while you were living it up with your fancy woman in Munich and Stuttgart. I couldn't stand it any longer so we packed a few clothes and took the train here."

Roger looked like he was dying to ask why Berndt hadn't paid the rent, but with all these women around let it go.

"We arrived in Duisburg just after midnight," she continued. "We found the club just as it was closing. Luckily the manager was still there. He said he had let you go home early and kindly drove us here." She looked around with an expression of deep scepticism. "And here we are."

Smiling bravely, she waited for a reaction. Surprisingly, Eva was the first to respond.

"And you've come to the right place," she said, smiling. "Let me fix some lemonade for your two boys, and maybe a glass of wine for you? Then presently your husband can take you to your room upstairs."

At about the same time as Roger took his family to their room, customers began drifting in and the ladies returned to their separate tables. We watched with interest as the new arrivals ordered drinks and began making eye contact with potential companions. Before long a cosy tête-à-tête, discussing price and sexual predilections, was struck up while more drinks arrived. Negotiations completed, the happy couples headed upstairs.

"My God, we really are living in a knocking shop," I remarked to no one in particular.

"Shame, I quite fancied the blonde," John said.

"You unsavoury fellow. The woman's on the clock, she does it for money."

"Well you'd know all about that," he said mischievously.

"If you're referring to Munich, I didn't know their professions at the time," I replied stiffly.

"Well none of these ladies are going to give you a freebie, or even offer it to you at cost price," Wolfgang stated frankly. "Eva's very nice but you can see she's running this place with a rod of iron."

Our drinks were finished so we said goodnight to Eva and went upstairs.

Apart from the unorthodox goings-on where we lived, there wasn't much to distract us that month, so it gave John and me the opportunity to work on some original songs. We had the offer from Rich and Randy in the back of our minds, and we had made a few stabs at composing rock songs that would work in the US. Now we were trying to write something that would be popular in towns like this, and it was a daunting prospect.

The German music scene in the seventies was generally split between the electronic krautrock bands like Kraftwerk and Tangerine Dream on one side and simplistic pop and *schlager* on the other, served up by impossibly good-looking chaps with carefully coiffured hairstyles, fake tans and halogen smiles. Personally, I couldn't see us fitting into either category. Eventually, we threw together a few ideas and played them to the band. Everyone seemed keen so we rehearsed a couple and started to play them on stage.

After the Bayerischer Hof it was nice to once again mix with the audience, but if the Munich crowd were hip and glamorous, the Silberpalais crowd projected distinctly less sparkle. This was a hard-working industrial town which was reflected in the clientele. Guests arrived early, ordered beer or wine and were gone before midnight approached, leaving only the ever faithful *freunde der nacht* to wind the clock down to two a.m. Friday and Saturday were more lively, and the club was busy from opening until closing time, but even though there were a few attractive ladies in the audience, no one in the band fancied the prospect of taking them home to our cosy little brothel.

During the second week we had a surprise visit from the Transylvania Express. They were still an odd bunch but so friendly and enthusiastic it was nice to see them again. With our improving German skills, we were also capable of following more of the conversation, which was certainly colourful when listening to Dan the saxophone player. He was the one Wolfgang and I had chatted to in Munich and was just as lecherous now as he was then. His twinkling eyes made a quick inventory of the women in the club, his gaze resting on an older lady with unusually large breasts.

"Man oh man, look at the engineering on that!" he exclaimed, puffing furiously on his pipe.

She noticed him staring and smiled back tentatively. He in turn switched his amorous gaze onto full power. If the intention was seducing her into bed with his eyes alone, he was doing a decent job of it. But before he could take things to the next level, her friend said something and they prepared to leave.

Smiling regretfully, she winked at him as they walked past and he called out, "Good night, sexy lady. Sleep carefully. There are dangerous dreams out there."

Swiftly he returned his attention to the few remaining ladies but didn't see anyone he fancied so prepared to leave, but when Roger told him we were living above an escort bar and would be going back there for a celebration, he quickly changed his mind.

In Germany, it's popular to toast a birthday boy or girl on the stroke of midnight. On this particular midnight John would be turning eighteen so it called for some particularly heavy-duty celebrations on our part. First we had champagne and schnapps with the staff at the club, then we took the party back to The Lady Bar where the working girls had sweetly decorated the place with bunting and ribbons. As they welcomed John with a winsome version of *Happy Birthday*, I think the Transylvanians thought it was their birthday too.

I made my way over to the bar and found Donald drinking alone. He was doing that more and more often these days so I asked him how everything was. He shrugged and continued to stare across the room.

"It's problems at home. Margit hates it when I'm away touring and now she's threatening to leave unless I come home."

"How will you solve that? We're going to Essen after this and a month in Ruhpolding and Munich in October."

"I know," he groaned. We stood quietly watching the proceedings in the bar for a few moments, then he said, "She's coming to Essen for a few days so I hope that might improve things. The trouble is, she loves her job in that stupid bar, otherwise she could come on tour with us like Mausi has."

I remembered the bar where she worked and her über-tactile style with the customers and decided I couldn't be as easy going about it as he was. But of course I didn't say that to him. Instead I said, "Don't worry. I'm sure she can do without you for two months and you'll be home again in December."

He nodded and attempted a smile. "Yes of course. It'll be fine."

CHAPTER THIRTY-SIX

When You're Hot, You're Hot

For the second part of August, we would be playing in Essen at the San Francisco nightclub. Essen isn't much more than a stones-throw from Duisburg so while John and Wolfgang went with Kassy in the VW, Roger and his family crammed into the back seat of the Merc behind Donald and me. As we entered the city centre, we were delighted to see our posters on a number of small billboards which delighted everyone. We were less pleased however to see almost as many posters for the Timelords who were playing at the Corso in nearby Dortmund.

"Oh brilliant! It's their night off tonight. I just bet they'll be there at the San Francisco telling everyone about that wonderful evening in Munich," Roger moaned.

"So what?" Donald said. "It was a cheap trick on their part. It's our show tonight and if they do come to see us we'll give them something to remember."

Being a Monday, and San Francisco the only club open offering live music, it was already busy by the time we arrived. It was another 'in' club in the style of the Happy Night and it had a reputation locally for its innovative interior with tables built into San Francisco-style street cars.

Wolfgang had spotted several bands in the audience and thought a couple of club owners and promoters were there. Apart from the musicians, the majority of the crowd appeared to be staff from other clubs and bars enjoying their night off.

Walking out on stage, I noticed the guys from Transylvanian Express at one table and Karl and the Blue Tramps at another. Between them was a long table seating a large group of Indonesian musicians. I recognised some of the guys from the Timelords – and even a couple of faces from the band I had seen so often at The Blue Door club in Munich back in March – but I didn't know the others.

Kassy noticed me staring and said, "The ones on the left are the Tielman Brothers and beside them are three guys from The Rhine River Union. I see the Timelords, although I don't see Jimmie." He glanced over at the entrance and made a face. "Forget that. The bastard's just been timing his entrance."

We watched with wry amusement as Jimmie made a big show of table-hopping, noisily greeting guests as he weaved his way around the room. Anyone would have thought it was him who was performing this evening. Strangely though, I got the impression some of the people he was pressing the flesh with weren't as enthusiastic about it as he was.

He turned his attention to the musicians' tables, giving everyone a big, presidential wave before coming to a sudden stop, his smile frozen in place. He was staring warily at Karl who was leering at him like a cat eyeing a particularly tasty mouse. Negotiating a swift, tactical withdrawal, Jimmie made a sharp about-turn and hurried over to the Indonesians. While this was going on I was delighted to see Heidi and Dagmar arrive with some friends.

Back on stage, a very determined-looking Roger announced: "Righto chaps, there's more spies out there tonight than at a KGB awards dinner. Let's make sure we give them something to remember."

Over the next hour we played our best numbers and gave it everything. The vocal harmonies sounded spot on and instrumentally we had never been tighter. The audience were enjoying it too and as it was mainly made up of professionals nobody danced, which made it feel like a concert. Each song was followed by enthusiastic applause which spurred us on to try even harder. By the break we knew we had just played one of our best sets and were interested in gauging the response from the audience.

First I went over to Heidi and her friends to say hello. She was dying to tell me about an exciting new job she had been offered in Barbados. I was delighted for her as she had always said it was her ambition to work in exotic places, but I knew I was going to miss her very much. She was one of the few bright spots while working up here in the Ruhr Valley. After arranging to meet the following day I joined the others in the band as they went around greeting the musicians in the audience.

It was good to see Karl again and to meet the Blue Tramps, who were quick to compliment us on the sound of the band. After passing by the Transylvanians and going through the usual courtesies we went over to the Indonesians' table.

Everyone ceremoniously shook hands and John and I were introduced to the ones we hadn't already met. The Tielmans were extremely friendly and generous in their praise, but the guys from the Timelords were less forthcoming. They seemed more interested in chatting to each other.

This changed when an older gentleman came striding over, hastily followed by a waiter loaded down with sekt bottles and glasses. The old man introduced himself as Herr Dietmeier, the owner of the San Francisco. Apparently a big noise in the Ruhr Valley, he also owned a number of other clubs and bars. The musicians around the table knew him and were immediately respectful.

"*Meine herren,*" he said in a loud voice while the waiter poured glasses of sekt for everyone. "That was one of the best sets I've heard in this club for a long time."

The Indonesians had gone quiet.

"I'd been told a number of different things about The Statesmen but I wasn't at all prepared for such a professional performance. A well thought out repertoire and beautiful vocal arrangements." He looked pointedly around the table, his eyes coming to rest on Jimmie, who had found a spot on the ceiling requiring his attention. "*Ja*," Herr Dietmeier continued, "not at all what I was expecting. Boys, I hope you will all join me in a toast – The Statesmen Singers."

When we got back to the dressing room, Donald asked Roger, "Well? I bet you're glad the Timelords are here for that, and to chew on a little humble pie."

"A little?" Kassy said. "Those bastards had to devour a whole bloody Indonesian *rijsttafel*!"

Roger looked fit to burst. "Yes indeed," he said, beaming with satisfaction. "Never again will that bullshit artist insult The Statesmen." He turned to the rest of us. "This is a great evening for the band, gentlemen. An important evening, and it's just the beginning."

The next day I met Heidi for lunch. She was leaving for Barbados at the end of the month but was determined we keep my German lessons going until then.

"That's really good of you," I said. "I don't know why you're wasting time on such an undeserving case as me."

"No! I heard you last night. You've started to become quite fluent and I like to think I helped a bit."

She was being way too kind as I was still plodding along.

Having learned a couple more languages since, I've come to the conclusion there are three stages in the learning process. Stage one is where you learn to speak some phrases and can deliver more than you can understand. You know how to ask where the post office is but you don't understand the answer. Stage two is when you begin to understand a fair bit but haven't grasped the vocabulary well enough to join in with a grown-up conversation. You understand more than you can speak. Stage three is when your level of understanding and expressing yourself are roughly on par. Unfortunately, I'm sure I was still stuck somewhere between stage one and two.

We arranged to continue our afternoon sessions, this time on

Tuesdays and Thursdays in another *konditorei* just around the corner from the club.

The San Francisco was a nice gig: the audience were fun and seemed to like us a lot. The playing times were from nine p.m. until two a.m., so not too brutal, and the band apartment was decent and just upstairs from the club. Roger had found a cheap hotel for his family so we didn't see much of them. Spending the hottest month of the year in another industrial city wasn't our first choice, but it was comfortable enough and the following month we would be going down south to the Alps.

Then towards the end of the second week, Margit came to visit Donald. She had been by once or twice in Worms but this was the first time I remember her visiting us on tour. I got the feeling the others weren't deliriously happy about it. I asked Wolfgang why.

"Because she's difficult. After one night here she'll get bored and start to make him jealous."

That was being optimistic. She arrived during the afternoon and came along to the club in the evening. As there were no other ladies present that we knew, she had to sit on her own while we played. During the first ballad she was invited up to dance by some oiled smoothie, wearing enough aftershave to put the Dortmund bog attendant out of business. I'd seen him a few times before, hanging around at the bar, always on the lookout for a quick one-nighter.

He was all over her and she didn't work too hard at keeping him off, making a couple of helpless gestures towards the stage, giggling and flirting outrageously. At first Donald was smiling indulgently, like he did when we were watching her at work. After a couple of songs, and the guy getting more and more intimate, Donald became seriously pissed. The break arrived and our guitarist was off that stage faster than a whippet on amphetamines. Margit urgently whispered something to the guy and he disappeared even faster.

The following evening she decided she would go out on her own. She didn't arrive back at the apartment until three a.m., which woke the rest of us up and caused a minor argument. Unfortunately it carried on in the same vein for the rest of the week: she got bored and tried to make him jealous. By the final evening it had come to a head.

We had finished the last song and were starting to pack up the equipment when Donald suddenly turned to the rest of us and announced:

"Boys. I can't do this anymore. This constant touring is ruining my relationship. I'm sorry but I quit."

We all stared at him in disbelief. It was Roger who responded first. "Donald that's crazy. We're finally getting somewhere. Why would you possibly quit now?"

"He's right," Wolfgang added. "We've worked hard for this. Why fuck it up now?"

"I know! I know. But she means more. And I will lose her if I am never home."

Maybe one or two of the others had an inkling this was coming but I was shocked. For me he was an integral part of our vocal sound, and apart from that he was a lovely guy. Roger tried to get him to cool down and promised that we'd take a one-month break after Munich, so there would be plenty of time to spend in Stockstadt.

It seemed as though he was starting to reconsider when Kassy unhelpfully told him to "man up and control his woman".

This resulted in some sharp words between them and the short story is that Donald packed his equipment into his car, grabbed Margit and his case and drove off into the night.

PART SEVEN

RUHPOLDING

CHAPTER THIRTY-SEVEN

Ain't No Mountain High Enough

Stepping off the train in Ruhpolding, we were all of a sudden in a completely new world. Gone was the grey, industrial landscape of the past four weeks. What replaced it was a vista so enchanting, so absolutely magical it could have been created by Disney for a movie. The air was clean and pure, the light sharp and intense and the scenery took your breath away. Majestic mountains stood in solemn attendance around a picture-perfect Alpine village, sitting snugly in the centre of an emerald-green valley. It dozed contentedly in the early afternoon sunshine, as though patiently waiting to welcome five tired and dishevelled musicians.

John and I gazed around admiringly while Mausi and the kids noisily assisted Roger in getting their luggage off the Munich train. After Donald's hasty departure, we were inconveniently left without transport. Essen to Ruhpolding was about a seven-hour car journey and the plan had been to drive through the night. Urgently requiring a new plan, we made enquiries and found there was a night train coming down from Copenhagen en route to Munich. From there we could get a commuter train out to Ruhpolding. It was all done by the skin of our teeth, but we managed to get to the station with about twenty minutes to spare. In the meantime Wolfgang and Kassy were driving down in the VW.

It looked like it was going to take Roger some time to get

organised, so we picked up our bags and began walking into the village centre. Coming the other way was a group of young American tourists talking excitedly about the Olympics. We took the opportunity to ask them if they knew where Cafe Markl was.

An attractive blonde girl stepped forward and said, "Yeah, we go there most evenings. It's got live music of sorts and we like to dance, although the dance music isn't great." She looked directly at me with interest. "Will you guys be going there tonight?"

"Yes, we're the new band so hopefully you'll be dancing to us tonight. And we do play good dance music."

"Great! A British band, how cool."

They pointed out the road where the club was situated and we said we'd catch up with them later.

We carried on down the main street, turned a corner by the Sparkasse bank and there, in the distance, was the VW parked beside a building that looked like the club – Cafe Markl. No sign of the Mercedes, so I guessed Donald hadn't changed his mind.

We spotted Wolfgang with Kassy and, surprise surprise, Sonja. What was she doing here? Oh God! Mausi and Sonja. I desperately hoped we weren't going to be sharing an apartment. Wolfgang seemed to read my mind.

"I can see from your expression that you were not expecting so many guests," he said, chuckling mischievously. "But no worries, the three of us are in that little cottage over there." He pointed across the road. "It has three small bedrooms and is actually very nice. Roger and his family and Kassy and Sonja will be staying up that hill in a guest house." He pointed towards some wooden buildings halfway up a mountain. I quietly asked what she was doing here.

"Her ex-husband takes their kids for a few weeks each year so she can have a vacation. She plans on being here the whole month."

Roger arrived with his family a few minutes later and was given a quick update. He looked down the road hopefully.

"No Donald?"

Wolfgang shook his head. "No. When we picked up Sonja in

Worms we drove through Stockstadt and had another talk with him. It's that bloody woman. He's pussy whipped. She doesn't want him to tour anymore so he's going to look for a job on Monday. He's still talking about becoming a dentist."

Roger looked surprised. "He won't just step into that job. He'll have years of studying first."

Wolfgang shrugged. "Whatever. He'll wake up one day and realise his mistake."

We entered the club and looked around. I guess it was what you would expect in the mountains: wall to wall pine, bench tables and wooden beams – the full Alpine experience. There was one large room with a wooden dance floor in front of a small stage. To one side was a cosy bar area with comfortable armchairs, some furry rugs and a wild boar's head grinning down approvingly from one wall.

A door behind the bar opened and Herr Markl entered. Once again he was dressed in full Bavarian regalia, his one concession to the summer weather being a short-sleeved shirt. He greeted us warmly enough, although he did remark on the loss of Donald. Roger assured him that it wouldn't affect the band's performance or the club's entertainment one jot.

"Herr Markl, you won't notice he's not here," he declared. "Two guitarists aren't necessary when we have such a guitar virtuoso as Steve." I quickly glanced at him but he continued, unperturbed, "Yes, a disciple of the Django Reinhardt school of virtuosity with just a taste of Jimi and Eric." He warmed to his theme. "And maybe a soupçon of Chet and Les Paul…"

Markl hadn't a clue what he was talking about and impatiently butted in, "*Ja, ja*, but can he play a decent polka?" He looked hard at Roger. "In fact, can any of you?"

"Can we play a polka? You jest," Roger blustered. "If it's polkas you want it's polkas you'll get. But sensing that the audience are going to be tourists, shouldn't we be widening our appeal with an eclectic mix of international hits?"

This hit a nerve with Markl, who became animated. "No! That's wrong. That's exactly what you shouldn't do." He glanced around suspiciously and lowered his voice. "The tourists bring no money. They dance and sip one beer the whole evening. My regular customers, they're the ones you should please and they want Bavarian music." He beamed triumphantly. "So I'm delighted you have such a store of polkas."

And with that he left.

CHAPTER THIRTY-EIGHT

Me and You and a Dog Named Boo

The accommodation was at least a pleasant surprise. It would have to double as a dressing room for the whole band, but apart from that, the bedrooms were cosy and it was literally only twenty steps to the club.

After unpacking, we showered and changed then took a little walk around the village. We dropped in at the Hotel Zur Post and had coffee. It was buzzing and full of young Americans, with a smattering of Brits and French, many of them here for the Olympics.

"It's going to be really easy to ignore all these people's requests and just play Bavarian music," Wolfgang said sarcastically.

"We don't have more than a handful of that stuff," I said. "So whichever way it goes, Markl is going to be an unhappy doggy. Might as well just start as we mean to go on with our usual repertoire and get the unpleasantness with him out of the way early."

Walking back up the road to the club, we were overtaken by Roger and Kassy on a couple of bikes.

"Too fucking far to walk from where we're staying. It's halfway up there." Roger pointed in the general direction of the range of mountains to the south. "But there was this bike rental shop next door, so here we are."

He affectionately patted the handlebar, obviously enjoying the novelty of it. I didn't say anything but wondered how much fun it would be cycling up a mountain in the dark after a few rounds of schnapps.

It was still an hour before the club would open its doors but we headed over there to meet the staff, and maybe even get some food. The first people we came upon were Markl and a lady who I imagined was his wife. She was about ten years younger than him, possibly in her early fifties, but wore a permanent expression of boredom which did nothing to increase her appeal. They were seated in the bar area eating dinner and while they were eating kept stopping to lavish praise and tiny morsels of food on a small, yappy dog.

Roger raised an eyebrow. "Oh God, this is going to be fun," he whispered. "OK men, give me some operating room. Let's try and scrape some of the permafrost off these two with the old Roger charm."

He strode in and declared, "Herr Markl, you sly dog. You didn't mention you would be dining with Miss World this evening."

Bowing in her direction, he smiled obsequiously while she inspected him briefly without expression. Languidly she turned her attention to the rest of us, lit a cigarette and slowly exhaled.

He continued obliviously, "A delightful honour, *fräulein*, we've seen all your movies. And what a beautiful dog – isn't it a Jagdterrier? It's been my favourite dog since childhood."

Her face briefly defrosted a couple of degrees while Markl immediately became interested.

"*Ja.* Exactly, a Jagdterrier. Fifi Nous is our *liebling*. She is the child we could not have."

In the meantime little Fifi Nous had become interested in one of John's platform shoes and was pulling on the zip. Unsure how to react, he tried gently nudging her away, but she was tenacious and wouldn't let go.

"*Ja,* Fifi is still just a baby," Markl explained. "She can sometimes be a little excitable but that's because we believe – maybe, just maybe – that she was trodden on or, *um Gottes willen,* kicked by a customer."

He laughed incredulously. "Impossible to believe when you see how *wunderschön* she is, but there are bad people everywhere." His eyes narrowed and darted around suspiciously as he paused for a moment. "More than likely some *scheiße tourist*."

He continued to stare at us thoughtfully while his wife, appearing totally bored with the conversation, blew smoke rings into the air. Just then Fifi Nous broke the spell by giving John's shoe one final yank. The zip came flying off and the dog scampered triumphantly away with it in her mouth.

"*Mein Gott!*" Frau Markl shrieked. "She'll choke to death. Helmut, do something."

She aimed a recriminating glare at John, who reacted furiously.

"Fucking hell, Roger, they were a new pair of shoes!" he trilled. "Tell the old bat she owes me forty-nine marks."

Markl also seemed to feel it was John's fault but calmed down when the dog promptly returned, apparently none the worse for wear. Before she could start on his other shoe we hurriedly made our excuses and left them to their dinner.

Heading towards the kitchen, Roger switched off the charm. "Fucking horrible little rat. I can't stand small dogs. Give me a big, fuck-off German sheepdog anytime."

John remarked, "Yeah, and I'm so glad you told them that when we were in there."

"You've got to choose your battles carefully, John my boy. No point in firing your big guns too early."

John made a face and said with some finality, "That dog comes near me again it'll get the whole artillery right up its arse!"

And that's just about what happened next.

We entered the kitchen and introduced ourselves to the staff. Waiters and waitresses were busily organising glasses while a chef was preparing small Bavarian specialities. The club didn't have a restaurant but you could order various sausage dishes and small plates of schnitzel and pork in the bar. After introductions were made the chef kindly offered to make us something for dinner.

While he was preparing the food, we got chatting and it became evident that the Markls weren't popular employers and the dog was pretty much loathed by everyone. The chef was particularly vocal.

"The fucking dog just comes in here and takes a piss and a dump wherever it pleases; they never discipline it. I'm supposed to clean it up then cook something delicious for the customers. Next time I'm going to fry up some of that shit for the Markls' evening meal and see how they like the taste!"

We were picking up our dinners and preparing to take them over to a table when the swing door flew open and a waiter came bustling in, followed closely by Fifi Nous, snapping at his heels.

"*Geh weg, scheiße hund!*" he yelled.

Fifi Nous spotted John and, wagging her tail, she happily dashed over to him, going straight for his other shoe, grabbing hold of the zip with fierce determination. Balancing a full plate of food in one hand and a glass of Coke in the other, John attempted to push her away with his foot. Finally he lost his patience, took a step back and planted his right foot under the dog's arse, performing the kind of drop-kick a rugby player would have been proud of.

Unfortunately, at precisely that moment the Markls walked into the kitchen. Frozen in time and space they watched open-mouthed as the dog flew majestically in a wide arc across the room, landing unceremoniously in a pile at the feet of a startled waitress. The dog looked surprised, both Markls screamed while the rest of us just looked on expectantly.

Frau Markl was the first to react. Dropping her cigarette and grinding it fiercely into the floor, she scooped up the dog and hurried out, shouting incoherently to her husband who was trailing after her.

The chef, who was beaming with delight, calmly reached for a bottle of Asbach and said, "I think that calls for a round of drinks, gentlemen. *Prosit* and welcome to Cafe Markl!"

CHAPTER THIRTY-NINE

Betcha by Golly, Wow

After dinner we got changed in the cottage and returned to the club which by now was full of happy holidaymakers. Markl didn't have a disco but was piping some bland background music that sounded like Bert Kaempfert through a small stereo system. A group of locals dressed in the same Bavarian attire as Markl were standing in the bar area, while our host was behind the bar pulling pints and chatting with them. From the dark look he aimed in our direction I imagined he was complaining about what bastards we were to little Fifi Nous. Whatever it was, the rest of them were staring at us with interest.

As we tuned up he came out from behind the bar and made his way over to the stage.

Roger went to meet him and began, "Herr Markl, many apologies for the incident in the kitchen, but—"

"No explanations, Herr Kapellmeister," he said briskly. "A man who hates dogs…" He looked witheringly at John, who was busying himself around the organ. Markl turned back to Roger. "*Ja*, a man who hates dogs is a man who hates life." He shot another hard look at John. "However, now it is about you performing and making a success of it. Remember your first obligation is to my *stammgäste*, my regulars. Ignore the tourists."

And with that he marched back up to the bar.

I noticed the American group we'd spoken to earlier had arrived.

The cute blonde waved and I winked back.

Roger appeared to be considering something; he turned on his microphone and announced in English: "Good evening, ladies and gentlemen, and welcome to Cafe Markl in beautiful Ruhpolding. We're The Statesmen Singers and we'll be here Monday to Saturday from nine p.m. until one a.m. playing the latest hits and the favourites you love." He smiled cheerfully in the general direction of the bar and continued, "Most of our repertoire is international hits so if you're looking for something Bavarian, you might want to try one of the bierkellers up the road. There are enough of them. Now, here's Kassy and *It's Your Thing*."

This was greeted by cheerful applause from sections of the audience and bemused looks from the bar area. Markl had stepped out from behind the bar and looked furious. By contrast all of us on stage were grinning from ear to ear. The dance floor quickly filled up as we played one dance hit after the other. We only had to play four sets so it was easy to keep the tempo up.

For all his moaning, the Americans were buying heaps of drinks, ordering food and also sending trays of beers and schnapps up to us on stage. We reached the first break feeling we had done a good job. The audience liked us and Markl was selling his drinks. Was he happy? Not a bit. He came charging over, looking very much like Schmiegel during one of his bad-tempered outbursts.

"Herr Kapellmeister! What did I specifically say? Do not defer to the tastes of a few American tourists. Play Bavarian popular music. You will now kindly follow my instructions."

"No," Roger replied.

"*Bitte?*"

"No. You booked us after seeing us in Worms and you knew precisely the type of music we performed. We're playing that music and it's exactly what this audience wants." He looked over to the bar and Markl followed his gaze. "And I would also guess that the Americans are drinking at least as much as your guests in there, so I don't understand the problem."

Markl was rapidly calculating the situation. He couldn't fire us because we had a contract and nowhere in it did it state that he could choose what we played. Furthermore, it was still the summer season so he wouldn't easily find a replacement band. He stared at us thoughtfully for about a minute, then abruptly swung around and stomped off back to the bar.

John was delighted and said, "That's more like it, Roger. England, 1 West Germany, 0."

Roger was smiling grimly. "Yes, that's settled his bollocks for now. But men…" He raised a cautionary finger. "Let's not give him any excuse to kick us out. As long as we don't start being late, pinching drinks, booting the rat into touch…" He looked at Wolfgang, "or turning up drunk, we should be OK."

We were reflecting on this when I got a tap on the shoulder. It was the American blonde.

"Hey, you guys are great. Much better than the last lot. They just played a load of boring German stuff. Wanna come over and join us?"

At the end of the evening, Roger and Kassy took off on their bikes while the rest of us joined the blonde, whose name was Jeannie, and her American friends in a late-night bierkeller down the road. That was my first introduction to Jägermeister. At the time it wasn't an 'in' drink by any stretch: there were no Jägerbombs or chilled dispensers. It was drunk at room temperature by solid gentlemen wearing lederhosen, green trilbies and sensible shoes. That didn't mean the drink was any less potent though. After all the beer we had already consumed, the rest of the evening passed by in a blur. The result being that I woke up the next morning to bright sunlight slanting through the window, with another hangover from hell and a blonde American snoring softly beside me.

She slowly opened her eyes and smiled. "Whoops. How did I get here?"

"Courtesy of a bottle of Jägermeister, I think."

"No no. You seduced me with that British accent."

"I did?" I said with mild surprise. "I would have enjoyed the seduction a lot more if I could remember it. Were we great together?"

"Don't worry, my honour's still intact. We both fell asleep straight away. But I'm wide awake now. Want to try again?"

She winked playfully and started to take her knickers off, then stopped, looked under the duvet and frowned. "Oops! Wrong time of the month. Guess we'll have to give that a rain check."

"OK. Need me to do anything?"

"Yeah, could you go down the road and see if you can buy some tampons somewhere? I'm leaking rather badly."

I threw on a shirt and some jeans and went off in search of a shop. Luckily, there was a chemist at the end of the road so I popped in there and bought a packet and hurried back. Another big smile greeted my return.

"Wow, it's true what they say about you Brits. You are gentlemen."

"Absolutely. We also get hungry. Want to go and get something to eat?"

We strolled into the centre of the village, chatting casually about this and that, and had a late breakfast at the Hotel Zur Post. The restaurant was filled with diners watching the Olympics on a couple of TV screens.

Jeannie laughed. "Heck, I totally forgot I have a ticket for today. You are a bad influence on me. Made me forget what I'm here for."

"But how would you get there?" I asked.

"The group I'm with. It's part of a package and we have tickets for certain days and events. A bus leaves each day around eight a.m."

I raised an eyebrow. "Well I guess you would have made it if you had gone straight from the bar."

"Yeah, instead I went straight to your bed," she said giggling. "Not a bad choice."

We found a table and ordered breakfast while watching the sport on TV; 1972 was swimmer Mark Spitz's year – he won a record-breaking seven gold medals. As we ate our eggs he was competing in the 100 metres freestyle.

A little while later, an English couple from the previous evening walked past. They recognised me and complimented the band on our music.

"Playing again this evening?" they enquired.

I nodded. "Yea we're here all month. Monday to Saturday."

"That's brilliant. Until your band arrived, the only music you could hear in the village was Bavarian folk music. Very nice, but…"

Jeannie joined in. "That's what I've been telling him. Guys in shorts with accordions and trumpets." She frowned and pinched me playfully on the arm. "I mean, really? Much more fun now."

After breakfast she showed me around the village. It was another hot day and the temperature must have been up in the thirties. We found ourselves by one of the cable-car stations and the thought of cool mountain air felt inviting so we bought a couple of tickets and boarded the car. The journey would take us to the top of the Rauschberg which, at around 1,600 metres, was a mile high and the tallest mountain in the area.

Leaving the village far below, the cable car ascended silently for about ten minutes until we slid smoothly into the station at the summit. After getting our bearings we followed the other tourists along a footpath through some woods to an attractive inn with a sunny terrace, and there we found Roger with Mausi and the kids, and Kassy and Sonja. Roger jumped up from his seat.

"Stephen, dear boy! What a delightful surprise. And the beautiful lady from last night. Come and join us."

They had a sheet of paper in front of them with a list of Donald's songs on it.

Roger saw me staring and explained cheerily, "Just divvying up Donald's songs. I'm taking over *Celebrate* and *Love the One You're With*. Kassy's doing *Morning Has Broken*. Fancy *The Lion Sleeps Tonight*?"

"No not really. Fancy the quick way back down the mountain?"

He grinned wickedly. "Thought so. I'll try and push it onto John."

After a quick drink we left them to it and took a walk along one of the mountain paths. Quite suddenly she stopped and pulled me to her and kissed me intensely.

When we parted she looked into my eyes and whispered, "I'm happy I missed that bus today."

CHAPTER FORTY

What's Going On

I woke up to someone banging on my door. It sounded urgent. Groggily I got up and opened it to find Wolfgang standing there looking angry and upset.

"What's wrong, Wolly?"

"It's the fucking Arabs! They've attacked the Olympic Stadium and they're killing people. Fucking bastards. It's terrible."

I was confused. Someone killing people at the Olympics? Shit! Jeannie was there today.

"What!? Where? When did you hear this?" I asked anxiously.

"Just now on the radio. It's on all the stations. Come on, we need to find a TV."

"Let's go down to the hotel. They've got a couple of TVs in the dining room."

John came staggering out of his room looking dazed. "What's all the racket about?"

Wolfgang told him what he knew so far and we all rushed off to get dressed.

A little later we entered the Hotel Zur Post. The news had spread quickly around the village and the dining room was full. Sombrely we watched the grim scenes from the Olympic Village live on TV.

The terrible events that took place during the early hours of 5 September 1972 are now well documented. Eight armed militants from Black September, a faction of the PLO, arrived at the Olympic Village on the outskirts of Munich and scaled a perimeter fence. Carrying assault rifles and grenades the Palestinians entered the building housing the Israeli delegation to the Munich Olympic Games. Bursting into the first apartment, they took a group of Israeli officials and trainers hostage. In another apartment, they captured a group of Israeli wrestlers and weightlifters. When the Israelis fought back, the Palestinians opened fire, killing two of them. The rest of the group were subdued and taken hostage.

Negotiations were underway between the terrorists and the German authorities. The Palestinians were demanding the release of political prisoners in Israel and safe passage for themselves to a country of their choice. The Games were still proceeding as usual, but after pressure from different sources they were later suspended, and there was an ongoing discussion about whether they should be abandoned altogether. I kept thinking about Jeannie and her friends who were somewhere in the Olympic Stadium. My God! I hoped they were OK.

We came to the conclusion it was going to be impossible to get a table in the restaurant. As we hadn't had anything to eat yet, we decided to carry on down the road to a smaller guest house Wolfgang had recently discovered.

The news from Munich wasn't getting any better. Despite their experiences with Baader-Meinhof, the German police appeared badly prepared when it came to terrorist attacks. The authorities were allowing camera crews free access to film the ongoing events and to broadcast the images live on television. The Germans didn't have a military anti-terrorist outfit like the British SAS, so it was the local police who were preparing a rescue attempt. Bizarrely, they made their preparations to break in and free the hostages live on TV, while the terrorists were able to tune in on their own TV, see it and react accordingly.

We watched in real time as one of the kidnappers peered from a balcony door while a police officer in combat gear stood on the roof less than 6 feet away from him, preparing for the assault. This prompted the terrorists to threaten to kill a couple of the hostages unless the police retreated from the area. Eventually the police stood down.

It was all getting too much for Wolfgang, who was feeling the pain for his country. As events unfolded, and one setback after another dogged the Germans, he let forth a stream of vitriol at the TV and ordered a round of Jägermeisters.

"Wolly, remember what Roger said," I warned. "We need to be on our best behaviour at this place and getting drunk before we start playing—"

"Yeah, OK," he said grudgingly. "Let's just have this one and go for a walk. It's too much for me to watch our police make such a fuck-up of everything."

Back outside we realised most of the day had already gone by, so we took just a short walk then made our way back to Cafe Markl. They had a TV on and Markl and the staff were glued to it. Roger, Kassy and Sonja were also watching.

"Bad show, eh?" Roger remarked.

Wolfgang looked at him grimly and asked, "Anything new happened? Last time we watched, Inspector Clouseau appeared to be in charge."

"They're talking about letting the kidnappers take the hostages to the airport. It's only speculation by the TV people, but it would be seriously fucked up if they let those bastards leave the country."

Markl was listening and responded stuffily, "Herr Kapellmeister, instead of second-guessing our police force, maybe you should be preparing for tonight's show? By playing a couple of good German songs, which would make your orchestra much more attractive to all of the audience, instead of just a few tourists."

That evening the mood was more muted than usual. Only about half the number of guests turned up and those that did seemed more interested in watching the TV screen by the bar than dancing to us. Despite that, Markl insisted we should perform.

Back in Munich, events were moving quickly as the terrorists and their hostages were transported by helicopters to an air force base where it had been promised they would be assisted to leave the country. By around eleven p.m., we gave up playing as everyone was crowded around the TV. The pictures from the air force base were dark, so there wasn't much to see, but we heard gunfire and explosions and knew some kind of rescue must be taking place. As the situation developed, Wolfgang and the other Germans became convinced their police force were finally doing something positive. Some loud braggart was even boasting about Germans knowing how to deal with *die Araber*.

After what seemed an eternity, but was probably an hour, information seeped out that all the hostages were safe and the terrorists had been killed.

The atmosphere in the bar immediately changed to one of wild celebration. Markl was pouring beers for everyone and even managed to be pleasant to us. Roger suggested we begin playing again and we continued until around two a.m. when Markl signalled that we should wind it down. After that the party broke up. As I hadn't heard anything from Jeannie, I went to bed soon after and had a decent night's sleep.

Unfortunately, by morning everything had turned around again and the true nightmare of what had happened at Fürstenfeldbruck Air Base was revealed.

The police had completely underestimated how many terrorists there were and sent a group of snipers to ambush them. They miscalculated and sent too few. They also hatched a plan to disguise police as flight crew, who would wait on the plane and surprise the terrorists, but at the last moment they inexplicably decided not to proceed.

The whole thing was an utter disaster and the result was that all nine Israeli hostages were killed by the terrorists while they sat in the helicopter that had brought them from the Olympic Village. Five of the terrorists were also killed and three captured, while one West

German policeman died. The three terrorists who were captured were later, to the further shame and embarrassment of the West German government, released after a Lufthansa flight was hijacked.

Jeannie came around a little later. She appeared remarkably unfazed by yesterday's terrible events and asked if I fancied a quick trip over to Salzburg.

"Isn't that in Austria?" I asked.

"Hope so. At least it was the last time I checked. It's only an hour away and apparently really worth a visit. And before you ask, I've rented a car. So?"

Two hours later we were parking a little blue Opel in a small side street somewhere below the castle. The city occupies both banks of the Salzach River and is dominated by the impressive Hohensalzburg castle, which sits on a hill above a perfectly preserved old town. Like Munich it's dotted with elegant buildings in the Baroque style and a healthy portion of palaces and churches. If you ignored the modern dress of the crowds thronging the narrow streets you could have been back in the eighteenth century, as little else had changed.

We exchanged some deutschmarks for Austrian schillings, purchased a guidebook and explored. Mozart was born, and lived, in the town for much of his life so we began at his birthplace in the Getreidegasse. The house was now a museum containing many original furnishings and musical manuscripts from when the Mozart family lived there. After that we visited the cathedral before taking the lift up to the castle. The views from up there were just knock-out. You could see every part of the city but beyond that, the sheer beauty of the mountains surrounding us was simply stunning.

Next up was a handsome drum called the Mirabell Palace. Unfortunately we were running short of time so we had to restrict our visit to the gardens which, laid out in a similar formal style to the Hofgarten in Munich, were also very attractive. A large lawn area – flanked by colourful flower beds and an intriguing assortment of stone goblins and larger heroic statues from mythology – led to the impressive Horse Fountain, which was the stage for the *Do-Re-Mi* song featured in the movie *The Sound of Music*.

We sat down on a grand flight of steps and she said, "Shame we're leaving on Saturday, I'm going to miss Ruhpolding." She squeezed my leg. "I might even miss you a bit too." We were quiet for a few moments then she continued, "You know, if you take that offer from those army guys there's no reason this has to end on Saturday."

"Why? What did you have in mind?"

"Philly is a lot closer to Austin than Germany is. You never know, if you play your cards right I could come down at weekends and carry your guitar."

"Why? You think I need a roadie?" I joked.

"Oh no. I'd be much more than that. A kind of roadie and groupie all wrapped into one," she teased.

"A sort of 'roapie' you mean?"

"That's right, and every night you'd get an erotic 'gropie' from a sexy 'roapie'."

"Now you're sounding dopy. Come on, you need to get me back to Germany."

"OK, Mr Mopie," she said with a playful pout. "Just don't say I didn't make the offer."

As we walked back to the car I realised how much I was going to miss her. Maybe she was right. If we took the job offer from Randy and Rich we could see each other again in the U.S.

CHAPTER FORTY-ONE

Suspicious Minds

That evening when I entered the club Roger was deep in conversation with Markl. On seeing me, he made a quick excuse and came over.

"Evening, Steve. Glad you turned up. You saved me from another skirmish with that nutter."

"What now?"

"Same old bollocks, but this time he's trying to say that we're not playing the international hits the audience want to hear."

"He's just playing mind games with you. The man knows diddly squat about popular music; probably thinks *A Walk in the Black Forest* is still number one."

He nodded but looked uneasy. "Yeah, maybe, but I get the feeling he's got something up his sleeve." He looked towards the door. "Ah, here's Kassy with Sonja."

Sonja hadn't been around too much since we'd been here. She preferred staying at home with Mausi watching TV. Tonight she had made herself up and looked very fetching in a black pantsuit. Kassy got her a drink and they found a small table close to the stage. We were about to start when an unusually upbeat Markl came strutting over, clutching a stack of paper and some pencils.

"Herr Kapellmeister, following our earlier conversation, I have a most excellent solution." He beamed at each of us and allowed a dramatic pause before elaborating. "Why don't we ask the audience themselves what they wish to hear?" We all nodded cautiously while Markl continued, "I have come up with what I believe is the perfect plan. I will distribute paper and pencils to each table and our valued guests can write song requests on them." His smile became distinctly more steely. "And you will then play them."

With that he hopped off the stage and hurried around to each table, dishing out paper and pencils.

When he had finished he returned to the stage and said, "Now please ask the audience to write their music requests on the paper and I'll shortly collect them."

With a resigned shrug, Roger turned on his mike and asked them in English and in German to write down their requests and we waited for Markl to collect them all.

Grinning like a wolf, he came back to the stage with the pile of papers and handed them to our bandleader who by now was biting his lip nervously.

"Herr Kapellmeister," he said triumphantly. "Now let's see what music the audience actually wants to hear."

And with that, he swaggered back over to his cronies at the bar and proceeded to bask in his own cunning.

We all looked inquiringly at Roger, who was staring at the pile with interest.

"Silly bugger didn't bother to look at them before handing them over," he said chuckling to himself. "Gentlemen, watch and admire." With a sweeping gesture of his arm, he switched on his microphone and announced: "Good evening, ladies and gentlemen, and welcome to Cafe Markl. Tonight is request night and Herr Markl has kindly gathered all your requests together and I have them here before me." He paused to look at one of the notes. "Let's see the first one. Ah yes, it's an old Statesmen classic – it's Kassy and *Sex Machine*."

After the song was finished he picked the next piece of paper.

"I see we have a Stephen Stills fan in the audience," he said with mock surprise. "Especially for that fan, here's *Love the One You're*

With."

And so it went on. Before each song he would take an exaggerated look at the next paper and introduce something from our usual repertoire. It took about four songs before Markl realised his blunder, but by then he was stuck behind the bar serving customers. Between pulling pints, he was craning his neck desperately, trying to see if anyone in the audience was complaining, but unfortunately for him they were too busy dancing and having a good time.

When the break arrived Roger couldn't resist sauntering over to the bar and complimenting a stone-faced Markl on his brilliant idea.

While we had been playing, another American girl had been dancing in front of the stage making eyes at Kassy. I had seen her a couple of times before, but I don't think he even noticed her. During that first break he certainly started to take notice, because Sonja was furious with him.

"Why was that girl staring at you the whole time? And why are you staring back? Bastard!"

Kassy couldn't believe it and exploded, "Are you crazy?! Roger, John? Have any of you seen me staring at that girl?"

Expressions of innocence all round didn't stop Sonja.

"Ha! You men always stick together. What about that time in Stuttgart with that Gypsy whore?"

Oops. I could see where this was going so I slipped away to the bar. A few moments later Roger and John joined me. We ordered some beers and Roger became unusually businesslike.

"Boys, I know I haven't been focused enough recently because of Mausi and the kids being here, but tomorrow that all changes. I'll call Bachmann and I'll get him to book a studio in Munich next month for us to record the new songs."

That sounded interesting. It would be nice to have a real project to work on.

A couple of minutes later, Kassy came over looking irritated.

"Fucking woman. What's wrong with her? And who's that damn

girl who keeps staring at me? What a pile of shit!"

At that same moment Jeannie arrived with her friends. She made a beeline straight for the bar and eagerly kissed me on the lips.

"Jeannie, I bet you don't get angry and jealous if another girl smiles at Steve."

She looked surprised. "Of course not, Kassy. I don't want to be together with a guy no one else fancies. Besides, jealousy is overrated."

"You are the perfect woman," he said. "Leave this guy and marry me."

We were all laughing so loudly no one realised Sonja had quietly joined us. She turned sweetly to Kassy, who almost jumped out of his skin.

"Marry who, Kassy?"

CHAPTER FORTY-TWO

Goodbye to Love

Jeannie visited the Olympic Stadium on the Thursday, so we didn't see each other again until Friday, which was her last full day in Ruhpolding. The weather wasn't as hot as it had been so we rented a couple of bikes and rode to one of the neighbouring lakes: the Chiemsee. It was further than we thought so when we got there we stopped for lunch at an attractive, flower-bedecked inn. After finding a corner table in the bar and ordering a couple of Cokes the conversation drifted back to where it had left off in the Mirabell Gardens.

"OK Mr Mopie, I hope you're ready for some red-hot passion tonight."

"Oh, I don't know. I think I'm washing my hair," I said casually.

Reaching over, she grabbed my ear playfully. "Leave it dirty." She kissed me softly on the lips and ran her fingers lightly over my groin. "Oh my word!" she murmured. "Look who's just woken up."

"Not here," I exclaimed in mock horror. "We're in a restaurant."

"Yeah, and I'd like to order the bratwurst please – hold the dressing."

After lunch we did a couple more kilometres around the lake. There were dozens of sailing boats out on the water and with the mountains in the background it looked perfect. In fact, it looked exactly how I had imagined Stockstadt would look when we were driving from the airport all those months ago.

I checked my watch and realised it was time to cycle back to Ruhpolding. I liked Jeannie; she was fun and didn't take herself too seriously. If we were going to the States next year it would be great to keep in contact.

Back at the cottage, however, all thoughts about America were thrown up in the air as there, on the bed, was a letter from Astrid.

I quickly tore the envelope open and scanned through the letter, before reading it again more carefully. Someone must have written it for her as it was in English. She knew we would be at the Arcadia next month and had made up her mind that she would come by to say hello. Her feelings for me were still strong, but she had been hurt by what happened that night. She was however prepared to listen to my explanation and we could see where we would go from there. The only slight dampener was that she would be away on a nursing course during the first week, but would come by as soon as she got back.

A few minutes later, John came bursting in. "Hey, did you see that letter for you? And we've got one from Randy."

"Oh. Anything new?"

"Yes. He and Rich have got their papers and they get out of the army on the fifteenth of December. They'll be home and ready to begin work by the beginning of January." He was quickly calculating. "We finish in Munich on the thirty-first of October which gives us two months to get the visas sorted. I guess we do that at the US embassy in London.

I stared one more time at the letter in my hands. "Wow, so it's happening."

He looked at me curiously. "Not getting cold feet, are you?"

"No, absolutely not. No fear. We can't carry on doing this forever." Carefully folding the letter, I reminded him, "But we've got that recording next month."

He continued to study me and said, "Yea, well if it turns out great we can of course revisit the plans."

* * *

Many guests would be returning home this weekend so the club was busy and by midnight you couldn't move for the crush of bodies on the dance floor. Once again Sonja was there keeping a watchful eye on Kassy, who could hardly look at the audience without her checking out who he was looking at. Roger couldn't resist a small jibe.

"Must be wonderful to be so much in love, Kass."

"Fuck off Roger. Just wait till we get to the Arcadia and Mausi gets her beady eye on Gina."

Apart from that particularly happy couple, everyone else in the club was having a great time. Even Markl was starting to accept that we weren't doing such a bad job as he was busier than ever pouring drinks and smiling happily at the tourists. He even appeared to be flirting with one American blonde female. She in turn raised her glass of beer in a toast and lewdly winked at me.

After we finished playing, Wolfgang and John decided to visit the late-night bierkeller down the road. Jeannie and I were going to have an early night as she had to meet the others at the bus stop at eight a.m. One of her friends was taking her case from their hotel so all she had to do was to be at the bus stop a few minutes before eight.

Smiling invitingly, she whispered, "Let's go to bed."

I'd like to report that we then proceeded to enjoy the kind of earth-trembling sex that she would still be feeling the effects of when she got off the plane in Philly. But unfortunately not.

After a couple of attempts, and my friend downstairs not rising to the occasion, she asked in a small voice, "Is it me? You don't want to?"

"No, Jeannie, you're just perfect. This is all about me."

I told her about the letter and everything about Astrid. When I finished I thought she would be all pissed off and storm out, but she was gentle and calm.

"It's OK. Maybe it's one of the things I like about you, that you need the right emotions in place before you make love to a woman. I don't want to be a one-night stand or a quick fuck. If you're meant to be with Astrid that's my loss. If not, you'll come to me."

Wow, this woman was perfect and as usual I was being a complete tosser. We lay there in the dark and talked for a bit then drifted off to sleep. Unfortunately neither of us had set an alarm clock so I think it was the sound of the boys returning home that woke her up. It was already light.

"What time is it?" she whispered urgently.

I reached over and found my watch. Suddenly I was very awake.

"Shit, it's ten past eight! We've got to run."

We hurriedly dressed then rushed out of the cottage and down into the village. It was almost a kilometre to the train station where the coaches left from. By the time we got there, there was no sign of a coach or any of her friends. She looked at me apprehensively.

"Oops. You might be stuck with me after all!"

Just then a middle-aged gentleman, dressed smartly in a Bavarian-style suit, walked out of the station and approached us.

"Is your name Jeannie?" he asked in English.

"Yes, that's right."

He glanced at his watch and decided: "OK, we must hurry. I have a small Cessna down at the airfield. If we leave now I can get you to Munich Airport around the same time as your friends get there in the bus."

She looked puzzled. "Excuse me for asking sir, but who are you and what's a Cessna?"

"My name's Manfred and I've got a small private plane. I often fly between here and Munich airport. Your friends were worried about you so the hotel phoned and asked me to be on standby in case you turned up." He glanced at his watch again. "But we must hurry. The airfield is about five hundred metres down that path. Oh, and your suitcase is just inside there. Maybe your friend can carry it for you?"

I grabbed the case and we hurried off down the path. After a couple of minutes it flattened out into a large field where four or five small planes were parked. We made our way over to one that already had its doors open. We stopped and she turned to face me.

"You've got my address and my phone number. Please promise you'll contact me if you're coming?"

I looked into those wide, blue eyes, which for once looked serious, and found myself nodding. I really was going to miss her and as we kissed and said goodbye I could feel a lump in my throat. She gave me one last, fierce hug, let go and climbed into the plane. I stepped back as the engine started and watched quietly as they taxied to one end of the field. As they hurtled past I could see her waving like mad. And then they were gone.

CHAPTER FORTY-THREE

Something's Burning

For the visitors who did leave that weekend it was a well-timed departure as the weather abruptly turned autumnal. After wearing T-shirts and shorts we were now hurriedly wrapping up in layers of pullovers and enquiring about heating for the cottage.

At first Markl tried to make out the weather didn't warrant such wild extravagance, until Wolfgang dropped a hint that if we all got colds we wouldn't be able to perform. The next day Markl appeared with two oil heaters, explaining that a third one was broken and being repaired. When we complained that one of us was going to have a cold room, he simply suggested that two of us double up in one room. Having got used to sleeping alone, we decided to take it in turns to have a night without heating.

During the next few weeks there were still a lot of tourists in the audience, but now they were of the sportier alpinist variety who spent their days climbing and hiking. An exception being two females from the Twin Cities in the US who had got the dates of the Olympics mixed up. John was chatting with them during a break and as I was walking past I heard part of their conversation.

"So, John, you're saying there are no more Olympics this week? Damn! That guy who sold us the trip in Saint Paul told us it was going on all month."

"No, I'm afraid not. It finished two weeks ago." He saw me and called out, "Steve, come and meet Barb and Paula. They came here expecting to watch Olympians in action and have ended up with us. I told them the best I could probably do is ladies' breaststroke. What's your speciality? Cock-a-doodle egg and spoon?"

Barb raised one eyebrow and responded sexily, "Mmm, make mine over easy."

She was a vivacious brunette with a great sense of humour and full of fun. By contrast Paula was much quieter. She had long, blonde hair like Jeannie but otherwise she was a pale imitation of the girl I'd recently said goodbye to. There wasn't going to be any romance, but as I hadn't been around much for John recently I would happily make up the foursome if they wanted me to.

The girls were staying in the village until the end of the month, then they were off to Munich for the annual Oktoberfest, so it looked like we would be enjoying their company for some days to come.

After we finished playing we took them to the usual late-night *kneipe* at the end of the road. Wolfgang tagged along with one of the waitresses from the club and before long was in his element, handing out drinks and explaining to the Americans about the many different types of schnapps. Endless rounds of Jägermeister, Sour Fritz and various other brands – distilled from herbs or fruit – passed our lips and by closing time we were all definitely the worse for wear. As Barb was keen to go home with John, I offered to walk Paula back to her hotel.

A combination of too much alcohol and neither of us having a clue where the hotel actually was resulted in us walking aimlessly around in circles for what seemed like hours. When we did find it, we were both freezing cold so she invited me in for a cup of tea. Her room was wonderfully warm and as it was my night to go without the heater, I was more than happy to accept the offer of Barb's bed.

The following morning Paula had breakfast waiting on the table when I woke up. She had been out to buy fruit, croissants, juice and coffee so we had an enjoyable meal and must have sat for over an hour chatting about this and that. She told me about some guy she had recently broken up with and I told her about my screwed-up love life, which extracted a few more shrieks of laughter than I thought was entirely appropriate. For all that though, she was a good listener and it was nice to talk to a female and get her perspective.

The sky was still a clear blue when I left but the temperature had dropped, so I hurried back through the village. Approaching the cottage I was puzzled to see what looked like feathers and smoke coming out of an open window in Wolfgang's room. I was just trying to figure out what it was when the front door burst open and John came sprinting out. Apart from a pair of bright-orange, bollock-sculpting speedos, he was naked.

"Morning John," I called out breezily. "Off for a run? You might want to consider some clothes, it's a bit chilly."

Seeing me, he abruptly stopped and shouted, "Quick! There's a fire in Wolly's room. Check if Markl's got a fire extinguisher."

Without waiting for an answer he shot back into the cottage while I ran across to the side of the club where the Markls lived and banged noisily on their door. It was answered almost immediately by Markl and the yapping dog. I was about to explain the emergency, but seeing the urgent look on my face and the cloud of smoke and feathers somewhere over my shoulder, he understood something was wrong.

"*Mein Gott*! Fire! The house is on fire!" he shouted.

"Yes, I know that," I said impatiently. "A fire extinguisher. Have you got a fire extinguisher?" With the rat making such a racket I don't think he heard me, so I urgently repeated the question: "For goodness sake man, have you got a fire extinguisher?"

Finally he made a move. He rushed back into the house and moments later returned with one under his arm. In the meantime John had gone to get Barb and together they were supporting a groggy Wolfgang, who was in his underwear. As we approached them Markl was incandescent.

"You!" he roared, pointing at John. "First my dog, and now my house!"

In reply John just gave him a dirty look and charged back into the cottage – a move I thought was extremely brave under the circumstances. When he came back out again he was pulling a smoking duvet behind him. We put it on the road and stamped on it while John went back in one more time to check nothing else was burning and – for the sake of modesty – to put some clothes on. Luckily it was only the duvet that had caught fire, so once that was outside the immediate danger to the cottage was over.

When everyone was dressed, Wolfgang explained: "Sorry boys. I fell asleep and the duvet must have come against the heater. When John woke me up the room was full of smoke and feathers." He looked accusingly at Markl, who was now looking less sure of himself. "Those stupid oil heaters are totally unsuitable for those small rooms, you cheapskate. If it wasn't for John, I would be dead!"

If not racked by guilt, Markl was at least appearing to look uncomfortable and in a rare moment of contrition disappeared into the club and reappeared moments later with a tray of cognac.

The month made its inextricable way towards October and as the weather closed in we really started to feel we were up in the mountains. Three brand-new electric heaters had been installed in the cottage so we were at least comfortable at home, but journeys into the village were few and far between.

By now everyone knew each other so Barb and Paula were sitting at the band table most evenings together with Sonja. It was an odd bunch. Sonja was sitting there hawk-eyed checking on Kassy, Barb and John were playing the part of young lovers, while Paula and I were the two friends making polite conversation and generally filling in the time. Markl had come to accept that we would not be the kind of band he wanted us to be, so left us to it. It was a sensible move as there were still a lot of tourists in town and the receipts in the cash register kept him happy.

Rehearsals were back in the program but they weren't a satisfying experience. None of the songs we had composed totally suited Kassy or Roger's vocal styles. We had been trying so hard to come up with something commercial enough for the German pop charts, and the songs worked well enough on stage, but Kassy's soul voice and Roger's jazzy blues style didn't fit. It was a shame that Donald wasn't around as he had the most appealing pop voice out of everyone. Anyway, we stuck to it as Bachmann had booked a day in a studio in Munich the following month.

Randy wrote to us again, keeping us up to date about the plans for the new band in the States. We instinctively knew that if we had any chance of a recording career, it was going to be there but we both had guilty feelings about leaving The Statesmen so soon after Donald.

Then all of a sudden that decision was taken out of our hands.

It was the final Saturday of the month and the club was heaving. A couple of tour busses had arrived earlier, bringing over a large group of twenty-somethings of mixed nationalities from nearby Berchtesgaden and now there was a great party atmosphere on the dance floor. During the first break Kassy was sitting quietly with Sonja when an attractive Dutch girl walked past, said something to him in Dutch and blew him a kiss.

He replied playfully in what I imagine was also Dutch. It was all innocent enough but this time there was no blazing argument; Sonja just got up and left.

Next morning Roger came by early and woke us with the news that Kassy was planning on leaving the band.

"It's Sonja," he explained. "She's just blown this jealousy thing out of all proportion. The poor bloke can't even smile at the audience without her having a tantrum. Anyway, he's decided she's more important than the band so after Munich he's quitting and moving back to Worms."

We contemplated this while Roger expanded on some thoughts he'd been having since getting the news.

"Maybe it's time to think about a new line-up with a couple of brass players. I could take over lead vocals and with a couple of horns in the band we could get all those luxury ski hotels in Switzerland." He thought about that for a moment. "You know this might not be such bad news. It may even be an opportunity."

John interrupted him with our own announcement. "Actually, Steve and I have had another offer. It's to join a new band forming in the States next year. We hadn't made any final decisions, but if Kassy is leaving it's best if we jump off at the same time."

All at once the air went out of Roger. He was quiet for a couple of minutes, then he asked, "Look, can't we just hold back on this? We're going to the studio in a week or so. If it turns out good I think Kassy will change his mind. And you guys aren't crazy enough to leave if our record career is about to take off?" He pushed the point home. "Let's all see what happens next month before we make any final decisions. I won't say anything to Kassy about this conversation. Let's hope he'll reconsider after we've made the recordings."

After all that had occurred, I couldn't imagine for one moment that Markl was going to miss us when we left. He was undoubtedly looking forward to a festival of tonsil-flapping mayhem in October, but he surprised us all by mentioning he had been negotiating with Bachmann for us to play again next August. Who would have guessed that? Whatever happened, though, I doubted John and I would be back.

Barb and Paula were moving with us to Munich. They had booked a hotel not far from the Arcadia where they would be staying before flying back to the US. As they had a rental car they were giving John, Wolfgang and me a lift, which was great as it would have been a very tight fit in the VW. But whichever way we got there I didn't care. We were on our way back to Munich.

PART EIGHT

CAFE ARCADIA

CHAPTER FORTY-FOUR

Yesterday Once More

It was like coming home and going on holiday all at the same time. Welcoming and familiar, but still full of excitement and possibilities. After the recent cooler weather in the mountains it was nice to feel the heat again as the city was enjoying an Indian summer. And with the annual Oktoberfest in full swing there was a party atmosphere on the streets.

Barb and Paula's hotel was only a couple of blocks from the Arcadia so they dropped us off at the club before continuing on to there. The first person we bumped into at the top of the stairs was Ivo – cigarette in one hand and glass of something in the other.

"Welcome back, boys. It's splendid to have you all here again. All that our regular guests have talked about this past week is the return of The Statesmen Singers to their spiritual home – Cafe Arcadia! And where's my old friend Roger? I know one little lady who is looking forward to him coming back."

It might be wise for him not to mention that to another little lady who would be arriving shortly.

When they did show up, I could see Ivo wasn't expecting the large entourage that noisily came trooping up the stairs. Without missing a beat he enquired who the attractive females and beautiful kids were. Sonja blushed coquettishly while Mausi eyed the place with suspicion and Roger made introductions. They got the kids organised around a table and Ivo called a waitress over to offer them some soft drinks.

A few moments later, he came over to us and whispered, "How long has Roger been back with his wife? Does she know about Gina?"

Wolfgang shrugged and answered, "If he's back with his wife it's because of Gina. She really fucked with him."

I got the impression Ivo didn't know all the details about their split as he looked nonplussed. Wisely, he moved the conversation on and addressed the whole band.

"It's fantastic to have you all back here again. Shame about Donald but… c'est la vie!"

"Well put, Ivo," replied Roger. "No point in being sentimental – and the five of us are better than ever. Hey, we're even making a hit record later this month. OK, chaps, let's get the gear up as quickly as possible. I want to take Mausi and the kids to the hotel. I got a decent price for the month at the same place as your American ladies."

After getting ourselves settled into the band apartment, Kassy took Sonja over to the *hauptbahnhof* to catch her train back to Worms while John, Wolfgang and I had dinner in an Italian place a few doors from the club. When we returned to the club Roger was already sitting at the bar looking miserable.

"What's wrong, Roger? You don't look happy," I asked.

"Yeah. If it wasn't bad enough that all the troops want to jump ship" – he looked accusingly at John and me – "that crumpet of yours, Steve, has offered to babysit a couple of evenings so Mausi can come and watch us play."

"She's not my crumpet, thank you very much," I objected. "She's the friend of John's crumpet. Anyway, what's the problem with that?"

"Gina," he said bluntly.

Ah yes. If Mausi was there she might make some kind of scene. But by the looks of it, both ladies were absent tonight, so that was a problem for another evening.

* * *

At eight p.m. we climbed on stage and began the first set. During the opening song the last few months just dissolved. It was as though we hadn't been away at all. Most of the regulars were already in their favourite places: Pavel on his usual seat at the bar, Hans and Werner chatting happily to Ivo and Claudia while Bernhard and Christoph – dressed in matching, eye-catching, off-the-shoulder cocktail gowns – shared a bottle of Asti Spumante in one of the booths. A couple of the tables by the dance floor were occupied by the same ladies who were often there back in March. Nothing much had changed.

As we began the second set after the break, Gina arrived together with a female friend. For a long moment she stopped by the door to listen to the band. She was smiling but I felt there was a certain sadness in her expression. Finally she joined her friend at the bar.

Roger was biting his lip in consternation so Kassy asked, "Anything special you want to play?"

"No thank you," he said briskly. "John. Let's hear something from you. What about *You've Got a Friend*?"

And so it went on for the next hour. Everybody else sang something while Roger moodily worked away on the drums. Then as the clock struck midnight Gina sent up a tray of Asbach with a request for *I Am I Said*.

Roger took one look at the tray, ignored the drinks and screwed the request up into a ball. "Steve! I think it's a *Superstar* moment."

I gave him a pained look. "No, that's not bloody fair. The woman wants to hear you." I looked around for support. Fortunately, it was very quickly forthcoming.

"Come on Roger, sharpen up," Kassy urged. "It's a request and it came with drinks. We don't ignore those."

Reluctantly Roger nodded and announced into the microphone, "*Und jetzt, meine damen und herren,* for the lovely lady who broke my heart, here's something slow and painful from Neil Diamond.

And that just about set the mood for the rest of the night.

CHAPTER FORTY-FIVE

Cracklin' Rosie

We had planned to visit the Oktoberfest with Barb and Paula the following day. Situated in a huge park called the Theresienwiese, it's of course world famous as the first and biggest of the now-popular *bierfests*.

John was staying with Barb in her hotel, so I had breakfast with Wolfgang and Kassy and then we walked over to the hotel to meet them. They were already down in the reception when we arrived and so was Roger and his family. Roger was arguing with Mausi about something.

"No, I don't understand why it's not a good idea for me to come tonight," she said firmly. "It'll make a change as I haven't watched you play for ages and Paula is being so kind by staying here with the kids." She smiled malevolently. "And it'll be just lovely to finally meet your fancy woman."

Roger stared daggers at her and bit back, "And I've already met your fancy man and there wasn't much that was fancy about him. Fucking poisoned dwarf."

He turned his attention to us. "Ah, Boys! Welcome to my little corner of hell. Happy you could join us. Apparently we're all going to the orgy of beer together, and I think I'm going to need a particularly stiff one."

As it was relatively close by we walked to the Theresienwiese, heading back down the Bayerstraße passing the Arcadia and the *hauptbahnhof*. When we arrived at the park it was already humming with happy revellers – many dressed in traditional Bavarian garb and guzzling beakers of frothy beer. We headed off to the fairground and watched while the kids went on a couple of rides. It was a nice family moment but it wasn't long before Roger became restless.

"Come on, chaps," he said. "Let's leave the ladies and kids to enjoy the fun of the fair while we repair to one of the tents and swag down a brace of beers."

It was only about eleven a.m. but the tents – which were huge pavilions – were already doing a brisk business. Inside it was a similar layout to the Mathäser with hundreds of people thronged around long trestle tables while buxom ladies in low-cut *dirndls* and other Bavarian finery dished out litre steins of the local Münchener brew. There was also the customary brass band pumping out a spirited soundtrack of drinking melodies. We found some seats at one of the tables and Roger ordered five big ones.

When they arrived he took a sip and groaned, "Oh God… I'm not looking forward to tonight. You've seen what Mausi's like. She's a coiled cobra just waiting to strike and commit savagery in the name of love. I tell you boys, being a sex god isn't all it's made out to be."

From the smirks on the other boys' faces the possibility of some excitement to break the monotony of a long evening at the Arcadia was appealing. Even if it meant a pile of shit coming down on one sex god's head.

Actually, nothing much went down that evening: Mausi sat with Barb and behaved herself. Shrewdly Gina served the booths by the bar and let someone else work the tables closer to the stage. She couldn't resist stopping to listen, though, whenever Roger sang one of his ballads, and he took full advantage of that by pointedly directing those songs at Mausi, who looked both surprised and delighted.

Someone who did have a problem however was John, when Rosie turned up unannounced. He hadn't seen her since July but I think she took it for granted he would be together with her while staying in Munich.

Roger watched her as she crossed the room and grinned wickedly. "Ha! Welcome to my world, young John," he exclaimed, his voice oozing schadenfreude. Step on in, the water's wonderful, ha ha!"

John gave Rosie a quick wave and busied himself around his organ while she found a seat at the bar.

As the break approached he leaned over and asked, "Er, do me a favour, Steve. Can you go and have a quiet word with Rosie? Tell Barb it's an old girlfriend from school and she'll be gone by the weekend, so if she could come back next week?"

I stared across the room to where she was sitting expectantly at the bar.

"If you insist. But I should advise you I haven't been too clever with jobs like that of late. You may recall my recent lack of success with Kassy's friend in Stuttgart."

"Don't worry, Rosie's a lot easier than her. Just lay it on with a trowel, how much I'm missing her."

When the break arrived I made my way over to the bar and said hello to Rosie. She was polite but a bit surprised.

"Hello, Steve, nice to see you back in the Arcadia. Where's John? Why isn't he coming over?"

I stared at something just above her shoulder. "Yeah," I began. "He's absolutely desperate to see you Rosie. Been talking about it since July. Unfortunately he's had a surprise visit from an old school friend – completely out of the blue. She's broken up with her boyfriend, and you know John… Always the gentleman, he's trying to be as polite as possible." I was struggling but went on doggedly, "She leaves at the weekend. Any chance you could come back early next week?"

"Really? Next week? How very generous of him," she pronounced, with all the warmth of a deep-freeze unit.

She stared at me speculatively for what seemed an eternity then got up and walked purposely across the room to where John was sitting with Barb.

Smiling brightly, she said in a loud voice, "Hello, John, lovely to see you too. Oh, and that reminds me... fuck off and find somebody else to keep your bed warm in Munich! Bastard!" With that she turned and stalked out.

Barb was the first to react. "A friend, John?" she asked sweetly.

Looking more than a little flustered, he mumbled something unintelligible, excused himself and came over to me at the bar.

"Wow, you handled that well," he remarked acidly.

"Yes, I thought so too. It needs a little fine-tuning but I think I've got this whole bullshit-excuse-for-errant-lovers spiel off to a fine art now."

He looked at me for a second and then we both burst out laughing.

Roger joined us. "What are you two giggling about? Anyway, chaps, big day tomorrow with this recording session. Time to make a couple of hits."

CHAPTER FORTY-SIX

Look What They've Done to My Song Ma

The Union Studios were located in a large, detached townhouse in a posh suburb of Munich called Solln. In many ways it was similar to studios in London, like Abbey Road, although unsurprisingly it felt a bit formal, more like the BBC. The recording rooms were large but uninspiring with high ceilings and bright utility lighting. Technically though, it had all the goodies, with brand names like Studer, Neumann and Telefunken plus an impressive array of keyboard instruments, amplifiers and percussion – so it would definitely do the job.

We didn't need our amps so we carried in Roger's drums and our guitars and got ourselves organised. A quiet chap named Wolfram came down and introduced himself as the *tonmeister*, or chief sound engineer. He arranged the microphone positioning and got each of us to play a little to adjust the recording levels.

When he was ready we ran through the first of the songs then went up to the control room to listen to the balance. Wolfram was sitting behind his mixing desk directly across from a slim, dark-haired girl who was loading tape into a sixteen-track recorder. Mmm, not bad. That was certainly a big difference between here and the UK. In Munich the tape op was a striking young minx. Back in London it would have been a callow youth of doubtful hygiene and a severe case of acne. I should know, I had been one.

I wasn't sure why, but she seemed strangely familiar.

I was just thinking of something clever to open the conversation with when she said, "Hello. I thought I recognised the band. I saw you play at the Bayerischer Hof a couple of months ago. A few of us from the studio were there together with Peter Maffay."

Of course. They had sat at Yolaro's table and later I bumped into her in the hallway.

We went back into the studio and worked on a song called *Goodbye Caroline*. We played it through a couple of times but something didn't feel quite right. Although we were comfortable playing together, here in a cold, spiritless studio we had lost the spark that made us good on stage. There was nothing wrong with the way we played the track, it just lacked that indefinable piece of magic.

I don't think I noticed at once, but when we had the background recorded and started adding some small overdubs the growing suspicion it wasn't happening dawned on me. It was the same with the vocals: they were competent enough, but we sounded just a little tired. Maybe the late nights were taking their toll and we should be recording at night? Of course that's what a lot of bands did in London. Whatever the excuse, it wasn't working out the way I had hoped.

Up in the control room Wolfram and the attractive tape op, whose name was Ingrid, were more upbeat.

"Nice song. Is it a cover of an English record?" she asked.

"No! Not at all. We have our own in-house hit factory and you're hearing it here first." Roger beamed with pride at John and me and then got a little carried away. "Worked with The Beatles, you know, and now hardly a day goes by when they aren't knocking out hits up at the band apartment."

She smiled mischievously. "That must be handy."

We went back down and tried the next track, which was a slower ballad called *My Friend Jo*. Once again, it was OK but nothing special. I felt deflated and it must have shown because when we took a break Ingrid came over to cheer me up.

"Hey, Steve. You don't look happy."

"Sorry, I'm not sure I'm hearing any hits," I replied.

She nodded and said, "You just have to see these as demos. The songs are really catchy so all you probably need is a good producer to make the most of them."

"Yeah, but we're running out of time. We're going to break up at the end of this month if we can't get something out of these recordings. John and I are going to join a band in the States." I became aware of something I hadn't realised before and heard myself saying, "And I was kind of hoping if this went well we would stay here."

At the end of the session we returned to the Arcadia. The other three seemed happy with the day's results but I knew John was thinking the same as me. After we had carried the gear back upstairs he took me aside.

"We've got to face it, this isn't a recording band and this middle-of-the-road pop isn't what we set out to do. With Rich and Randy we can write the kind of songs we like, and they've got the right voices to carry it."

Reluctantly, I nodded in agreement. "Yeah. It would have been nice if it had turned out better, but it wasn't great."

As I was saying this I remembered with a tingle of excitement that Astrid would be home next week.

Later that evening we were pleasantly surprised to see Ingrid and Wolfram had come by for a drink. At the break we went over and joined them at the bar.

"See?" Ingrid said. "We think you're so great we want to listen to you again live."

"Yes indeed," Roger said. "Take the chance to see us here while you can. Next time we're in Munich it'll probably be on the TV."

"On the six o'clock news for murdering the drummer?" John enquired drily.

Before he could reply, Mausi entered the club and headed over to the table where Barb was sitting. Roger, still fretting about any potential confrontations with Gina, quickly left us to join her. Soon after that, the others went over there too.

Ingrid looked around the room with interest. "Cool place. A bit different to the Bayerischer Hof. What do you do when you're free?"

"We only started a couple of days ago, so we haven't had much chance for any free time yet." Some mad devil then decided to take control of my tongue and I heard myself say, "And I'm waiting for my girlfriend to get back from some nursing course."

Her face remained impassive, although her eyes betrayed a slight disappointment. "That will be nice for you, having your girlfriend back again."

I then rather bizarrely added: "Actually, I'm not sure if she still is my girlfriend because she caught me in bed with this English trombone player…"

Now she looked totally confused and stuttered, "Oh, sorry, I didn't realise…"

"Shit! No, I didn't mean…" Oh fuck, could someone please stop me? Conveniently, before I could say anything even more stupid, she brought the conversation around to music and the band.

"No worries, we came here to listen to the band live. Hearing you again, I get the feeling you're more comfortable playing black music, so you can get more out of Kassy's voice."

She was right, but I reminded her sourly, "If we want to have a record career in Germany we need to be more like these bloody German *schlager* people: Rex and His Barking Dildo, Heino, blah blah."

She nudged me lightly in the ribs. "Naughty boy. No. Look at artists like Les Humphries. He's English, lives in Hamburg and has adapted the style of the Edwin Hawkins Singers. We Germans are receptive to Anglo-American music and I think if you modelled yourselves more on bands like The Stylistics or The Delfonics it could work well. And you and John could write something more in that style."

Certainly food for thought. I glanced across at Roger who was making his way back over to us. At the same time Gina was bringing him a song request with a tray of Asbach. Maybe she said something flirty, I'm not sure, but all of a sudden Mausi was out of her seat. She stormed over to them shouting: "You! You stay away from my husband! I know all about you."

Roger pleaded with her to be quiet and sit down but her blood was up and she was having none of it.

"I knew she couldn't stay away from you. I just knew!"

When she had finished shouting, Gina quietly turned around and walked off, leaving Mausi looking rather sad and pathetic.

I felt sorry for Roger and said so to Ingrid.

She was sympathetic but replied, "His wife sounds like she's going through a bad time. There has to be a reason for someone to get in that state."

I didn't feel in the mood to tell her about Redeye. I kind of liked the way she wanted to stick up for the loser, even if it was someone like Mausi. I looked earnestly at her and said, "The trombone player."

"Huh?"

"The trombone player. She was a girl in an orchestra and I didn't do anything with her. It's complicated but…"

She smiled ever so sweetly and leaned over and kissed me softly on the cheek.

"Why didn't I meet you before?" I said, with just a tinge of sadness.

"You did, don't you remember? Anyway, no more flirting, mister, you've got a girlfriend and I've got a job to go to in the morning so I need to get home."

CHAPTER FORTY-SEVEN

I Saw the Light

The weekend came and went and we said goodbye to the American ladies. While John was sad to see them go he didn't waste any time getting back in touch with Rosie. I thought after the scene in the club he might have his work cut out, but sure enough a few days later she came to the Arcadia. Initially she played hard to get, but when he aimed a couple of his songs at her, they were back together before midnight.

The same evening there was a letter waiting for me from Astrid. She was delayed a couple of days as her mother hadn't been well but would see me at the club on Friday evening. Around the same time we received a message from Ingrid. The acetates of the recordings were ready and she'd drop a couple round at the club on Friday. I wasn't sure I wanted her and Astrid to meet. Not just yet anyway. But there was nothing to be done about it as the band were eager to hear the recordings.

When Friday arrived I had my excuses for Stuttgart all neatly rehearsed in German and by the afternoon was prepared for whatever the night would bring. A little later at the club we had just got changed into our stage clothes when Ingrid arrived and found a seat at the bar. She handed Roger one of the discs which he immediately put on the club's stereo. Unfortunately, just as I suspected, it sounded wooden.

Ingrid saw my reaction and said softly, "Remember, it's only a demo. You can do better than this."

I sighed and nodded. Roger and Wolfgang were both smiling.

"Sounds good, huh?" they both said.

"Yeah, sounds great."

At that moment I needed something to lift my spirits and hopefully someone would be arriving soon who could do just that.

And all of a sudden there she was, standing in the doorway looking drop-dead gorgeous. John spotted her first and went over and gave her a welcoming hug. Her hair was a little longer but she still had the fringe, which framed her beautiful eyes. Her makeup was impeccable and she was wearing a tight-fitting black dress that set off her figure perfectly. I hurried over to the door, stopped a few feet in front of her and waited for one of us to make the first move.

She looked deep into my eyes and smiled warmly, then said something in German. At least I thought it was German. Whatever it was, I hadn't understood a word and asked her to repeat it a little slower. Cripes, what kind of language was she speaking? I hadn't misheard anything; she had an accent thicker than mud. I shot an anxious glance at John, transmitting a 'help' message with my eyes, but he was shaking his head in confusion. He hadn't understood her any better than I had.

Grinning horribly, I stood there silently as she began waffling on about something else. It wasn't just the thick provincial accent, this vision of loveliness appeared to be a simpleton to boot. She was coming out with some inane nonsense about our romance being ordained in the stars, then abruptly changing the subject to something about a love story in a soap on TV. I couldn't believe it. Why hadn't somebody told me I had been squiring a half-wit around Munich? People hadn't been smiling at us, they'd been shrieking with laughter!

As I write this I know how unreasonable it sounds, but please put yourself in my position for one moment. You see a gorgeous woman across the room. She smiles invitingly and comes over to say hello. You open with something warm and witty and in reply she says: *"Och laddie, ay havnae been doon hair sunce ya left toon. Och but look at yer ya big lummock. Ye havnae changed at all. Come an guv ma a kuss afore a wet masel wuth lust an disahrr."*

I just stood there and stared. The cruel unfairness of it all. I could have wept. I didn't of course. I put a brave face on and pretended everything was fine. I bought her a glass of wine and found a table. God, she looked just beautiful when she kept her mouth shut. Trouble was she couldn't. She started lathering away again and I found my attention drifting across the room to Ingrid who was still sitting at the bar talking to Kassy. She must have noticed me staring as she turned and smiled, but then she paid her bill, blew me a kiss and left.

Reluctantly I turned my attention back to Astrid, who was sharing another demented confidence. I gave up and turned off.

Somehow the evening dragged by and at closing time I realised I was going to have to come clean with her as she would be expecting me to go back to her home. While getting changed I made up my mind that I would be totally straight. It would be horribly unkind to lead her on. Expecting an uncomfortable scene, I went back into the club and was surprised to see her already standing at the door with her coat on. Staring at the floor, avoiding my gaze, she said she understood I was no longer interested. She probably also said something about the moon being made out of Bavarian cheese, but I was just so sad and disappointed I simply nodded and watched her go.

After that there was very little keeping me in Germany. Munich had lost its sparkle and it was time to move on. I think Kassy sensed that nothing was going to come of the record and was already sorting out a job in Worms. It took Roger and Wolfgang a little longer but when Bachmann came back with a lukewarm reaction to the record they accepted the days of the band were numbered.

* * *

A couple of evenings later I noticed Marlene sitting at the bar. It was the first time I'd seen her since the Bayerischer Hof and as usual she looked hot and sexy. She winked and blew me an amorous kiss. I was just coming around to the idea that I should ditch my high ideals for one night when Ingrid unexpectedly arrived. This time she was together with a male friend. From his appearance he was undoubtedly purebred German *schlager* material with his shoulder-length blonde hair and Mediterranean tan. At break time I joined them at the bar. His name was Udo and sure enough he was an up-and-coming singer.

I made polite conversation with them and was just about to go over to Marlene when Ingrid asked, "How did everything go with your girlfriend?"

I shrugged and said, "I'm afraid it didn't."

"Why? She looked lovely."

I didn't want to tell her the real reason as she would no doubt think I was even more of an idiot than she already believed.

"I realised she wasn't the right woman for me," I said, omitting any details.

I was about to leave when she asked, "Steve, can we talk?"

Udo had spotted a couple of fans and drifted off down the bar to speak to them. She saw me looking in his direction.

"It's OK. Udo is gay." She giggled. "Very gay."

I sat down on one of the bar stools and waited for her to begin.

She said, "When I saw you at the Bayerischer Hof I had this totally mad urge to go up and tell you I fancied you. And when you came to the studio I realised that I more than fancied you, I wanted to have you. That's why I dragged Wolfram here." She laughed nervously and continued, "And I'm afraid I still want you. Any chance I can tempt you back to my place tonight so I can finally have you?"

By now I was grinning like an idiot. "Yes please."

Suddenly Munich was wonderful again. It was a town for lovers and for the first time in ages I was one. She had an apartment a few blocks from the studio in München-Solln and we spent all our free time there making love. She was fun, she was sexy and her interest in music was as big as mine. It was perfect.

Back at the club we had a surprise visit from Jimmie, who was free this month. That evening at the San Francisco might have made him a little more respectful, but he couldn't resist asking where Gina was and if Donald's departure hadn't affected the quality of the band. Before anyone could say anything she came around the corner.

"Jimmie. What are you doing here?" she asked in a not altogether friendly voice. "I thought you were in Amsterdam."

He grinned cockily and said, "Hey baby. I wanted to come down and see how my favourite lady is."

"Well a lady doesn't like surprises like that," she said blankly. "Next time, call first."

He then squarely put his foot in it by asking, "Why, baby? You back with Roger?"

She appeared to be making her mind up about something. "No I'm not. But since he's been back I've realised I made a big mistake back in May." It sounded like she was no longer talking to him but to Roger, who was standing at the bar listening in silence. "I don't know if he wants me back, and I don't deserve a second chance but…" She looked straight at Jimmie. "What I do know is… I don't want you."

With that she walked over to serve some customers.

All eyes turned to Roger, who was staring thoughtfully at her across the room. Finally he turned his attention back to the rest of us and said to Jimmie, "Don't ask me, mate, I only play the drums." He glanced at his watch. "OK men, let's go and make some music. Hey Jimmie. Fancy coming up and doing a song with us? We do a lovely version of *Ruby Don't Take Your Love to Town*."

Jimmie raised an eyebrow, laughing drily. "Maybe another time Roger."

Shortly after that he left.

CHAPTER FORTY-EIGHT

Never Can Say Goodbye

The end of the month approached and John suggested we should go over to the *hauptbahnhof* and book our tickets for the journey home. Since the recording session he had been concentrating on our move to the US and was impatient to get going. We bought two tickets and reserved a couchette each so we could sleep on the way. With the ticket in my pocket the reality that we were leaving all of this behind hit home.

Without a job in Germany there was no point in discussing alternative options, so I didn't even bring it up with Ingrid. We enjoyed the time we had together and didn't talk about the future. Then on the morning of our last gig, as we were sitting at her kitchen table, she started crying. At first it was a few gentle tears but then the floodgates opened and she was racked with sobs.

"I'm sorry Steve, I really am. I don't want to be like this." She furiously wiped away the tears. "It's just that the last few days have been perfect and I can't bear the thought of you leaving me now. I'll be alright in a minute."

After that we didn't say anything more about it. She put on a brave face and I just accepted the fact that I was leaving.

Our last night was a Tuesday which was a shame as the beginning of the week was always quiet. It would be a bummer to finish our German adventure playing to an empty house. We arrived earlier than usual but were surprised and indeed delighted to see the club was packed. Roger asked Ivo what the occasion was.

"It's you guys," he said, laughing. "The Statesmen Singers. Rumour spread it was your last night together, and I guess everyone just wanted to come and say goodbye!"

All the staff were busy serving tables but when she spotted us Gina came over and quietly asked Roger if she could have a word. A little later as we were getting changed Wolfgang asked him what it was about.

"She wants us to get back together again. Says she wants to quit this place and come with me."

Wolfgang looked sceptical. "You trust her?" he asked. "She's fucked you around once already."

"I don't know Wolly, but maybe she does mean it. She just sounds a lot more genuine this time and you heard what she said to Jimmie."

"So what did you say?"

He shrugged. "I said I'd think it over." He turned to the rest of us. "OK boys, it's our last night together. Let's at least make it one to remember."

By two thirty a.m. we were dead with exhaustion. We had played our hearts out and the audience had responded by keeping the dance floor full all evening, applauding loudly after each song and keeping the band all jollied up on beers and schnapps. After the final song we all looked at each other dumbly, realising this would be the last time we would be standing together on the same stage. Kassy saw the expression on my face and came over and gave me a hug. Then we all ended up hugging each other. It had been an unbelievable ten months and although many evenings had been distinctly less lively than tonight, the whole experience had been unforgettable. But now we would be moving on.

The plan was to meet at eleven a.m. and pack the gear so Kassy and Wolfgang could drive it back to Herr Knapp's shop. Roger and his family would be taking a train up to Stockstadt while John and I would take the train to London. Ingrid had asked for the day off work so she could come with me to the Arcadia and then on to the station to say goodbye.

We arrived promptly at eleven. The first person we bumped into was Gina. From her expression I guessed she hadn't got the answer she was hoping for from Roger. He was packing up his drums so I went over to join him.

"Morning, Steve," he said brightly. "I told Gina it's not going to happen, I'm staying with Mausi. It's not perfect but it's my family. Oddly enough the last couple of months have been good while she and the kids have been along. Anyway, it looks like her mother has found us an apartment in Lübeck so we can get out of Stockstadt. With hindsight, Wolly should never have moved there either. It was a bloody miserable place for people like us and we paid the price for it. We're going there now to sort all the shit out and then we're leaving." Theatrically he put a hand around his throat, "Let's just hope that Redeye's a bad shot."

The other three arrived shortly afterwards and we set about dismantling the equipment.

Roger and I were carrying his drums downstairs when I found myself asking him, "If I decided to stay here, what are the options? I mean, what are you and Wolfgang going to do now?"

He studied me quietly for a moment then said, "Well it's a damn sight easier if there are three of us. We only need an organist to get some gigs. I had thought of contacting Bachmann when we get back to find some other musicians, but if you're thinking of staying I can call him now and hear what he's got for us."

I stood there and thought about it. Actually, I guess I had been thinking about it non-stop for the last week. I looked at Roger and realised that life would be less colourful without him around. He could be irresponsible and pretentious but since I had met him he had never been anything but supportive and full of enthusiasm.

I thought about Wolfgang and realised that even though his world had been falling apart for most of the time we'd been here, he had never once been unkind or less than caring about the two young *Engländer* he had been living with.

And there was Ingrid. I didn't know where our relationship was going, but leaving now would be difficult. Roger was looking at me carefully.

I nodded. "Yeah, give him a call."

I went back up to speak to John. Oddly enough, he wasn't terribly surprised.

"I guess I knew you were getting cold feet and she's great, so why not? And maybe it's good you're still here so there's a door open for me if it doesn't work out in the States."

I was about to tell Ingrid when Roger came hurrying out of the office all excited.

"Great news. Bloody brilliant news in fact. Spoke to Bachmann and one of his other bands is splitting at the end of the year and, would you believe it, it's a boy and girl singer and an organist who are looking for bass, guitar and drums. Ha! Switzerland here we come."

"What's he talking about?" Ingrid asked.

I looked at her carefully. "How would you feel about me staying?"

She stared at me long and hard, then rested her head on my shoulder and whispered "Yes please."

The VW was packed and we were all there on the pavement looking at each other, not quite knowing what to say.

It was Kassy who broke the silence: "We'd better be off before the traffic gets bad. Wolly, you ready?"

We all shook hands for the last time and they climbed in to the VW and left.

Mausi and the kids arrived just as we were saying our farewells to John. We had come a long way since that beer beside Windsor Bridge, and I wanted him to know how grateful I was he had given me the chance to accompany him on the journey.

He put his hand up. "I know. You don't need to say anything. Just remember to leave that door open." He grinned and rubbed his hands together. "Righto boys, that train is waiting." He hugged each of us and was gone.

Roger turned to me. "We've got November free and we need to meet the new people down here in December to start rehearsals. So enjoy your vacation, because next year's going to be busy, busy, busy!"

We said our goodbyes and Ingrid and I watched as they made their way down the Bayerstraße. Mausi was berating him about something and with the two small kids buzzing around his legs it wasn't the rock star image I had once imagined, but it still felt pretty good.

As they disappeared from view Ingrid squeezed my hand gently and said, "Come on. Let's go home."

Credits

Excerpts from *Green Green Grass of Home* CLAUDE PUTMAN JR., CURLY PUTMAN Warner/Chappell Music, Inc.

Excerpts from *Ruby Don't Take Your Love to Town* MEL TILLIS, Cedarwood Publishing

Excerpts from *Ride A White Swan* MARC BOLAN, Westminster Music PRS

Excerpts from *My Way* PAUL ANKA, Chrysalis Music

Excerpts from *I Gotcha* JOE TEX, Tree Publishing Co. BMI.

www.ingramcontent.com/pod-product-compliance
Lightning Source LLC
La Vergne TN
LVHW011910080426
835508LV00007BA/326